Transactions of the American Philosophical Society
Held at Philadelphia for Promoting Useful Knowledge
Vol. 86, Pt. 5

PREHISTORIC SETTLEMENT

OF THE PACIFIC

Edited by Ward H. Goodenough

AMERICAN PHILOSOPHICAL SOCIETY
Independence Square ❧ Philadelphia
Second Printing, 1998

Copyright © 1996 by the American Philosophical Society for its *Transactions* series. All rights reserved. Cover illustration: Lapita bowl from Malo, Vanuatu, found by John Hedrick. University of Pennsylvania Museum of Archaeology and Anthropology, Negative #128585. Used with permission.

Library of Congress Catalog Card No.: 96-84050
ISBN: 0-87169-865-X
US ISSN: 0065-9746

CONTENTS

PREFACE

The papers in this volume result from two, back-to-back symposia. The first, on "Human Settlement of the Pacific," took place at the Autumn General Meeting of the American Philosophical Society in Philadelphia on November 12, 1993. The second symposium, entitled "The Settlement of the Pacific Islands," was held on the next day at the University of Pennsylvania Museum, preceded the evening before by Ben Finney's address "Colonizing an Island World."

We are grateful to the American Philosophical Society and to the University of Pennsylvania Museum for hosting the symposia, and to the latter for travel funds for the participants. We wish also to thank Randolph S. Klein of the American Philosophical Society and Patricia Goodwin and Bridget Sobel of the University of Pennsylvania Museum for their help in arrangements. We are also grateful to Carole LeFaivre-Rochester of the American Philosophical Society for editorial advice.

Ward H. Goodenough
October 15, 1994

PREFACE

About the Contributors

JIM ALLEN holds the Foundation Chair in archaeology at La Trobe University in Melbourne, where he is also Australian Research Council Senior Fellow. A graduate of the University of Sydney, he received the Ph.D. from the Australian National University at Canberra in 1969. He was on the faculty of the University of Papua New Guinea and then the Australian National University before going to La Trobe. He has published extensively on his researches into the prehistory of Papua New Guinea and, more recently, the late Pleistocene sites of Tasmania.

ROBERT BLUST is Professor of Linquistics at the University of Hawaii, where he received his Ph.D. He held teaching and research positions in Australia and the Netherlands before returning to Hawaii in 1984. His linguistic field research has been in Sarawak and the Admiralty Islands. Author of many papers and monographs on Austronesian linguistics, he is currently funded by the National Science Foundation to produce a new and greatly enlarged comparative dictionary of the Austronesian languages.

KWANG-CHIH CHANG is John E. Hudson Profcssor of archaeology at Harvard University, where he received his Ph.D. in 1960. He was a professor at Yale University for many vears before returning to Harvard. He has done field archaeology in Taiwan and northern China. Author of a number of books and monographs, he has received the Wharton Drexel Medal of the Universitky of Pennsylvania Museum, and is a member of the National Academy of Sciences.

BEN FINNEY is Professor of Anthropology and department chair at the University of Hawaii. He received the Ph.D at Harvard in 1960. Well known for earlier work on social and economic change in the Pacific, he has for the past 30 years pioneered an unusual approach to Polynesian prehistory: making replicas of voyaging canoes and taking them on test voyages over the legendary sea routes of Polynesia, on which he has written several books. More recently he has also been investigating the impact on humans of the exploration and possible eventual colonization of space.

WARD H. GOODENOUGH is University Professor Emeritus at the University of Pennsylvania, where he joined the faculty in 1949 immediately after receiving the Ph.D. at Yale. Author of several books and monographs, he has done ethnographic and linguistic research in Micronesia and Papua New Guinea. He is a member of the National Academy of Sciences and the American Philosophical Society.

PATRICK V. KIRCH is Class of 1954 Distinguished Teaching Professor of Anthropology at the University of California, Berkeley. After receiving his Ph.D. at Yale in 1975, he was on the research staff of the Bernice P. Bishop Museum in Hawaii and then was Director of the Thomas Burke Memorial Museum of the University of Washington before going to Berkeley. He is the author of a number of books and monographs dealing with his archaeological researches in Hawaii, Tikopia, and Niuatoputapu in Polynesia and the St. Matthias Islands in northern Melanesia. He is a member of the National Academy of Sciences.

I. INTRODUCTION

Ward H. Goodenough
University of Pennsylvania

WHILE exploring the Pacific, Captain Cook, was amazed to observe that the inhabitants of the widely scattered islands of Polynesia all spoke what were almost mutually intelligible dialects. Clearly, he observed, they were one people with a common ancestry. They lacked writing and metal tools, yet they managed to build and sail large double-hulled vessels and had been able to settle virtually all of the habitable islands of the central and eastern Pacific. The spread of Polynesian speakers that so amazed Captain Cook had, we now know, occurred during the first millennium of the common era, the immediate origin of the spread being from the Central Pacific region made up of Fiji, Tonga, and Samoa. It was the most recent chapter in a much larger and even more intriguing story.

The Polynesian languages, together with Fijian, comprise but one sub-sub-subdivision of one of the world's geographically most wide-spread groups of historically related languages, known as the Austronesian language phylum (Figure 1). This phylum moreover contains many more specific languages than any other known language phylum. There are close to 1,200 of them, and they are distributed from Taiwan in the north, throughout the Philippines, Indonesia, Malaysia, westward across the Indian Ocean to Madagascar, and eastward along the north coast and offshore islands of New Guinea to the Bismarck Archipelago and all the Pacific islands of Melanesia, Micronesia, and Polynesia out to Easter Island, not far from the coast of Chile, more than half way around the world.

Historical linguists have demonstrated that these languages are all derived from a common ancestral language, spoken around seven thousand years ago. They testify to a geographical diaspora by sea of what was once one people, a diaspora that is without parallel in human history until the spread of Indo-European languages from western Europe over the world that began in the sixteenth century. Where was their homeland? What was their culture? And what were the concerns that motivated their great maritime spread from its outset somewhere between five and six thousand years ago and thereafter?

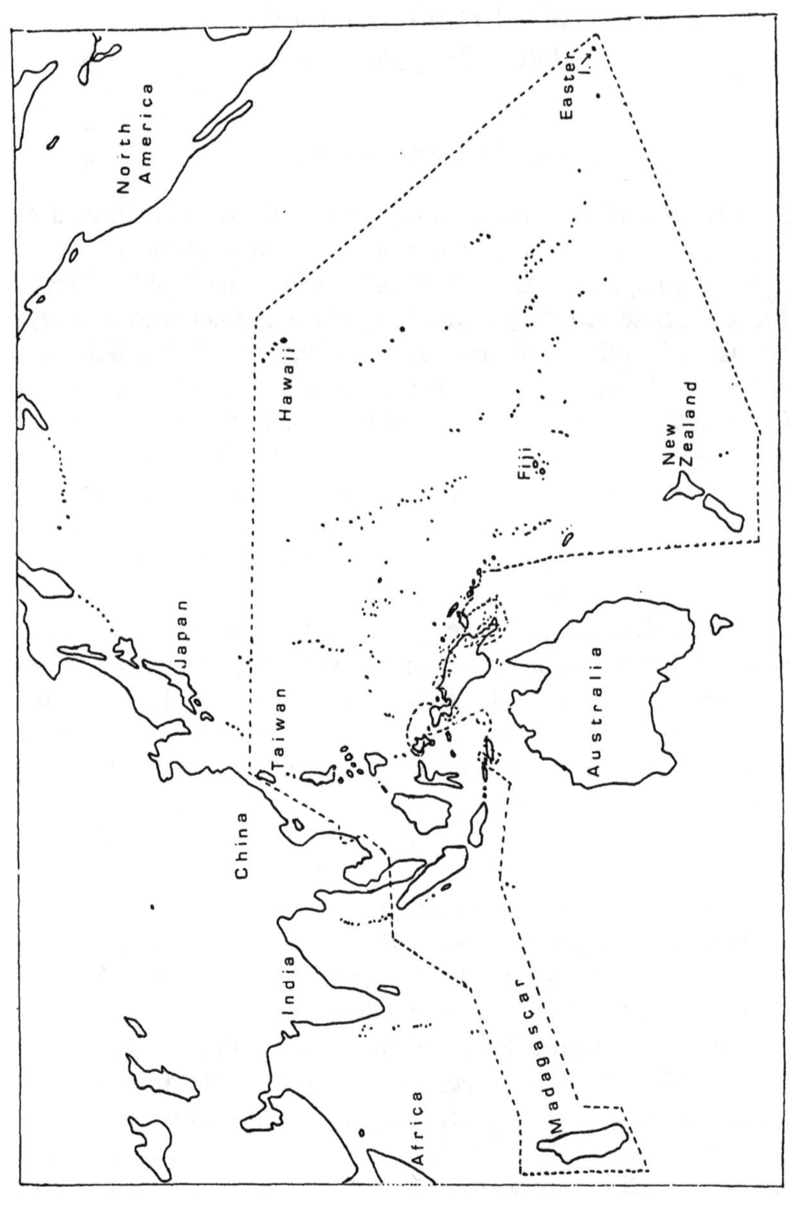

Figure 1. Present area of Austronesian languages.

Speakers of Austronesian languages appear to have originated in the province of Fujian in China and the nearby island of Taiwan. In the course of their great diaspora, they became the first humans to settle Madagascar and were also the first to settle the islands of the outer Pacific in Micronesia, Polynesia, and Eastern Melanesia. But other peoples already were present in the rest of the vast region where we now find Austronesian speakers: namely, the Philippines, mainland Southeast Asia, Indonesia, New Guinea, and Western Melanesia (including, at the very least, the Bismarck Archipelago and the Solomon Islands). The part of Indonesia that is west of Huxley's line and lies on the Sunda shelf (Borneo, Bali, Java, Sumatra) had been inhabited by humans, beginning with *Homo erectus*, for more than a million years. About forty to fifty thousand years ago, people from western Indonesia crossed Huxley's line into eastern Indonesia (Allen, this volume, chapter 2). By thirty thousand years ago they had settled New Guinea, Australia (including Tasmania), and Western Melanesia. The history of much of the region that is now inhabited by Austronesian speakers has involved interaction by Austronesians with these older populations. The nature and results of this interaction differed considerably from region to region.

In the Philippines, western Indonesia, Thailand, and the Malay Peninsula, evidence regarding pre-neolithic inhabitants is scant. What there is indicates the presence of a sparse, tropical forest, hunting and gathering population without knowledge of horticulture. Neolithic cultures were first introduced into southern Thailand and the Malay Peninsula in the second millennium B.C. by people with cord-marked and tripod pottery that had a clear family resemblance to the pottery associated with Austronesian speaking peoples from southeastern China and Taiwan (Bellwood 1993).The few survivors of the older populations, such as the Semang, did not preserve their lan-guages (Parkin 1991). In the Philippines likewise, the first neolithic cultures were introduced from Fujian and Taiwan in the third millennium B.C. (Bellwood 1985). Only a few groups of Negritos, who now speak Austronesian languages, remain as a legacy of the older, non-Austronesian inhabitants (Reid 1994a).

In eastern Indonesia, by contrast, non-Austronesian languages continue to be spoken in Halmahera, Alor, Pantar, and Timor (Foley 1986); and the physical appearance of Austronesian speakers suggests considerable intermarriage in the past with the older inhabitants, who were darker in skin color and rather different in facial and other features from the later Austronesian speaking immigrants. Most of New Guinea and all of Australia remained non-Austronesian speaking, and there are surviving enclaves of non-Austronesian speakers in the Bismarck Archipelago and the Solomon and (possibly) Santa Cruz Islands (Figure 2). This region where Austronesian immigrants were interacting and intermarrying with an older indigenous population, archaeology shows us, was more heavily populated by people who already had their own domesticated food crops and a water transportation technology that permitted inter-island trade in the Bismarck Archipelago (Allen, this volume chapter 2).

Thus it was that in the Philippines and western Indonesia, Austronesian immigrants effectively swamped out a sparse indigenous population, but in eastern Indonesia and western Melanesia this did not happen. There the Austronesian immigrants were not dealing with a few technologically backward people. Interaction necessarily took place on a more equal footing (Bellwood 1980). In the 4,000 years of that interaction, the Austronesian languages have come to prevail through most of island Melanesia, but not in New Guinea except for some coastal areas. Genetically, there appears to have been a thorough mixing of the once disparate gene pools, with markedly different results as to skin color and other physical features in different areas. This mixing of genetic heritages and its genetic effects were much less advanced than they are now when Austronesians began to settle the Central Pacific and Micronesia in the second and first millennia B.C. Thus we have Polynesians and Micronesians, each in their own ways, appearing to be different in physical characteristics from their fellow Austronesian speakers in Melanesia. We no longer need to speculate, as anthropologists once did, about separate major migrations into Melanesia and Polynesia to account for these differences. They are what we would expect, given the circumstances that Austronesians encountered when they began to establish colonies in the already more heavily populated parts of eastern Indonesia and Melanesia.

Around 1500 B.C., the first settlers of the Central Pacific Islands of Fiji, Tonga, and Samoa, from whom the modern Fijians and Polynesians are clearly culturally and linguistically descended, brought with them a distinctive pottery style, called Lapita. This style is also known from sites in Vanuatu, the Solomon Islands, and the Bismarck Archipelago. These sites are regularly on small islands or peninsulas in distinctively maritime contexts. Since bearers of Lapita pottery into the Central Pacific were without question speakers of an Austronesian language, it has been reasonable to associate Lapita pottery sites in Melanesia with Austronesian speakers. These Melanesian Lapita sites also date well back in the second millennium B.C. What is remarkable

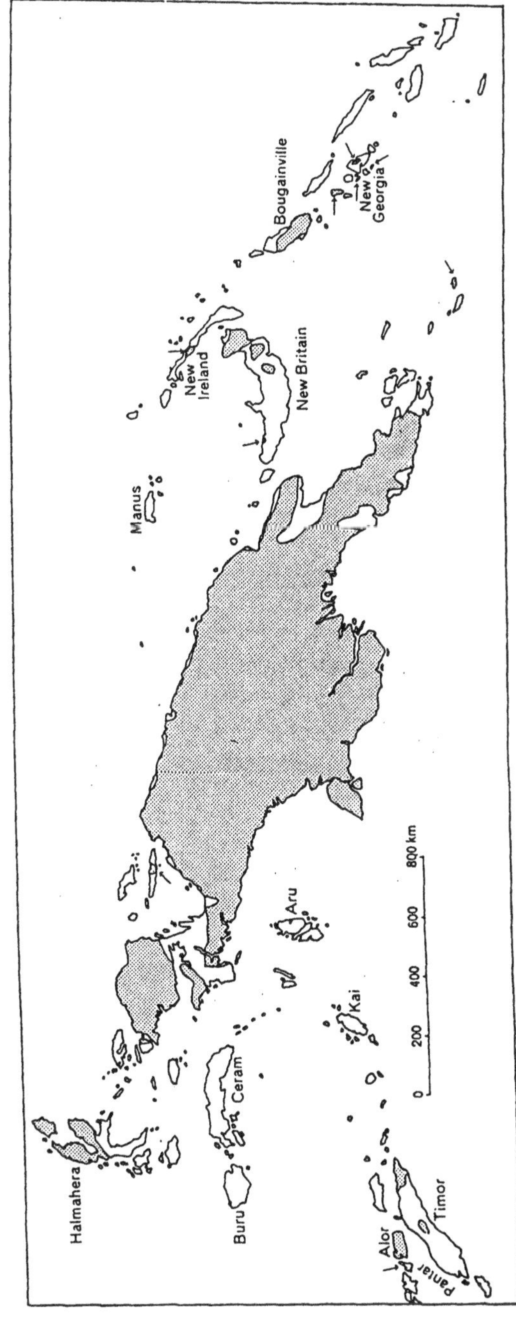

Figure 2. New Guinea and adjacent islands, showing present distribution of Non-Austronesian (Papuan languages) (stippled areas and arrows) and Austronesian language (white areas). After Map 2 in William A. Foley, *The Papuan Languages of New Guinea*,, © Cambridge University Press, 1996. Reprinted with permission of Cambridge University Press.

about the Lapita sites is the narrow span of time in which they first appear in both Melanesia and the Central Pacific. The spread of Lapita peoples seems to have covered this wide area within a few hundred years.

There has been considerable debate as to whether the Lapita style was brought into Melanesia by immigrant Austronesians or evolved in the Bismark Archipelago on a pre-Austronesian cultural base. It is possible that the style developed in the Bismarcks in the context of early interaction between immigrant Austronesian and the older inhabitants. It is clear that the Austronesian immigrants came into Melanesia, for their languages are very much there; and it is clear that Lapita pottery is associated with the first settlers of the Central Pacific, who were unquestionably Austronesian in language. The conclusion is inescapable that Lapita pottery, which spread so quickly over a wide area of the Pacific, owed that spread to movements of seafaring peoples, most of whom, if not all of whom, were Austronesian speaking. Because of this, it is easy to assume that the appearance of Lapita pottery marks the earliest coming of Austronesian speakers to Melanesia. There is, of course, no necessary reason that this should be so, and there are some stray bits of evidence that it may not be so, to which I shall return below.

Where scholarship now stands in its efforts to recover this great story in human prehistory is the topic of these papers. They will address six questions: *(1)* What is archaeology beginning to reveal about the pre-Austronesian inhabitants of New Guinea and Western Melanesia (Allen, chapter 2)? *(2)* What does historical linguistic research tell us about the location of the probable homeland of the Austronesian speaking peoples and their ancestral culture as revealed by vocabulary that can be reconstructed for the ancestral language (Blust, chapter 3)? *(3)* What does archaeology tell us about this probable ancestral homeland as it was five to seven thousand years ago, and what does that suggest about what may have given initial and perhaps continuing impetus to the Austronesian diaspora (Chang and Goodenough, chapter 4)? *(4)* Does archaeology give us clear evidence as to when Austronesian speakers were present in Melanesia and the rest of the Pacific, and if so what does it tell us about their way of life (Kirch, chapter 5)? *(5)* What are we learning from experimental voyages with replicas of ancient Polynesian sailing vessels about how Polynesians–and presumably their Austronesian forebears–were able to travel eastward into the previously uninhabited areas of the Pacific against the prevailing winds and currents (Finney, chapter 6)? *(6)* What can we now begin to entertain as hypotheses about the older and wider linguistic and cultural affinities of the ancestral Proto-Austronesian people (Blust, chapter 7)?

As we hope you will be able to see, the outlines of a coherent story are beginning to emerge, but so far only the outlines. Most of it has yet to be learned. There are some intriguing puzzles in the data now available to us, as well. For example, how is it that we can reconstruct a word for 'sugar cane', *CebuS, in Proto-Austronesian (Blust 1984-5), spoken in Fujian and Taiwan 6000 years ago, and yet botanical evidence seems to indicate that it was first domesticated in western Melanesia (Warner 1962)? And how is it that we have evidence of domesticated pigs in western Melanesia two thousand years before the earliest Lapita pottery (Allen, this volume)? Pigs could not have come from hunters and gatherers in western Indonesia and southern mainland southeast Asia. China is where we have evi-dence of them this early, and pigs were known to proto-Austronesians.[1] Was there, then, already a voyaging corridor of trade extending from western Melanesia to eastern Indonesia and from there northward to Taiwan and China prior to the earliest Lapita pottery? Were Austronesians involved in that trading corridor? There is linguistic evidence to suggest that there may have been.

In much of Melanesia there are Austronesian languages that appear to be separated from one another and from Fijian by about the same time depth. These include the languages in the Meso-Melanesian cluster of Ross (1988) together with those making up the Eastern Oceanic subgroup of Geraghty (1983). These languages extend from the central north coast of New Britain through New Ireland, the Solomon Islands, on out to Fiji and Polynesia. They appear to include the languages of most of Micronesia, as well. If we add the Admiralty Islands and St. Matthias Islands to the region spanned by these languages we embrace the area over which Lapita sites are distributed. In this regard these languages show the kind of relationship to one another we would expect if a group of closely related dialects had spread rapidly over this region at about the time we associate with Lapita remains (Pawley and Green 1984).

There are two other major clusters of Austronesian languages in western Melanesia: the Papuan Tip cluster and the North New Guinea cluster (Ross 1988). The latter extends from the central northern coast of New Guinea eastward and south to the Huon Gulf, including the offshore islands, the Vitiaz Strait islands and the bulk of western and southern New Britain. Whereas the Lakalai and Bulu languages of northern New Britain, both in the Meso-Melanesian cluster, have respectively 28 percent and 25 percent shared retentions of basic vocabulary with Fijian, Lakalai has only 15 percent and 12 percent shared retentions with the neighboring Bebeli (Kapore) and Mangseng languages (Goodenough 1961:115).[2] These last two languages belong to the Whiteman group (Chowning 1976), which has been assigned to the North New Guinea cluster by Ross (1988).[3] Similarly, Fijian shares only 13 percent retentions with Mangseng. Though more evi-dence is needed, this difference suggests that the Whiteman languages (and perhaps the entire North New Guinea cluster) are much older in their separation from the other Austronesian languages in Oceania, as their geographic location also implies. The distribution of Whiteman languages throughout the interior of New Britain by contrast with Lakalai and other languages in the Meso-Melanesian cluster, which are all largely coastal, suggests greater age in New Britain as well.[4]

It may be no coincidence that Bebeli is located in the immediate vicinity of the source of Talasea obsidian, which was traded in Melanesia long before and well after the Lapita period. It may be no coincidence that the languages of the North New Guinea cluster are distributed over the area from which sugar cane appears to have originated and where the pig makes its first appearance into Melanesia. And it may be no coincidence that the North New Guinea cluster of languages is distributed along what Terrell (1994) has suggested to be a pre-Lapita trade corridor. It is possible that Proto-Austronesians were engaging in small-scale, long-range trade with older non-Austronesian communities in eastern Indonesia for a thousand years or more before they began their major colonizing expansion into the Philippines, western Indonesia, and northern Melanesia. Evidence as to the diffusion of loan-words in Austronesian languages suggests that eastern Indonesia may have been an older center of influence than western Indonesia (Mahdi 1994). Here, indeed, is a challenge for further research.

Even with the best of evidence, constructing the story of what happened in prehistory necessitates making inferences from archaeological, linguistic, and ethnographic data. These inferences require attention to what we otherwise know about human behavior and about social and economic processes. Something to bear in mind is that the exploration and settlement of places away from home may be driven by a need to escape from a bad situation such as over-population, scarce resources, or defeat in war; but it may also be driven by what look like opportunities to be exploited, as in trade. All of these factors were probably at work at one time or another in the course of the Austronesian dispersal.

In any event, travel overseas can be accomplished only by those who have access to overwater transportation and knowledge of seafaring and navigation. Wherever seafarers settle, if the land resources are extensive and good, they tend to give up seafaring and turn to exploiting the abundant local resources. None of the high island peoples in Micronesia, for example, have kept a knowledge of seafaring. Such knowledge has been maintained by people who live on the small, low islands of the atolls, where life is impossible without it. We must infer that the exploration and settlement of this vast region was carried on by those who continued to maintain a seafaring tradition: the fisherman and traders, the boat people, who derived their living plying the inter-island waterways and the rivers and coasts of the larger land masses, where growing populations provided markets for what only the seafarers could supply.

The lands surrounding the South China Sea have clearly been heavily engaged in a distinctively organized system of maritime trade for a long time (Hutterer 1977; Hall 1985). The ports of southeast China have been importing tropical forest products from the Indonesian islands and Malay Peninsula for at least the past 2,000 years, according to Chinese records (Wang 1953; Peters 1986, 1988). Malays and Indonesians have provided vessels and ships' crews in this trade. People from Indonesia were trading with India as well as with China, and there is reason to believe they were pioneers in the trans-Indian Ocean trade to Sri Lanka, Arabia, and East Africa. If we exclude the outer Pacific, we find that the regions occupied by Austronesian-speaking peoples have been actively engaged in mari-time commerce for as far back as we have historic record. Did such commerce have its beginnings back when the Austronesian diaspora began? If so, it may provide at least a partial insight into what motivated that diaspora from its inception.

NOTES

1. Two words can be reconstructed for Proto-Austronesian: *babuy 'wild pig' and *beRek 'domestic pig' (Blust 1984-5).

2. I suggested in that paper that the relatively close relationship of Lakalai and Solomonic languages to Fijian, in contrast with their relationship to Bebeli, might indicate back migrations from the outer Pacific similar to those that established the Polynesian outliers in Melanesia at a later date. That suggestion makes less sense than does the view that these are languages associated with the rapid spread of Lapita pottery in the Pacific, a spread that

occurred well after Austronesian languages had first been introduced to western Melanesia. The lexicostatiscal comparisons were done with the Tri-Institutional Pacific Program's basic vocabulary list of 215 items.

3. Ross (1988:163) has redesignated Chowning's Whiteman group as an Arawe/Pasismanua group within the Vitiaz division of his Ngero/Vitiaz main branch of his North New Guinea Cluster.

4. The paucity of shared innovations within the North New Guinea Cluster as a whole, noted by Ross (1988), also suggests that it goes back farther in time than Ross's other "clusters" among the Melanesian languages.

2. The Pre-Austronesian Settlement of Island Melanesia: Implications for Lapita Archaeology

Jim Allen
La Trobe University

Introduction

EAST of Southeast Asia, that area known as the Southwest Pacific consists of a series of islands, from continental size to atolls, which are separated from each other by ever increasing water barriers as one moves east. Understanding the human colonization of the Pacific involves solving the fundamental questions of when and how people crossed these barriers and how the barriers themselves were transformed into highways for long-distance communication. In particular, the spectacular seafaring and colonizing achievements of the Polynesians have seen Polynesian prehistory separated from other Pacific prehistories, and many, if not most, researchers still subscribe to the view that ancestral Polynesians were closely related linguistically and genetically to Southeast Asians. When, in the 1960s and 1970s, complementary archaeological evidence—a series of island village sites 2-3,000 years old, containing a distinctively decorated pottery, shell tools and jewelry, and a marine-adapted economy offering strong presumptions of an agricultural subsistence base–was found stretching down the Melanesian island chain from New Guinea to Tonga, the argument was effectively complete: the ultimate settlement of the remote Pacific, eastern Melanesia and Polynesia, during the last 3,000 or so years was seen as a distinct and separate event from the history of those groups who had settled the southwestern fringes of the Pacific at an earlier period. These archaeological sites, linked historically by their similar sets of distinctive artifacts, were seen as members of a single and closely related group named Lapita (after the first excavated site found to contain such an archaeological assemblage, in New Caledonia).

Groube (1971:280-1) initially raised objections to the simplicity of this rapid migration model which likened Melanesian Lapita sites to "temporary railway encampments," and Green (1979a:45) specifically referred to the Bismarck Archipelago, those islands immediately east of New Guinea, as a likely Lapita "homeland," where colonists with access to continental island resources learned the adaptive skills necessary to colonize the truly oceanic world of the Pacific. Research done in the Bismarck Archipelago in the last decade (Allen and Gosden 1991) has also begun to refine the simpler diffusionist models which saw Austronesian speakers sweeping rapidly and unimpeded out of Southeast Asia to carry agriculture, ceramics and other superior technologies and forms of social organization into the island world of the Pacific. While the notion of innovation and change being carried from superior cultures to inferior ones has been, and remains, a dominant model for reconstructing prehistory, the new Melanesian data now suggest that a more interactive model, involving interchanges between new arrivals and incumbent Melanesians, may be more appropriate. Indeed, the transmission of genes and Austronesian language(s) notwithstanding, it is no longer apparent in the archaeological evidence that we need invoke any significant migration to explain Lapita sites, although this is not to say that such migration did not occur.

Even if we allow that the occupants of Lapita sites arrived in Melanesia as migrants from somewhere west of New Guinea (see Kirch this volume), we now also recognize that they did not simply move rapidly through Melanesia into the remote Pacific. Many Melanesian Lapita sites continued in use for many centuries and show developmental sequences, particularly in ceramics. In addition, there are now scores of Lapita sites known throughout thousands of kilometers of the Melanesian island chain. Thus the demographics (specifically unknown but generally imaginable) needed to sustain a single Lapita migration, which also left in its wake many culturally distinct and enduring villages, alone indicate the improbability that Southeast Asian people arrived in what is now Western Polynesia unchanged linguistically, genetically or culturally. The notion that Lapita colonists remained separate from incumbent Melanesian populations as they progressed eastwards is also denied by Lapita sites in Melanesia, which show evidence of interaction in the presence and transportation of local raw materials such as obsidian. This volcanic glass has a long pre-Lapita history of local use and value (Summerhayes and Allen 1993), and local, non-Lapita ownership of the few major Bismarck sources must be assumed, unless control of these sources was acquired or taken from the incumbents, which itself implies interaction of some sort.

This paper thus attempts to contribute to wider Lapita debates by examining present evidence for the initial settlement of the Bismarck Archipelago and subsequent developments there up to the middle of the Holocene period, and thus prior to Lapita. The general conclusion reached is that if Southeast Asian colonists established Lapita sites they also encountered Melanesians who had long solved many of the problems of living on islands. It should be noted that the data now reviewed have also been synthesized as part of a longer paper elsewhere (Allen and Gosden in press), although the uses made of these data differ in each place.

Human approaches to island Melanesia

That Austronesian incursions into the Pacific form only one chapter of the wider story can be quickly established. Our human ancestors had moved to the edges of the Pleistocene Southeast Asian mainland by c.1 million years ago, but further advances eastwards were apparently stopped by sea barriers of at least 90 km, regardless of how low fluctuating sea levels fell at various times between then and now (Birdsell 1977; Irwin 1991; Chappell 1993). By at least 40,000 years ago modern humans transgressed this barrier, thereafter rapidly occupying all the single Pleistocene landmass of Australia and New Guinea and the nearer offshore islands.[1] Originally it was thought that these first sea crossings were accidental and rare; but recently Geoffrey Irwin (1991, 1992) and others have argued that they may have been deliberate, more frequent, and probably two way voyages. Irwin sees this region as a voyaging nursery which likely saw the very first developments of controlled sea travel anywhere in the world. While the western Melanesian islands were progressively occupied soon after Australia and New Guinea, the final Melanesian barrier, south and east of the main Solomon Islands chain where sea crossings significantly increase in difficulty and distance, was on present evidence not breached until c. 3,500 years ago by the bearers of Lapita material culture.

Movement into Australia and New Guinea required adaptations beyond the acquisition of basic sea skills; people moved from a tropical region dominated by animals such as primates and elephants and ungulates and large cats into one populated by marsupials, which stretched to a latitude of 44°S. By 35,000 years ago, at the very minimum, people were hunting wallabies in the peri-glacial uplands of Tasmania, and continued to do so through the height of the last Ice Age, along the very fringes of permanent glaciers. Apart from the Central Australian desert, people had occupied every major environmental zone in Australia and New Guinea by at least 35,000 years ago. The push into the nearer Melanesian islands was one episode in this great colonizing movement.

Earliest evidence from the Bismarcks

Crossing the Vitiaz Strait, which separates New Guinea and New Britain, provided no major impediment in terms of the water crossing, but it was nonetheless a significant journey for Pacific history. New Britain and New Ireland, the other large island in the Bismarck Archipelago, are larger and more geologically complex islands than many further east, but they are Pacific islands nonetheless. Today New Guinea possesses two species of anteaters, four species of tree kangaroos, seven species of bandicoots, nine species of wallabies and twenty-seven species of phalangers which reduce to one species of bandicoot, one species of wallaby and two species of phalanger across this single water barrier (Brendan Marshall pers. comm.). Bird species across this gap reduce from 265 to 80 (Green 1991a:494). This first experience of the reduction of species diversity on islands began a human learning and adapting process which, more than 30 millennia later, would help take humans into Polynesia.

Because only nine sites of Pleistocene age have so far been excavated in the Bismarcks they provide at best a disjointed view (Figure 3). Initially, excavations at Matenkupkum Cave on New Ireland led Gosden and Robertson (1991:43) to propose that the earliest settlers of New Ireland were likely strandloopers, held closely to the coast by topography and the location of food resources. Newer evidence has now refined this model. The oldest known Bismarcks site is presently at Yombon in West New Britain, c. 35 km in from the coast at an altitude of 500 m.a.s.l. Here Pavlides and Gosden (1994) have reported two dates of 35,570±480 BP and 33,600±670 BP which date stone flaking floors associated with the exploitation of local outcrops of high quality chert. These dates, which overlap at two standard deviations, are from identical stratigraphic locations more than 500 m apart. Each date is stratigraphically below a further Pleistocene date (32,630±400 BP in the latter case, 14,310±100 BP in the former) and all four dates are contained within the upper c.10 cm of a clay layer which, at both locations, is c.150 cm below the present surface. At each location the dating samples and artifacts, including struck flakes and a single retouched flake some 10 cm long, were initially sealed by 40 cm and 60 cm respectively of similar sterile deposits (a consolidated terminal Pleistocene-early Holocene tephra,

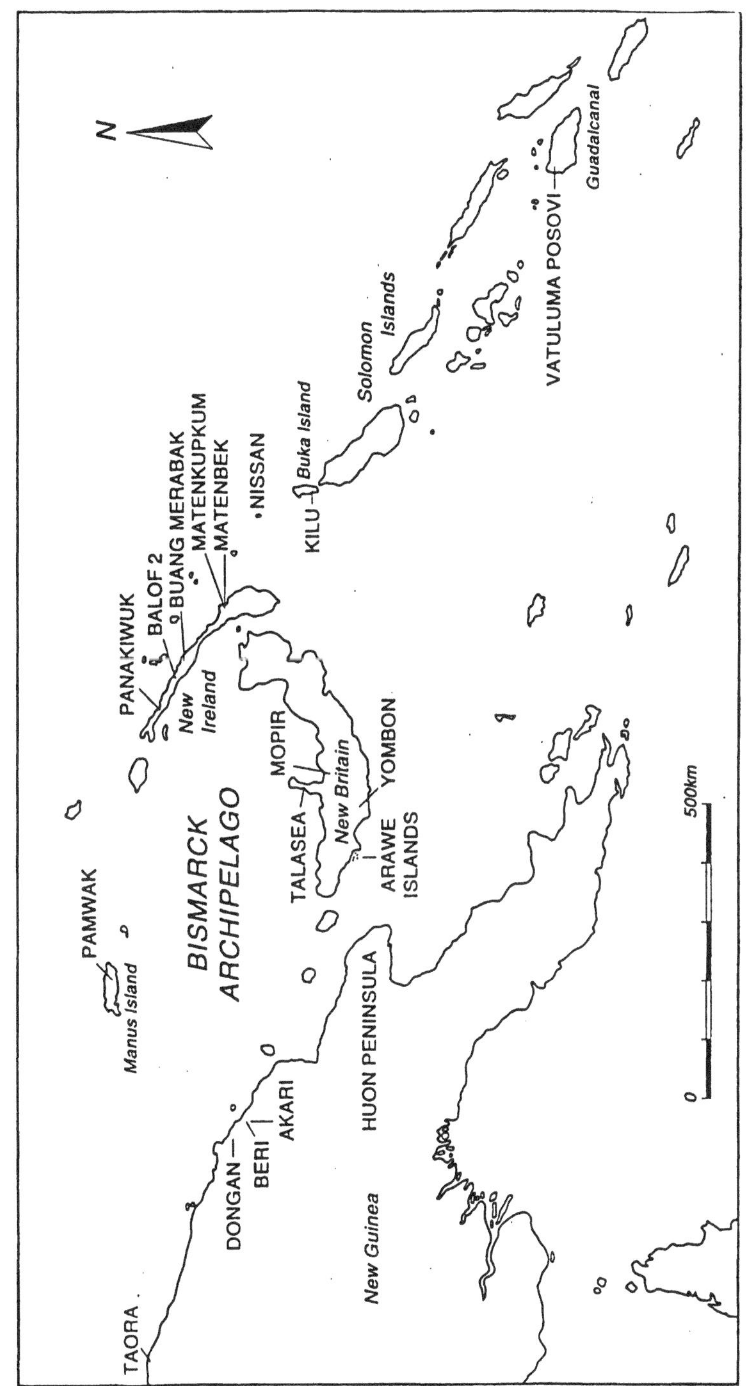

Figure 3. Location of archaeological sites mentioned in text.

and then clay) and subsequently overlain with a series of Holocene tephras and soils containing artifacts (Pavlides 1993).

Because the locations of these remarkable finds are so similar stratigraphically, so well sealed, and at such a distance from each other, the association of the dates and artifacts cannot be doubted. The demonstration that people had located and were exploiting this chert source by 35,000 BP indicates deliberate forays into the interior of New Britain and the repeated use of a valuable resource by this time. This is an area difficult of access and implies a good deal of exploration of New Britain prior to this date.

At Matenkupkum, previously published basal dates of c.32,000 BP (Allen, Gosdon, and White 1989; Gosden and Robertson 1991:29) have now been revised using newer techniques that minimize the uptake of atmospheric carbon during the preparation of samples. The oldest radiocarbon date from the site is now 35,410±430 BP (ANU-8179). While there is copious evidence of littoral exploitation of shellfish in these early layers and marine fish from the first occupation onwards, further analysis of the bird bones from the basal layers of the site indicate the exploitation of extinct forest birds. A greater frequency of lizards, snakes and bats also occurs in the earlier levels than in the later ones in this site. This, in turn, suggests that the earliest occupants of the cave foraged for food through a number of the local micro environments. Shellfish exploitation, as previously reported (Gosden and Robertson 1991:41), concentrated on the selection of large species with higher meat weights, especially the reef species *Turbo argyrostoma*. At the same time the large sizes of individual turbos in these early layers suggest that the local shellbeds were not heavily exploited for a long time. This is taken, in conjunction with other site data, to indicate only sporadic use of the site and its surroundings in this early phase.

Anita Smith's examination of the shells from the earliest levels of Matenkupkum (currently being prepared for publication) has now demonstrated that the modest lithic assemblage there was supplemented by shell tools. Heavily worked 'skeletons' of *Trochus* shells (probably T. *niloticus*) occur, reduced by flaking down to their thick central spines, and some of the large turbos have had a tab of shell, about the size of a thumbnail, removed from the body of the shell. Excavation recovered both the shells with holes in them and the tabs, and as yet their purpose(s) are not understood. Evidence from the nearby site of Matenbek (see next section) suggests that these tabs, which also occur there, were drilled out.

The early dates of these sites are complemented by a date of

31,990±830 BP from the coastal New Ireland cave site of Buang Merabak (Balean 1989:7) c.100 km northwest of Matenkupkum, but details of the site contents are not yet published. Human colonization extended at least into the northern Solomon Islands, where at Kilu Cave, on the southeastern coast of Buka Island, similar sporadic settlement of the cave took place between 28,740±280 BP and 20,140±300 BP (Wickler 1990:139). There, rodents, bats and reptiles constitute the vast majority of the faunal assemblage, while bird extinctions are also reflected in the faunal remains. The Pleistocene stone tools are mostly small unretouched flakes of a coarse-grained crystalline igneous rock, with lesser amounts of fine-grained igneous and sedimentary rocks, all thought to be locally procured. It is suggested that starch grains and crystalline raphides on some of the stone tools indicate the processing of root vegetables and in particular, the taro genus *Colocasia* (Wickler 1990:140).

To reach Buka directly from New Ireland, people needed to cross 180 km of open sea and had to sail out of sight of New Ireland before they could see Buka ahead. If the stepping-stone islands of Nissan and Feni were used, this distance would have been less, but the visibility problem would remain (Irwin 1992:23). In either case this was another significant water crossing which was achieved by c.29,000 BP at least. Wickler (1990:142) suggests, however, that Buka in the Pleistocene was on the edge of the Bismarcks sphere. He argues for minimal contact between the two regions until midway through the Holocene period. He suggests that a water gap of this size may have impeded regular two-way voyaging between the Bismarcks and the Solomons.

These data suggest that before 35,000 years ago people had settled New Britain and New Ireland and only shortly after had crossed into the northern Solomons. The Yombon data indicate purposeful exploration and patterned use of a valuable stone resource, while the coastal cave sites reflect not only an anticipated dependence on littoral resources, including fish and shellfish, but also the available terrestrial fauna including forest birds and root vegetables. The meager data imply population numbers large enough to create archaeological sites, but beyond this the sites themselves suggest only sporadic occupation. Currently this settlement seems to have involved small groups of mobile, broad-spectrum foragers; as far as the few archaeologically available sequences inform the situation, there was little change to this pattern for the following 15 millennia.

The terminal Pleistocene in the Bismarcks

Data for the period from c.20,000 BP to c.10,000 BP are both fragmentary and to some degree contradictory. One relevant question is the degree to which changes in the Bismarck archaeological record from c.20,000 BP are connected to the deepening last glacial maximum period at that time. In this region the most telling effect of the climatic shift was falling sea levels.It is probably no coincidence that sites like Kilu Cave were abandoned at this time and not reoc-cupied until c.9000 BP, when sea levels again approached their present height.

While Matenkupkum was not certainly abandoned at the height of the last glacial maximum, there was clearly less deposition from 20,000 BP to 15,000 BP (Gosden and Robertson 1991:33) but after c.14,000 BP deposition increased significantly. While this possible reflection of lowering sea levels is echoed at Kilu Cave, it is at odds with Matenbek, a second New Ireland cave in the same cliff line as Matenkupkum and only 70 m from it. Excavations there in 1988 (Allen, Gosden and White 1989:551) demonstrated that in the area of the test trench, the first cultural deposits were laid down between c.20,000 BP and 18,000 BP, after which cultural deposition in this area ceased until the Holocene. The possibility that earlier deposits exist in the area of the now collapsed cave mouth could not be tested with the time and equipment available. If the *prima facie* evidence is correct, and Matenbek was occupied as the adjacent Matenkupkum was being used less or not at all, then an explanation not involving lowering sea levels seems to be required for the lack of cultural deposition in Matenkupkum at this time. Eventual abandonment of Matenbek (and Matenkupkum?) at 18,000 BP could, however, still reflect falling sea levels. There are, as well, both continuities and differences between the earlier Matenkupkum and the Matenbek assemblages. Fish and shellfish, including numbers of large turbos, plus birds, bats, rats and reptiles occur in the Pleistocene layers of Matenbek, and in this sense they look similar to the earlier deposits from Matenkupkum. The same forms of worked shell also continue. The tabs of turbo shell, previ-ously described for Matenkupkum, continued to be manufactured at Matenbek, where better preservation has maintained semicircular indentations along the edges of the tabs and the holes in the shells, which indicate that they were drilled. Although this need not imply more than a hand-held awl (more direct evidence of drilling tools was not recognized in the excavated materials), it provides a further measure of the technical competence of these early settlers.

As well, two pieces of worked trochus which were recovered from these layers look very similar to the blanks for one piece fishhooks made from this shell species and commonly found in Lapita sites at a much later date, although until other examples are found one must remain skeptical about shell fishhook manufacture at this date.

However, two clear differences in the Matenbek Pleistocene layers are quite startling. The first is that from the earliest deposits onwards, and continuing throughout the Pleistocene occupation, the dominant terrestrial animal present in the faunal assemblage, using both NISP and MNI counts, is the phalanger, *P.orientalis*. This animal, non-endemic to New Ireland, is considered to have been transported there by humans. Subsequent animal transpositions are dealt with below, but the Matenbek phalanger bones are currently the earliest evidence for the occurrence of this species in the Bismarcks.

The second difference, again continuing from the bottom of the site through the Pleistocene layers, is the small but persistent presence of obsidian. In all, 37 pieces of obsidian were recovered from the Pleistocene layers of the test pit, of which 17 have been sourced using the PIXE-PIGME technique (Summerhayes and Allen 1993). Slightly more than 70% derive from the New Britain source of Mopir and the remainder from sources in the nearby Talasea area of the same island. The assemblage consists of very small flakes and tiny bipolar cores, both of which rarely exceed 2 cm in maximum dimension and 1g in weight. It is reasonable to see this small size as a result of intensive curation, which likely reflects the distance the site is from the obsidian sources — 350 km in a straight line, including a 30 km water crossing.

That neither obsidian nor phalangers occur in layers dated to or before 21,000 BP in the adjacent Matenkupkum site suggests that the Matenbek dates closely identify the time of both introductions to southern New Ireland. As well, the apparent absence of both these items in Matenkupkum before c.16,000 BP tends to confirm the hiatus in the deposition of artifacts in this latter site previously identified by Gosden and Robertson, as discussed above.

Some 200 km to the northwest, two more sites, Balof 2 and Panakiwuk, are both occupied by humans for the first time at c.15,000 BP. Between this time and the nominal beginning of the Holocene at c.10,000 BP, the human use of both sites is sporadic in the extreme, with small amounts of cultural refuse involved. In the case of Panakiwuk the presence of raptors in the cave and the remains of possibly natural animal deaths contributed to the assemblage in this period (Marshall and Allen 1991:84) although White *et al.* (1991:49) argue that this is not the case at Balof 2. Like the other sites discussed, human food remains predominantly comprise bats, rats and reptiles in this period.

Two aspects of these two sites are significant. First, both are non-coastal sites. Balof 2 is currently 2.7 km from the coast and Panakiwuk is 4 km inland. With Pleistocene sea levels lower, the sea would have been more distant, although given the steep submarine contours of this coast, perhaps never more than a further kilometer. The difference between the two sites is that while marine fish and shellfish occur throughout the Pleistocene levels of Balof 2, they are absent from the corresponding layers at the more 'inland' site. Second, both obsidian and phalangers are absent from these layers in these sites, with the exception of a single phalanger bone at Panakiwuk associated with a date of c.13,000 BP.

On Manus Island, the Pamwak rockshelter has c.2 m of cultural deposits beneath a secure series of dates back to c.12,000 BP (Fredericksen *et al.* 1993:146) and it is possible that the initial occupation of this site may have been 20,000 years ago or earlier. Colonizing Manus represents another significant sailing achievement. The lack of intervisibility between Manus and either mainland New Guinea or Mussau Island, plus the distances it is away from these nearest neighbors (200+ km), plus the reduced angle of Manus as a target destination (Irwin 1991:10-17), all mitigate against its accidental human colonization.

In summary, the lack of data again hamper any profound interpretation of human behavior in the Bismarcks between 20,000 BP and 10,000 BP. The appearance of phalangers at Matenbek at 20,000 BP suggests three interpretations. That phalangers were endemic on New Ireland and had not been taken by humans during the prior 15,000 years seems improbable, given that they can be captured easily and that hunting them requires no complex technology. That they were brought or traded into Matenbek, alive or dead, from elsewhere on New Ireland or from New Britain remains a possibility, but this might seem more likely if the numbers of animals potentially represented in the site were fewer or if the site was nearer to New Britain. That a breeding population of phalangers was established in the local area by this time seems to require the fewest assumptions. The dynamics of its establishment are a different question. Here a previous explanation (Allen,Gosden and White,1989:557) that this is an accidental byproduct of the human transport of live animals as food or pets which subsequently escape could readily account for the establishment of foreign species in new landscapes.

On the other hand the presence of obsidian in the earliest layers appears to represent trade in some form, since the round-trip distance from the known sources in West New Britain is 700+ km. This distance and the heavily reduced nature of the discarded obsidian flakes indicate some form of down-the-line exchange as the most likely method of transfer. Although only small amounts of obsidian were recovered from the excavation, the material seems to have been an important and persistent import into the site at this early date. Further north on New Ireland, Balof 2 and Panakiwuk appear to be beyond the range of this obsidian trade during the terminal Pleistocene. Phalangers are absent at these latter sites as well. Terminal Pleistocene occupation in these more northern New Ireland sites was sparse, but that they were occupied at all points to a changing configuration of human activities in New Ireland at this time. As more Bismarcks sites were occupied, relationships between 'territories' around the archipelago presumably also evolved structurally. Such a developmental model, involving considerations like boundary formation and the regularizing of across-boundary social relationships through trade, has many analogues in later Melanesian prehistory (Allen 1984; Irwin 1985) as well as in Melanesian ethnographic studies.

The settlement, at least by this time, of Manus Island and probably the Admiralty Islands as a whole, and also the Matenbek obsidian data demonstrate different aspects of apparently deliberate water crossings, the former in open sea and out of site of land, and the latter to and fro across the 30 km divide between New Britain and New Ireland. By 12,000 BP the evidence from the Pamwak site on Manus shows that obsidian was being transported from Lou Island, 35 km to the south, and imported *Canarium*, possibly from the New Guinea coast, also appears in this site from this time on (Fredericksen *et al.* 1993:146-7). In general in this period, local canoe travel and the transfer of distant resources probably integrated colonizing outposts into distinct spheres of interaction within the Bismarck Archipelago.

The early Holocene in the Bismarcks

While it may be a product of the data, the archaeological evidence from the Bismarcks suggests that as seas again approached their modern levels there were also more people in the region than earlier; new sites were occupied, previously occupied sites were reoccupied and discard rates in many sites rose dramatically. Panakiwuk was most intensively occupied between c.10,000 BP and c.8,000 BP. More than 70 percent of faunal remains and stone tools in the site were deposited at this time. A similar pattern is reflected in Balof 2 (White *et al.* 1991:56, tables

5-8). In Panakiwuk, in the middle of this period, marine shells appeared in significant numbers in the site for the first time, indicating an important change in its use which aligned it much more directly with coastal activities. In both sites phalanger bones were discarded regularly for the first time, although in far greater numbers in Balof 2 than in Panakiwuk. A single flake of Talasea obsidian was recovered from Panakiwuk in the 8000 BP levels, and a single flake occurred in Balof 2 at a similar period (White *et al.* 1991:tables 2 and 11). Further animal transpositions were also recorded at this time, with the large rat, *Rattus praetor*, occurring at Panakiwuk and the thylogale, *Thylogale brunii*, appearing at Balof 2. A piece of the endocarp of the tree nut *Canarium* was also recovered from Panakiwuk (Marshall and Allen 1991:88), while in Balof the early and late Holocene levels from c. 8000 BP onwards, contained 20 elasmobranch vertebrae and 13 shark teeth (White *et al.* 1991:54).

At Panakiwuk, in the midst of this activity, human occupation ceased for some 6,000 years. It is less clear whether Balof 2 was also abandoned at this time; however there is a gap of some 4,500 years between the dates for Horizons II and III. The excavators suggest 'minor breaks before and after c. 3000 BP' (White *et al.* 1991:48).

The absence of early Holocene deposits in Matenkupkum is possibly the result of deposits being cleared out of the cave by Japanese soldiers in World War II (Gosden and Robertson 1991:27-9, 30), although, equally, there is little to suggest that any major Holocene deposition occurred at the site. In 1988 a test square at the rear of the cave produced a radiocarbon date of 8650$\pm$70 BP and a single sherd of pottery was collected from the surface. In the adjacent Matenbek Cave, however, deposits dating to between 9000 BP and 6000 BP reflect significantly higher rates of deposition than in the underlying Pleistocene layers. Among interesting changes in this site at this time, while the obsidian assemblage maintained the same heavily reduced characteristics as the Pleistocene materials and derived in similar proportions from the same New Britain sources, in this period it occurred in significantly greater numbers and almost totally supplanted the use of local lithic materials. In addition, the small test pit also uncovered an earth oven, more shell tools, including a shell bead, and two fragments of edge-ground stone tools, probably axes.

While these aspects of material culture are somewhat early, they are probably less contentious in this context than two pig teeth, one associated with a date of c. 8000 BP and the other with a date of c. 6000 BP. The contentiousness arises because pig is an introduced animal in Melanesia which is normally thought to have been transported as a domesticated animal, which, if being fed by humans, also implies the presence of agriculture. However, the association of pigs, shell tools, earth ovens and edge-ground axes is a familiar one in later periods and thus lends limited contextual credence to the associated pig finds, despite the dates. Also, while terminal Pleistocene dates for pigs in the New Guinea Highlands have been questioned, mid-Holocene dates are generally accepted (see White and O'Connell 1982:187) and similar dates are now suggested for pigs on the New Guinea north coast (see below). On this basis, the transport of pigs to New Ireland in the first half of the Holocene seems at least possible, especially since other animals were being moved by humans in the Bismarcks before this time.

Intensive use of the Yombon chert quarry sites is reported, beginning some time after 7000 BP (Pavlides 1993 and personal com.), where both stemmed and waisted pieces were produced prior to c . 3500 BP. Similar artifacts made from obsidian also occur at this time in sites near Talasea (Torrence 1992:116). During this period Mopir obsidian was reaching the Yombon sites, but whether this was via land routes across a straight line distance from source to sites of almost 100 km or via the coast, a distance some five or six times further, is unknown.

Elsewhere, on Buka, the Kilu site was reoccupied c. 9,000 years ago and several new artifact classes were recovered from these layers, including shark teeth, reminiscent of the finds from Balof 2, but here with drilled suspension holes and pieces of ground *Tridacna* and *Terebralia palustris* shell. As well, endocarp fragments of Canarium spp. (possibly *C. indicum and C. solomonense*) occur in the site from 9000 BP onwards. A single phalanger bone from the site is the same age. A second Buka preceramic Holocene site, Palandraku, was occupied by 5000 BP and had shell beads and *Trochus* ring fragments in the preceramic deposits. Here the excavator allows that they may have derived from the overlying ceramic occupation, but the earlier Matenbek shell bead now raises the question of whether they might also be *in situ*. While no Bismarck Archipelago obsidian reached these Buka sites in the preceramic period, it did reach the intermediate island of Nissan where it was found, together with phalanger bone, in the Takaroi Phase site DFV, where occupation commenced shortly after 5000 BP. Site DFV represents the earliest evidence of the human settlement of this island (Spriggs 1991:232-3, 237, 240). Further afield in the Solomons on Guadalcanal, the site of Vatuluma Posovi has produced trochus shell armrings and fishhooks dating between 6000 BP and 4000 BP (Roe 1992:97).

Finally, from the nearby north coast of New Guinea a number of sites have now produced remains of tree crops and pottery dating to just after 6000 BP. Two sites west of Vanimo, Lachitu and Taora, have levels dating back to the Pleistocene and mid-Holocene respectively (Gorecki *et al.* 1991; Gorecki 1992). Pig is found at Taora from the base of the deposit, dated to 6,120±190 BP. Pottery occurs in a level dated to 5410±90 BP. Similar dates for pottery occur at the Beri and Akari sites in the Ramu River area (Swadling *et al.* 1989; Swadling *et al.* 1991). Although there are problems with the dates of the Akari site (Swadling *et al.* 1991:106), the association there of pottery, pigs and dates of c.6000 BP now finds support in the newer dates for pottery and pigs around Vanimo. Also important is the Dongan site which has produced a large range of plant remains preserved by the waterlogged conditions. These include *Cocos, Canarium, Pandanus, Aleurites, Areca catechu* and *Pometia pinnate* (Swadling *et al* 1991:Table 2) dating back to 5830±90 BP. As Swadling *et al.* (1991:103) note, this evidence extends tree cropping in Melanesia considerably beyond the Lapita period from which the earliest direct evidence of arboriculture had previously come (Kirch 1989). In the case of the domesticated species of the important food nut, *Canarium indicum*, this was in the lowland Sepik-Ramu Basin by 14,000 BP (Yen 1990:262).

This review of the salient data indicates that by the mid-Holocene the archaeological array represented by sites in the Bismarck Archipelago and the northern Solomons had taken on a much more familiar Oceanic Melanesian character, including: the widespread distribution of New Britain obsidian; plant remains which include the important species in Melanesian arboriculture, *Canarium;* the transportation and, in places, the establishment of breeding populations of animals which may include the pig; ground shell and lithic tools; shell and shark teeth ornaments; and earth ovens. Peripheral sites like Balof 2 and Panakiwuk were used more frequently or intensively, and contact between the Bismarcks and the northern Solomons apparently was re-established, as well as settlement being established on the intervening coral atoll of Nissan. When the other flanking islands off New Ireland were settled is not known, but it is reasonable to argue that if Nissan was occupied by the mid-Holocene, it is likely that they were also.

Conclusion

As many of the references cited in this paper indicate, the newness of most of these data make synthesis difficult. On the one hand they are very exciting, and suggest fundamentally different views of Melanesian prehistory from those previously advanced, while on the other they are frequently so radical that care is required lest too many sweeping revisions are made before more confirmatory evidence is available. The fragmentary nature of the archaeological record reviewed here cannot be over-emphasized. Despite this, two important and related conclusions seem to propose themselves. I begin with the chronologically more recent.

The period of the mid-Holocene is one of considerable change in island Melanesia, albeit with different developments taking place in different areas. On the New Guinea mainland, arboriculture is reflected earliest in the archaeological record by domesticated species of pandanus in the Highlands at 10,000 BP and, as mentioned, domesticated *Canarium indicum* in the lowland Sepik-Ramu Basin by 14,000 BP (Yen 1990:262). Because of this, the small amounts of *Canarium* husks so far recovered in terminal Pleistocene-early Holocene contexts in Manus, New Ireland and the Solomon Islands are therefore vital in documenting archaeologically the possible spread of plants into island Melanesia and their manipulations from the late Pleistocene onwards.

The possible early to mid-Holocene presence of the (non-indigenous) pig in New Ireland (and on the north New Guinea coast, where pig may be even older than the dates cited above— Paul Gorecki personal com.) equally hints at the possibility of developed root crop systems, direct evidence for which exists at Kuk in the New Guinea Highlands at 9,000 years ago (Golson 1991). As noted, claims have previously been made for pigs to be also present in the Highlands at 10,000 BP (Bulmer 1975:18-19; White and O'Connell 1982:187-9) so that their occurrence in coastal and island Melanesia in the early Holocene is not totally unexpected. Younger Highlands dates of 5-6000 BP for pigs have never been questioned, so that pigs were certainly in Melanesia well before the Lapita period. Also on the north coast of Papua New Guinea pottery existed some 2,000 years before Lapita ceramics, and its ultimate origin is unknown (Swadling *et al.* 1989:108-9). Swadling *et al.* (1989:109) also report a 5,000 year old, large, ground clamshell adze 300 km upstream from the mouth of the Sepik River. Thus, in this region and within the Bismarck Archipelago, shell tools were made and used in the mid-Holocene, as well as ground stone tools.

On this evidence, ground stone technology, shell tool technology, ceramic technology, horticultural technology and efficient sailing technology all occurred in Melanesia well before the advent of Lapita, rather than arriving with Lapita as was widely believed a decade or so ago. This is not to imply that some of these technologies did not change significantly with the appearance of Lapita sites. As Kirch's article (this volume) makes clear, they did. What we are led to reconsider, however, is that the general Southeast Asian ancestry of Lapita was previously argued on the basis that it had no local antecedents in Melanesia and thus must have arrived as a package from island Southeast Asia. This argument is now far from obviously true. As well, this argument has remained weak because no clear archaeological antecedents for the Lapita cultural complex have been documented west of Manus. Various claims for similar ceramic decorations there do not seem to have clear temporal priority over Melanesian Lapita sites (Spriggs 1989:607). The persistent view of one-way movement from west to east needs also to be challenged, especially now that Bismarck obsidian has been re-covered from the site of Bukit Tengkorak in Sabah, dated to c. 2000 BP (Bellwood and Koon 1989). As well, *Phalanger orientalis* occurs in East Timor perhaps 6,000 BP, and this animal must have been introduced from somewhere east of the Wallace Line (Glover1986:table 122).

The second and associated conclusion can be stated much more succinctly. Just as we appear no longer to need a Lapita migration from Southeast Asia to explain 'neolithic' developments in much of Melanesia, neither do we need a pre-Lapita migration from Southeast Asia to explain them. The interesting thing about the long historical sequence presently available from the Bismarck Archipelago is that, as fragmentary as the data currently are, they point to local adaptations and a long local developmental sequence.

At the same time, Polynesian linguistic evidence and to a lesser extent the genetic evidence point to a Southeast Asian connection, and Lapita provides the archaeological link out to Polynesia. In attempting to reconcile this paradox, Allen and Gosden (in press) have recently observed that the orthodox proposal of a migration out of island Southeast Asia which was forced by increasing population, itself the result of the development of agriculture, no longer accommodates the Melanesian data, which presently represent much of the earliest evidence for agriculture and associated technologies in the island Southeast Asia-Melanesia region. Instead, if growing spheres of activity in both Melanesia and island Southeast Asia intersected in the later Holocene, the resultant interactions of different technologies and experiences and genes may well have created the necessary impetus to launch the eastwards move across much wider water gaps into eastern Melanesia and western Polynesia. Such a reconstruction lacks the dramatic images of proto-Polynesian heroes and heroines sailing ever onwards into the rising sun, but it may be no less human for that.

NOTE

1. Currently, radiocarbon dates in Australia and New Guinea nowhere exceed c. 38,000 years. However, a different geochronological technique called luminescent dating is now producing dates for the human occupation of sites in Australia which are between 50,000 and 60,000 years old. Since most dates available at present are radiocarbon dates, here I continue to use the numbers they have produced, while recognizing that these numbers may significantly underestimate real calendar years (see Allen 1994 for a detailed discussion of this problem).

3. AUSTRONESIAN CULTURE HISTORY: THE WINDOW OF LANGUAGE

Robert Blust
University of Hawaii

Lexical reconstruction and culture history.

I AM GOING to delineate some things about the way of life of a prehistoric people for which we have no historical documentation and, with regard to some particulars, little or no physical evidence. Under the circumstances it would hardly be unreasonable to ask me how I *know* what I claim, or at the very least why I believe that it is true.

At a meeting of the Pacific Science Congress a decade ago, I heard a distinguished British social anthropologist who disapproved of what he called "conjectural history" declare in no uncertain terms that the only reliable guide to the prehistoric past is "scientific archaeology." As, the linguistic meat in an archaeological sandwich that you are being served with these papers, I must hasten to take exception to this statement. Collections of excavated artefacts are not science; rather, science is a system of theories and hypotheses that serves to explain the raw data of experience in terms of fundamental principles of generalization, parsimony, and predictability. Seen in this light the more durable parts of material culture that survive the punishment of time are only one type, albeit a focally important type, of raw data from which to reconstruct the human past. Indeed, because of the filtering effect of differential survival probabilities, exclusive reliance upon the archeological retrieval of prehistoric cultures may distort our reconstruction significantly, even for material culture. And, of course, with regard to such areas of nonmaterial culture as kinship and social organization, religion or folk taxonomy, archaeological evidence is either entirely lacking or can be used only for the most perilously tentative inferences. But archaeologists need not feel alone in their excursions into the dark shafts of prehistory. What some of us too often forget, and what I would like to remind you about, is that Man the untutored has been inadvertently recording the stuff of social and cultural history in his daily speech since long before the advent of writing.

At least since the latter part of the nineteenth century, when the celebrated Swiss linguist Ferdinand de Saussure adopted the term 'linguistic paleontology' to describe the use of cognate vocabulary as a key to the past, comparative linguists have recognized that an adequate understanding of the history of words is inextricably intertwined with the social or cultural usages with which those words have been associated. Consider the common English words 'pen' and 'clock'. Without entering into all of the details needed to treat adequately the history of either word in English, it is nonetheless instructive to note that the first word derives from Latin *penna* 'feather', and that cognates of the second word in a number of other IndoEuropean languages mean 'bell'. We know, of course, from documentary history that feather quills preceded metal pens as common writing implements, and that the ringing of church bells was the common means of marking time in medieval Europe before the invention of mechanical timekeeping devices. Even without this supporting evidence, however, we would be led toward much the same conclusion in order to reconcile the disparate meanings 'feather quill' and 'writing implement' on the one hand and 'bell' and 'mechanical time-keeping device' on the other, since in each case we are dealing with words of differing shape and meaning which ultimately derive from a single historical source.

The preceding examples make use of related words which differ in meaning to reach an inference about past cultural usages. Similar inferences can be reached on the basis of words which *agree* in meaning. Both types of related words have been used to reconstruct the prehistory of the Austronesian (AN) or Malayo-Polynesian language family, a collection of over 900 languages spoken from Madagascar to Easter Island and from Taiwan to New Zealand.

Austronesian culture history.

It is convenient to divide the linguistic study of culture history into two broad categories: 1. the problem of homelands, or centers of origin, and 2. the problem of determining the major features both of material and of non-material culture which characterized the society associated with a prehistoric language.

Although I can do no more than scratch the surface here, it is essential to note that any inference about the homeland of a language family which has a wide geographical distribution depends critically on the internal branching, or subgrouping, of the member languages. This consideration alone eliminates Madagascar as a possible homeland for the AN family, since Malagasy is rather closely related to certain of the languages of southeastern Borneo. Perhaps more significantly, it eliminates the vast region of the Pacific islands stretching east from New Guinea, since all but a handful of the AN languages of this area belong to a single well-established subgroup known as 'Oceanic'. A careful assessment of the available evidence has also convinced many scholars that all AN languages outside the 21 or 22 indigenous languages of Taiwan form an enormous subgroup, now commonly called 'Malayo-Polynesian'. By applying what is sometimes called 'the principle of least moves' to this subgrouping picture, it follows that the AN homeland was most likely on or near the island of Taiwan. From there, beginning shortly after 4000 B.C., some groups of AN speakers began to move southward into the Philippines. By perhaps 3000 B.C. the AN expansion reached the southern Philippines and at this point evidently split into two major streams of migration, one colonizing the large islands of Borneo and Sulawesi in western and central Indonesia, the other entering the northern Moluccas in eastern Indonesia. This latter stream, the hypothetical ancestor of what I call the 'Central-Eastern-MP' languages, also subsequently split, one branch moving southward into the central and southern Moluccas and the Lesser Sunda islands, the other following the north coast of New Guinea into the Bismarck Archipelago by, about 2000 B.C., whence it spread through island Melanesia, into Micronesia, and eventually to the farthest reaches of Polynesia.

A number of questions are sure to come to mind: how did these people accomplish this impressive feat of colonization millennia before the European Age of Exploration? What drove them to do it? What kind of economy, society and culture did they have, and how were these transformed as they spread into a variety of different environments? And, finally, who were the early AN people and where did they come from before they reached Taiwan?

It probably is impossible to separate these questions completely but let us begin with "how?" Although the evidence from Taiwan is fragmentary and inconclusive, since most of the native peoples abandoned the agriculturally favored lowlands to the Chinese before terms for boats could be recorded, it is clear that by about 3500 B.C. when AN speakers began to move southward into the Philippines, they possessed the outrigger canoe, perhaps the most seaworthy watercraft known in pre-modern times. As evidence we find widely distributed sets of related words not only for 'boat', but also for 'sail', 'paddle', and 'outrigger float'. With such canoes in use by the mid-fourth millennium B.C. (if not earlier) the seas of island Southeast Asia, with their relatively short sailing distances and numerous unsettled shorelines, offered almost unlimited opportunities for new colonization. By about 2000 B.C. this pattern of maritime migration and exploitation of coastal resources had been extended to the western Pacific, and within only a few more centuries, to Fiji and western Polynesia.

The chapter of human prehistory with which we are concerned consisted of a millennia-long migration of globally significant proportions, and it is perhaps futile to try to determine a single motive force as the driving cause. Why did Europeans emigrate to the New World? There were many reasons. Nonetheless there is abundant linguistic evidence that speakers of Proto-Austronesian around 4000 B.C. were agriculturalists who possessed both rice and probably more than one variety of millet. As such we are probably safe in assuming that they were capable of developing population densities far greater than those typical for hunter gatherers. The relationship of agriculture to migration has become a prominent theme in the recent archaeological literature, and although I myself do not believe that it was the only important factor determining the colonization of new territories, it will be useful to think of agriculture as the engine of migration in powering a sustained expansion of related peoples out of Southeast Asia and into the Pacific.

Culture loss.

One of the most intriguing consequences of the use of related, or cognate vocabulary to reconstruct AN culture history is that a simple model of unilineal progress in material culture becomes completely untenable. Based on the linguistic evidence, there can be no question that AN speakers in Taiwan around 4000 B.C.

1. cultivated rice and millet,
2. lived in substantial timber houses raised on piles,
3. had domesticated pigs, and dogs (which were important as companions of the hunt), water buffaloes, and perhaps chickens, although the evidence for the latter is indirect,
4. practiced true weaving, probably on a simple back loom,
5. used the bow and arrow,
6. made pottery, and
7. were familiar with some metals, including at least tin.

By the time the descendants of this cultural community reached the northern Philippines around 3500 B.C., the linguistic evidence shows clearly that they possessed in addition the outrigger canoe, a number of important root and tree crops including the yam, taro, banana, sago, breadfruit, coconut, and sugar-cane, the last of which they had brought with them from Taiwan. They probably also engaged in headhunting. By the time the descendants of *this* cultural community reached Fiji and western Polynesia just after 1500 B.C., they

1. had lost all knowledge of grain crops,
2. lived in reasonably well-constructed houses which, however, apparently were not raised on piles,
3. had lost the water buffalo, and perhaps the dog (which had no useful functions on Oceanic islands that lacked indigenous terrestrial mammals and was, moreover, in times of famine both a competitor for and a source of food),
4. had lost all knowledge of true weaving, coming to rely instead on bark cloth, and
5. had lost all knowledge of metals.

Although pottery survived in Fiji until modern times and was in use during the initial settlement of western Polynesia and the Marquesas Islands in the eastern Pacific, it subsequently disappeared throughout Polynesia. Similarly, although the bow was known in much of Polynesia, it had lost whatever value it once had as an instrument of the hunt, apparently never functioned in war, and was confined almost exclusively to sport.

Such a developmental picture, suggesting as it does an ongoing impoverishment of material culture, is jarring to many westerners, for whom the idea of 'progress' is unassailably basic and universal, and for whom the definition of progress is uncompromisingly technological. But the alternative to this conclusion—that the features of material culture in question were developed after the separation of the AN-speaking peoples of island SEA from those of Fiji and Polynesia—is impossible to maintain without ignoring or doing serious violence to the evidence of comparative linguistics. Moreover, archaeological and distributional evidence supports the general thesis that culture loss was not an unusual phenomenon in Austronesian culture history. To cite only one archaeologically salient example, pottery is found in the earliest culture-bearing levels in Tonga around 1200 B.C., shows stylistic deterioration after about 400 BC, and disappears around the time of Christ. Nearly two millennia later it was reacquired from Fiji, where it had survived throughout the more than 3,000 years since the common ancestor of Fijian and the Polynesian languages split and began to diverge.

Perhaps most remarkable of all, the very long-distance sailing technology that had enabled AN-speaking peoples to settle the remote islands of the Pacific, was lost independently in such widely separated areas as Easter Island, some 2,200 miles west of Chile, and on the high islands of Micronesia.

The types of material culture transformations that AN-speaking societies appear to have undergone in adapting to new environments in the Pacific are perhaps easier to understand if we realize that the food-producing resources of early AN speakers included not only grain crops, but also root and tree crops. Several decades ago it was fashionable to speak of an evolutionary sequence in the agricultural development of SEA societies which began with root crops and 'progressed' to grains. Whatever sequential developments may have characterized their earlier agricultural prehistory, it is now clear that speakers of PAN had at least rice, millet, and sugarcane, and that their descendants probably less than a millennium later had these together with the other root and tree crops that have already been mentioned. Speakers of PAN distinguished 'riceplant' or 'rice in the field', (*pajay) from 'husked rice' (*beRas). and each of these from 'cooked rice' (*Semay). All three terms have been preserved in many of the languages of island SEA and completely lost in the Pacific; however, the distribution of terms for 'rice' in SEA itself is complex. Rice is retained over much of eastern Indonesia, but in the Moluccas (the famous 'Spice Islands' of European colonial history) it is less important than the starchy pith which is extracted from the trunk of the sago palm and prepared in a variety of ways. As might be expected, this reduction of cultural importance has its reflection in language: the sago-producing societies of eastern Indonesia preserve only the word for 'riceplant' or 'rice in the field', which they extend to cover rice in all of its forms. What this comparison illustrates is that the complete loss of grain crops by AN-speaking societies as they moved out into the Pacific from island SEA is simply the most extreme expression of a type of adaptation that is seen in less extreme form in SEA itself. A sharp reduction in the importance of rice as against sago is also seen among the Melanau-speaking peoples of coastal Sarawak in western Borneo, while on the island of Botel Tobàgo off the southeast coast of Taiwan the economy of the Yami people was built on taro rather than rice.

Perhaps the most extreme form of cultural change that AN-speaking peoples underwent in island SEA was the complete loss of agriculture and of permanent settlements. In the early 1970s the popular press was treated to a feast of uninformed speculation about the 'original Filipinos', when a group of fewer than 30 individuals forming some seven family units was found living in a large cave on the southern Philippine island of Mindanao.

These people, known as the Tasaday, practiced no agriculture, made no dwellings, and used only the simplest of stone tools. Superficially the Tasaday appeared to preserve a materially less advanced way of life that had been altered by external contacts in all other Philippine ethnic groups. The problem with this interpretation is that it conflicted with the evidence of language. Not only is the Tasaday language closely related to the languages of various neighboring sedentary agriculturalists, but we have an obligation to explain the wide distribution in AN languages of cognate words for various aspects of grain agriculture, for weaving, and for pile dwellings with house beams, rafters, ridgepoles and the like. A far more coherent account of the linguistic evidence emerges if we assume instead that the Tasaday represent a small group of people who, for whatever reason, separated from a sedentary, agricultural community some generations in the past. Under such conditions it would be almost impossible to muster the manpower necessary to maintain swidden agriculture or the construction and maintenance of large pile dwellings, and a reversion to a hunting-gathering lifestyle would hardly seem surprising. Similar changes evidently happened in other parts of island Southeast Asia, as with the Punan or Penan of Borneo, the Kubu or Lubu of Sumatra, and the Kadai of the Sula archipelago.

Beyond the Austronesian homeland.

This brings us to perhaps the most difficult question of all: where was the ancestral line of Proto-Austronesian before it arrived in Taiwan? We know that the origin and early dispersal of members of the genus Homo was in continental areas, and that island environments everywhere have been settled from adjacent continents. There is archaeological evidence that Taiwan was inhabited during the Pleistocene, but from all indications it had only a sparse population of hunter-gatherers. Pottery appears suddenly on the island around 4,000 B.C., and it is of a manufacturing and stylistic type which can be fitted comfortably within contemporary archaeological cultures on the adjacent mainland of China in what is now Fujian Province. All of these observations suggest that Taiwan was settled by AN-speakers from the adjacent mainland of China, probably as the result of a gradual process that extended over a period of centuries.

During the 1970s and 1980s archaeological discoveries in the basin of the Yangzi River and the coastal regions near its mouth advanced our knowledge of the prehistory of pre-Han China in at least two very important respects. First, it became clear that rice was being extensively consumed, stored, and presumably cultivated by populations in the Middle and Lower Yangzi by about 6000 B.C., some two millennia before the AN settlement of Taiwan (Yan 1991). Second, at Hemudu (Figure 5) on the coast some 60 miles south of the mouth of the Yangzi River, the waterlogged, basal level of a habitation site was radiocarbon dated to between 5200 and 4900 B.C. (Bellwood 1985: 219). Because this site offered unusually favorable conditions for the preservation of normally perishable materials (as cordage and wood), it has proved to be a veritable goldmine of information not normally available in archaeological contexts. Briefly, the excavation uncovered a village of large rectangular timber houses (one of them 23 meters long by 7 meters wide) which were raised on piles. There is abundant evidence for rice, pottery, domestication of the dog, pig, chicken, cattle and water buffalo, hunting of various birds and such mammals as deer, rhinoceros, elephant and monkeys, while tools and other implements include hoes made of animal scapulae, matting and rope, stone adzes, pottery spindle whorls, which suggest that true loom weaving was practiced, and evidence for carpentry and boat building. Both the dating of this site and the content of its material culture fit very well with a hypothesis that it was part of a cultural tradition which spread southward during the fifth millennium B.C., first along the island-dotted coast of Zhejiang and Fujian provinces, and then in time to the large and sparsely inhabited island of Taiwan.

The extraordinarily rich material culture unearthed at Hemudu raises questions about the generally less impressive inventory of later archaeological sites in Taiwan. Was there significant culture loss during the initial migration from mainland China, or do the earliest known Neolithic sites on Taiwan conceal—or at least fail to reveal— what might be called an 'invisible culture' of perishable materials? For the archaeologist these are difficult, perhaps for now even unresolvable, questions, but for the linguist the answers are gloriously clear: PAN reconstructions for rice and millet, dog, domesticated and wild pig, water buffalo, weaving, matting, rope and housepost among others point to a material culture on Taiwan around 4,000 B.C. which appears to have been remarkably similar to that of Hemudu on the mainland of China a millennium earlier. In time, with luck, we may witness the discovery of an equally well-preserved site in Taiwan which confirms these well-established linguistic inferences. And when that time comes, I hope that I am still around to tell my archaeologist colleagues in a spirit of friendly rivalry "I told you so!"

4. ARCHAEOLOGY OF SOUTHEASTERN COASTAL CHINA AND ITS BEARING ON THE AUSTRONESIAN HOMELAND[1]

Kwang-chih Chang
Harvard University

Ward H. Goodenough
University of Pennsylvania

THE ISLAND of Taiwan is peculiarly important in the effort to identify the probable homeland of the Proto-Austronesians before they spread into insular Southeast Asia and the Pacific. Before the first arrival there of Han Chinese immigrants in the seventeenth century, Taiwan was populated exclusively, as far as we have evidence, by people speaking Austronesian languages. Therefore, if we can trace an archaeological continuum from that time back to some earlier time, a continuum that shows no evidence of having been disrupted by population movements into the island involving other language families, we can state with confidence that the archaeological culture or cultures in Taiwan at that earlier point belonged to the ancestors of the modern Taiwan Austronesians. We proceed, then, to examine the cultures of Taiwan at the early end of the continuum and their distribution outside of Taiwan. These cultures go back in time over 6,000 years. This time depth is significant in light of linguistic evidence regarding the Austronesian homeland.

At present there are up to three hundred thousand so-called aborigines in Taiwan. They still speak a variety of Austronesian languages. The mountain tribes (ethnic or language groups) remain largely unsinicized, but the tribes in the plains to the west have been heavily sinicized. The twelve unsinicized tribes, each still with its own language, are Atayal, Sedeq, Tsou, Kanakanabu, Saaroa, Amis, Paiwan, Bunun, Puyuma, Rukai, Saisiyat, and Yami. The heavily sinicized tribes include the Kavalan, Pazeh, Thao, Ketagalan, Luilang, Taokas, Papora, Babuza, Hoanya, and Siraya (Figure 4). The languages of all but the first three among these ten sinicized tribes are now extinct (Sung 1989, Li 1992).

Linguistically, the aboriginal Taiwanese fall into three groups:

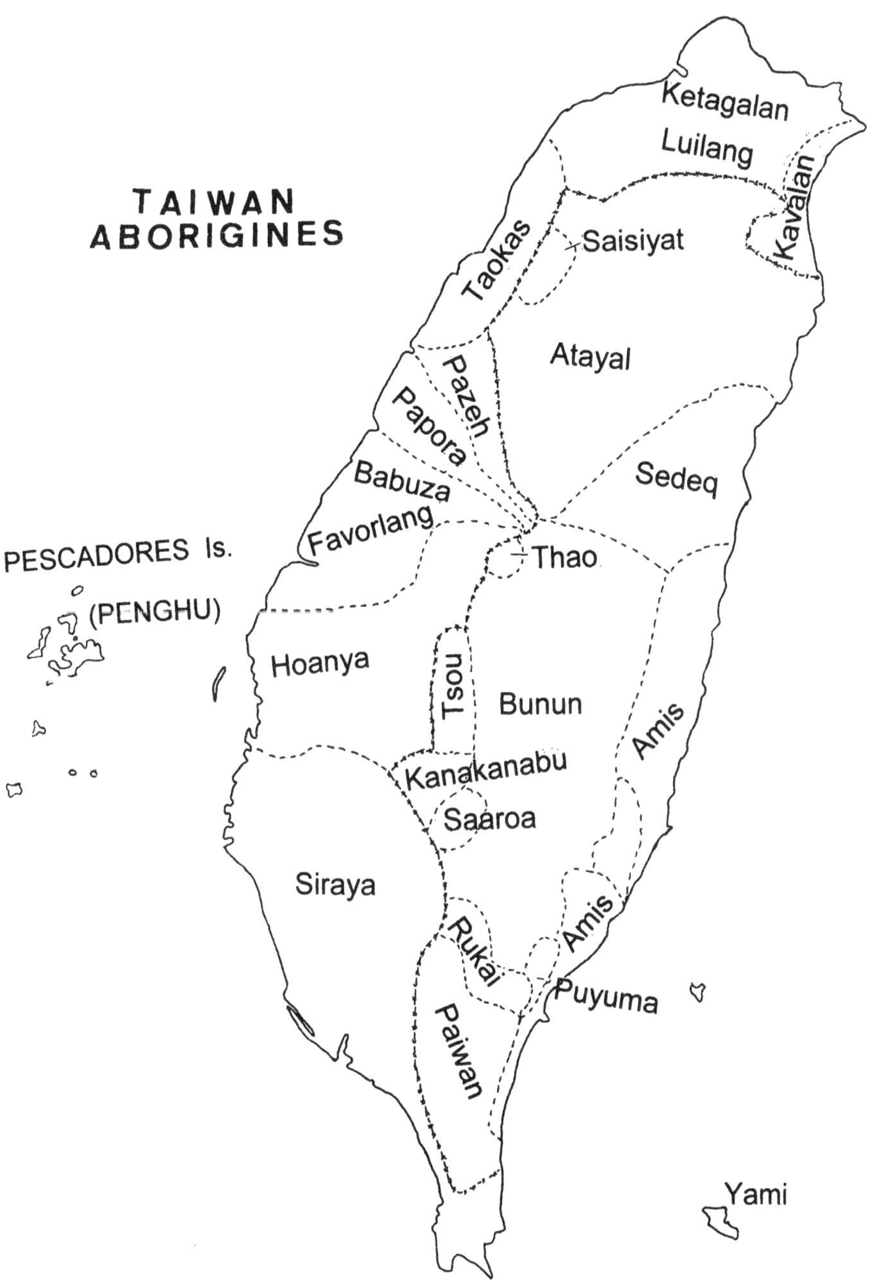

Figure 4. Map of Taiwan showing location of aboriginal tribal groups.

Atayalic (Atayal and Sadeq), Tsouic (Tsou, Kanakanabu, Saaroa, and possibly Rukai), and Paiwanic in two major subdivisions (I: Pazeh, Saisiyat, Favorlang, Thao, Paiwan, Puyuma, and possibly Rukai; II: Siraya, Bunun, Amis, Kuvalan, and Yami) (Sung 1989). These three groups are currently understood to represent three of the four oldest sub-phyla within the Austronesian language phylum (Blust 1980). The fourth sub-phylum, known as Malayo-Polynesian, includes all the other extant Austronesian languages, i.e. those not in Taiwan itself. Thus Taiwan appears to be geographically closer to the homeland from which Austronesian languages spread than any other place where these languages are still spoken.

The seventeenth century, when large-scale immigration of Han Chinese into Taiwan began, is the earliest point in time for which we have written evidence of the Taiwanese Austronesians. The immigrants left voluminous records of their encounters with the aboriginal tribes on the plains. As we go back from the seventeenth century, however, we find textual records becoming sparse and then completely unavailable. Archaeology has to take over. It is important to point out that archaeological data by themselves do not tell us what language the people who produced them spoke. If, however, the cultures of the people who now speak Austronesian languages can be shown to form a continuum going back through time, then we can infer that these earlier people spoke an older form of Austronesian. Without going into the details of the sequence of Taiwan's archaeological cultures (Sung and Lien 1989), we can simply state that they do constitute a continuum to at least 3200 B.C. and probably as far back as 4,500 B.C., the beginning of the Dapenkeng culture.

The Dapenkeng Culture

Dapenkeng (Ta-p'en-k'eng) is the earliest known archaeological culture in Taiwan associated with both pottery and agriculture. It has a wide distribution, ranging from the sites of Dapenkeng and Yuanshan (the lowest level) in northern Taiwan to Bajiacun (Pa-chia-ts'un) in south central Taiwan and the lowest level of Fengbitou (Feng-pi-t'ou) in southwestern Taiwan (Figure 5). Its material inventory (Chang 1970, 1986, 1989a; Huang 1989) includes:

(1) POTTERY. Fragile and heavily eroded potsherds, usually fragmentary, are thick, and gritty. Their color ranges from cream to dark brown. Large globular jars and bowls are the major shapes. Low and perforated ring feet are often found attached to the bottoms of the jars. The rims have medium flare, and many have a circumferential

ridge or carination below the lip. The entire body of each vessel is invariably impressed with cord marks, probably applied with a cord-wrapped stick or paddle, but the rim is never so impressed. Rim surfaces and, frequently, the upper part of the shoulder are decorated with incised designs composed of wavy lines and short parallel strokes, applied with a comb or shell. At Bajiacun, some of the shards were impressed with the external surface or the edge of molluscan shells (probably shells of *Anadara granosa*). Objects of clay or similar paste include spindle-whorls and pot-supports.

(2) PECKED PEBBLES. Only a small number of stone types are known to be associated with the cord-marked pottery. Among them worked pebbles are the most common. These are natural river pebbles, at most 20 cm. across, with pecked and flaked ends, sides, or circumferences, or all three. They were probably used as net sinkers.

(3) BARK BEATER. A fragment of a stone bark beater, for making barkcloth (tapa), with a polished and grooved surface was discovered from the Dapenkeng cultural level (lowest stratum) at the Yuanshan site (Chang 1989a:544 and 1989b:87).

(4) STONE ADZES. Most of the adzes, of a variety of rocks, are highly polished, asymmetrical of edge, and rectangular in cross section. A few have two small notches or depressions on a side, reminiscent of the "steps" of the stepped adzes in the subsequent assemblages at Yuanshan.

(5) POINTS. Small (ca. 4 cm. long) points of greenish slate are often found. They are invariably thin, flat, triangular, and perforated at the center.

Dapenkeng subsistence appears to have been based on a combination of gardening, hunting, and fishing. The relative importance of cultivated root and tuber crops in comparison with rice is, as yet, unclear. The transition from Dapenkeng to the next phase of prehistoric cultures involved numerous and significant changes. Whether these later cultures were developments out of the Dapenkeng or, indeed, were brought by new immigrants from outside Taiwan has been a subject of debate for many years (Tsang 1990). The current consensus is that the Dapenkeng population continued and contributed to the development of the later regional cultures as a result of intensive contact with cultures in nearby Fujian (Chang 1989a:544 and 1989b:94-95; Tsang 1990:9-11). As we shall see, it is probable that these outside cultures were associated with peoples who were also speakers of Austronesian languages.

Mainland Affiliations of Dapenkeng

Since Dapenkeng is the earliest culture in the archaeological continuum of Taiwan that can be identified as probably belonging to ancient speakers of Austronesians languages, Taiwan assumes great importance in regard to the source of the Austronesian diaspora, if not of ultimate Austronesian origins. It shows that Austronesians lived on Taiwan as early as 4500 B.C., almost two millennia before any archaeological evidence of Austronesian movements into Malaysia and the Pacific (Bellwood 1985).

As to the beginning of the Dapenkeng culture, there are no data to indicate that it originated within Taiwan, where preceramic materials are very sparse. Therefore, we must look to see if there are archaeological cultures identical with or similar to Dapenkeng in the neighboring areas, i.e., Japan, Korea, eastern and southeastern coastal areas of the Chinese mainland, and the Philippines. If such cultures can be identified, then we can begin to expand the possible homeland of the Proto-Austronesians from Taiwan to a larger area.

So far, no assemblages remotely resembling Dapenkeng have been reported from Japan, Korea, or eastern coastal China north of the Yangzi River. In the Philippines, in northern Luzon, we get a different picture. The archaeological data have been reviewed by Bellwood, (1985: 222-232). Pottery and other cultural materials are somewhat like those of the Dapenkeng and later Yuanshan (see below) cultures of Taiwan, but they do not seem to date reliably to earlier than 3000 B.C. Bellwood concludes (1985:232) that there was a southward movement into northern Luzon from Taiwan. Thus Luzon gives evidence of a southward spread of neolithic culture from Taiwan but cannot be seen as the source of the Dapenkeng culture.

The southeast coast of China, by contrast, shows cultures with strong affinities with Dapenkeng. Such similarity between cultures located in and on opposite sides of the Taiwan Strait is not surprising. It is noteworthy that this strait has a maximum width of 90 miles and an average depth of only 120-240 feet (450-96 meters) (Pearson 1989: 115-116). On a clear day, moreover, the mountains of Taiwan are visible to the naked eye on mainland China from the north coast of northern Fujian, a phenomenon mentioned as early as the sixth century A.D. in the *Sui Shu* (Huang 1989:71). These observations help explain what could have led people to move, given a means of transportation, from coastal mainland China to island Taiwan at such an early date.

Archaeological sites on the mainland showing similarities with Dapenkeng range from northern Fujian province, just opposite northern

Taiwan, southward along the coastal areas of Fujian and Guangdong, as far as the coasts of the Gulf of Tonkin (Figure 5). Chronologically many of these sites fall into the fifth millennium B.C., contemporaneous with Dapenkeng. The better reported sites are listed and briefly described in the Appendix to this paper.

These sites contain cord-marked pottery with comb and shell-edge patterns on the rims. Among the sites we also find worked pebbles, polished adzes, points with holes in the center, and grooved beaters for making bark cloth.[2]

The most significant of the mainland sites is, perhaps, Fuguodun on Jinmen Island (Quemoy), Fujian. Pottery designs on shards from this site show a statistical difference from those at Dapenkeng. The surface of many Fuguodun shards is cord-marked, but a higher percentage shows dentate stamping with shells. In the pottery from Dapenkeng, by contrast, cord-marked decoration predominates over dentate stamping. The two cultures are strikingly similar in other respects. At least one scholar (Chang 1989a:545) considers them to be two facets of the same larger cultural complex.

Thus, although the coastal assemblages of Fujian and Guangdong dating to the fifth millennium B.C. are not identical with Taiwan's Dapenkeng, a systematic comparison of both pottery and lithic inventories from the sites in Taiwan and the southeastern coastal areas of mainland China shows enough similarity to allow us to regard them as representing regional manifestations of a single cultural tradition (Chang 1989a; Huang 1989:80-81). We must bear in mind that archaeological research in Fujian and Guangdong has barely begun and that there is much in the Dapenkeng culture of Taiwan that remains unexplored (e.g., the highly important site of Bajiacun, as of this writing, has not yet been excavated). Nevertheless, the admittedly sparse data at hand point clearly to an ancestral homeland for Taiwan's aborigines in the coastal areas of southeastern China, most immediately Fujian.

Two large questions remain.The first pertains to the wider affinities and possible origin of this southeast coastal corded ware or Dapenkengian culture, and the second pertains to its subsequent fate, both on the mainland and in Taiwan. These questions bear importantly on our understanding of the homeland of the Proto-Austronesians and on the culture that their descendants carried southward into the Philippines, Indonesia, and the Pacific.

As to the first question, if the people of Dapenkeng are to be associated with speakers of Austronesian languages, we must conclude

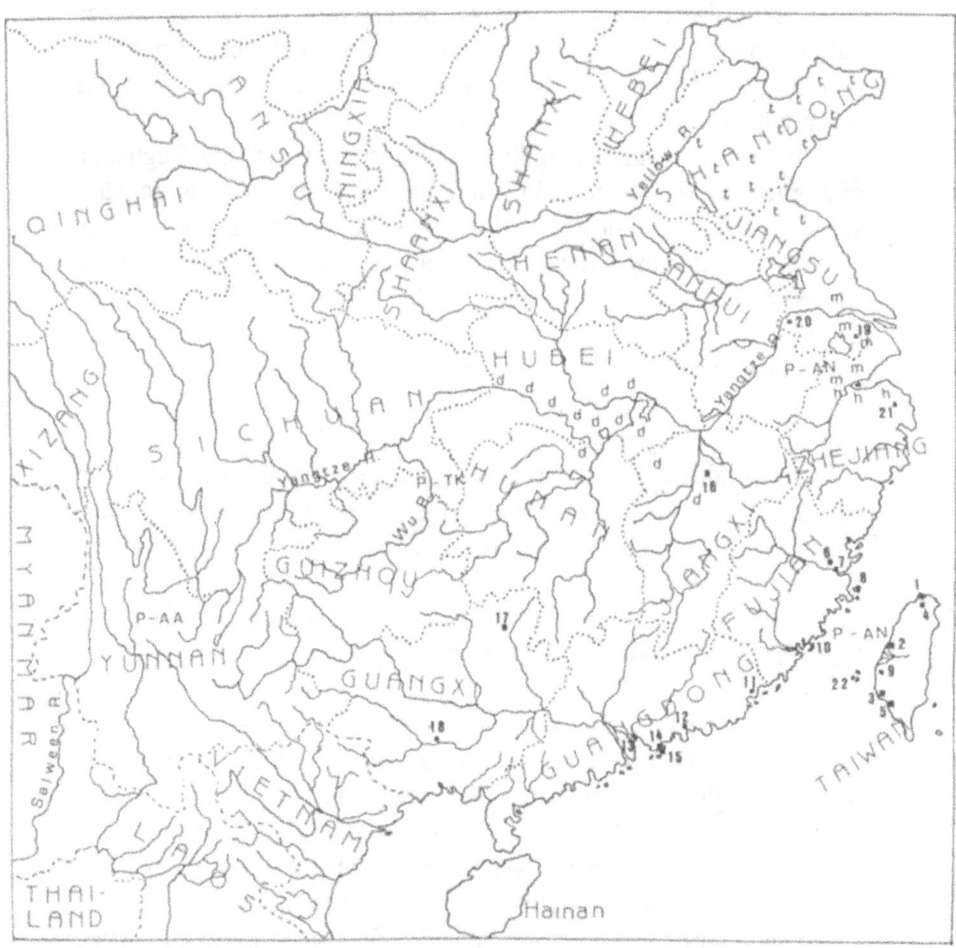

Figure 5. Map of South China. Archaeological sites: 1.Dapenkeng, 2. Yingpu, 3. Niuchouzi, 4. Yuanshan. 5. Fengbitou, 6. Tanshishan, 7. Xitou, 8. Kequitou, 9. Niumatou, 10. Fuquodun, 11. Chenqiao, 12. Northern Shakenq, 13. Panyu, 14. Xiantouling, 15. Dahuangsha, 16. Xienjandung 17. Qengpiyen, 18. Nanning, 19. Coaxieshan, 20. Beiyinyangying, 21. Hemudu, 22. Penghu. d d d = area of Daxi Culture sites, h h h = area of Hemudu Culture sites, m m m = area of Majiabang Culture sites, t t t = area of Dawenkou and Longshan Culture sites. P-AA = *suggested* regions of Proto-Austroasiatic languages, P- AN suggested regions of Proto-Austronesian languages, P-TK suggested regions of Proto-Tai-Kadai languages.

that the ultimate homeland of the Proto-Austronesians was on the mainland of Southeast China. Of interest in this regard are sites in Guangxi, at Nanning and Zengpiyan (Tseng-p'i-yen), and in Jiangxi, at Xianjendong (Hsien-jen-tung) (Figure 5). These sites also show related corded ware pottery with dates earlier than Dapenkeng and the corded ware sites in Fujian. The lower cultural level at Xienjendung has been radiocarbon dated to 6875 B.C. (Huang 1989:59). This wider, older distribution in interior South China of the corded ware neolithic cultures suggests that the Proto-Austronesians of the Dapenkeng culture shared in an older and more widespread cultural tradition in southeastern China. It appears to have been located in the early seventh millennium B.C. in the lower Yangzi basin, especially south of the Yangzi in the valleys of the rivers that fed northward into it, and to have been carried thence in the fifth millennium B.C. to the coastal areas of Fujian and Guangdong, and from Fujian to Taiwan.

This larger region of interior and coastal Southeast China corresponds to that occupied by what Chinese geographers of the later first millennium B.C. referred to as the Bai ('many') Yue peoples. Huang (1989), citing the work of Ling Shun-sheng, argues plausibly that Taiwan aborigines were a part of this larger group of Yue peoples. He also suggests that the Yue were largely, if not entirely, most probably speakers of Austronesian languages. That the Bai Yue were all or predominantly Austronesian is widely disputed.[3] But there is reason to believe that the Min Yue (Yue of the Min River region) of northern Fujian were Austronesian speaking. They remained independent from the rest of China well into the first millennium A.D., and there is historical evidence that an Austronesian language was still spoken in Fujian as late as A.D. 620 (Huang 1989:79-80).

Given that evidence shows a close cultural relationship between Dapenkeng on Taiwan and Fuguodun in Fujian during the fifth and fourth millennia B.C., given the reasonable inference that the associated peoples spoke early Austronesian languages, and given evidence, just cited, that an Austronesian language was spoken in Fujian as late as the beginning of the seventh century A.D., we expect that Taiwan, Fujian, and northern Guangdong would continue to share cultural traditions in subsequent periods. Indeed, this is just what we find.

First, in the latter part of the third millennium B.C., we find cultures, to be discussed below, appearing in northern Fujian and Taiwan with features diagnostic of what has been termed the Longshanoid horizon (Chang 1986). These are in turn followed by cultures in Fujian and Taiwan with geometric pottery in the first millennium

B.C. (Huang 1989). These changes reflected southern extensions of cultural influences from the lower Yangzi region, where the older Dapenkeng related cultures had developed into much more elaborated ones by as early as 5000 B.C.

Cultural Developments in the Lower Yangzi

Five hundred years before the Depenkeng and related coastal corded-ware cultures appeared in Fujian and Taiwan, their ancestral neolithic cultures in the lower Yangzi were undergoing considerable elaboration (Bellwood 1985:219). This region has been a major population center in China from prehistoric times and enjoyed a subtropical climate from 7000 to 5000 B.C. (Chang 1986:193-194). Two cultures in this region in northern Zhejiang are particularly important. They are rich in cultural remains, including organic remains usually lost to the archaeologist, which enable us to construct a fuller picture of the developing agricultural communities in this area. Significant for us, as just stated, is the relationship these cultures have with those farther south in Fujian and Guangdong.

One is the Hemudu (Ho-mo-tu) culture (Kaogu Xuebao 1978; Zhao and Wu 1986-87; Chang 1986) (Figure 5). Just to the south of Hangzhou Bay, it is represented by a number of sites, radiocarbon dated from c. 5000-4500 B.C. (Huang 1989:64), followed by later phases to c.3000 B.C. (Bellwood 1985:219-222; Chang 1986:208-212). The excavated site of this name was a village surrounded by forests, ponds, and rivers, with a vast and abundant supply of natural resources. Houses, built on piles with plank floors, were of frame construction involving sophisticated mortise-and-tenon joinery. Rice remains are everywhere. The people also ate bottle gourds, acorns, water-caltrop, and possibly fox nut. Leaf remains show that the climate at the time was still subtropical. Animal remains include monkeys, deer, elaphure, muntjiak, water deer, rhinoceros, elephant, tiger, bear, smaller mammals, and many kinds of fowl and birds.There are remains of alligator, turtle, and tortoise and, also, of fresh-water, estuarial, and marine fishes, most commonly the fresh-water carp. Animal bones included those of dog and pig, probably domesticated. Clay figurines show sheep as well. The cultural remains reveal not only a life based on farming, hunting, and fishing, but considerable wealth as reflected in the workmanship of arts and crafts.

Hemudu pottery is distinctive. The handmade ware is black, tempered with charcoal powder (from tempering with plant stems and leaves). It is thick and porous. The surface of the vessels was burnished, but was also commonly decorated with cord impressions and incisions. The most common type was the cooking pot, sometimes with a waist ring. Other forms were urns, bowls, shallow plates, basins, vessel lids, and pot supports. Flat and round bottoms were common, and there were only a few tripods. The assemblage looks like one that had its roots in the corded-ware tradition (Chang 1986:212; Huang 1989), being an elaboration out of it. "While the pottery tradition clearly has more variation in form than the Ta-p'en-k'eng [Dapenkeng] and Yuanshan cultures in Taiwan, it shows that the totality of potting knowledge found in the early island cultures was already present in this region a millennium before the beginning of Austronesian expansion" (Bellwood 1985:219).

The second of these two cultures is the Majiabang (Ma-chia-pang) (Figure 5), which with its later Songze (Sung-tse) phase dates from c. 4200-3000 B.C. (Bellwood 1985:219-222; Chang 1986:192-206). It is known from a series of sites between the Yangzi River and Hangzhou Bay, especially between the modern cities of Shanghai and Nanjing, in the area of lake Tai (T'ai-hu), but is also considered a successor phase to Hemudu, which was immediately to the south (Bellwood 1985:219; Huang 1989:65).

The Majiabang people built their houses on natural or artificially constructed mounds near rivers and ponds. Their rectangular houses were built with timber frames, using sophisticated joinery (as in the Hemudu), the floors paved with sand, molluscan shells, or clay. They were intensive rice growers, with two varieties of rice. Other plant foods included water-caltrop and bottle gourd.Their domesticated animals apparently included the pig, water buffalo, and dog, possibly also chickens (Bellwood 1985:222). They also subsisted by hunting, which the vast amount of animal remains shows to have been very important, as well as by fishing and gathering. They buried their dead in single graves, mostly in the prone position with only a few tools, ornaments, and vessels as grave goods. The custom of tooth extraction, also practiced in Taiwan, is evident from burial remains (Huang 1989:76).[4] Pottery was reddish or reddish gray. Round-bottomed pots with a ring at the waist predominated. Distinctive types were vessels with tripods and bowls or cups on pedestals. There were also shallow plates with carinated rims and a flat based, spouted water jug. There were clay pot supports, paddles, and animal figurines. Most pottery vessels had plain surfaces, but there were occasional red slips, hollow-outs, depressions, and incised designs. Of special importance is the fragment of textile (China's oldest) from the Majiabang site of Caoxieshan (Archaeological Institute 1984).

In the succeeding Songze phase, the extended burials were oriented with the head to the southeast, rather than, as before, to the north. There were more grave goods, and tripod vessels and pedestaled bowls were standard burial items. The tripod pot largely replaced the round-bottomed pot for cooking. Storage jars and urns were much more numerous. Pottery decoration was considerably more varied and sophisticated.

The Hemudu and Majiabang cultures are roughly contemporaneous with a series of highly developed neolithic cultures distributed westward along the Yangzi River. A culture much like later phases of Majiabang is known from a cemetery at Beiyinyangying (Pei-yin-yang-ying) near Nanjing, dating to about 3700 B.C. (Bellwood 1985:222; Chang 1986:206). Farther west are the Daxi (Ta-hsi) culture (Figure 2), from c. 4000 B.C. and earlier, and the later Chujialing (Ch'u-chia-ling) from c. 3000 B.C. They are known from the eastern border area of Sichuan eastward along the Yangzi and its tributary rivers through southern Hubei and northern Hunan. The Daxi culture is best known from the region of Lake Dongting (Tung-t'ing) in northern Hunan (Chang 1986:224).

All of these cultures appear to be outgrowths of the domestication of rice and the kind of settled life it made possible. Wild rice was native to the middle Yangzi basin, and the oldest date for domesticated rice comes from this region at the site of Pengtoushan in northern Hunan, dated perhaps as early as 6000 B.C. (Bellwood 1992a:161, citing Yan 1991). That domesticated rice was known as early as this farther west in the Three Gorges area of western Hubei and eastern Sichuan is suggested by recent archaeological work there showing pottery and stonework dating back at least to 5000 B.C. (Shenon 1994). These developments have important implications for the homeland and spread of two other major language groups in addition to the Austronesian. They are the Tai-Kadai and Austro-Asiatic language families, which may have a distant relationship with the Austronesian family, whose homeland area is ascribed by Blust (chapter 7, this volume) to more western reaches of the Yangzi valley.

We should note also that, as a major highway of trade and population movement, the Yangzi required rather sophisticated boat construction—whether outrigger or otherwise. The carpentry and joinery we find associated with Hemudu and Majiabang house building was of a kind that could have readily fashioned seaworthy vessels as well. The technology required for coastal transportation and for the settlement of Taiwan from Fujian may well have developed earlier in the context of riverine transportation.[5]

The Southward Spread of Cultural Influence

The Hemudu and Majiabang cultures were more advanced in agriculture, arts and crafts, and richness of cultural inventory than the contemporary corded ware cultures in Southeast China and Taiwan. In the period immediately following, we see northern Fujian and then Taiwan and other parts of Southeast China increasingly influenced by later phases of these cultures immediately to the north. It is not clear whether people from the Hangzhou Bay area migrated southward or whether the southern cultures adopted the technology of their more developed northern neighbors as a result of increasing commerce, but some significant movement of people probably accompanied commercial expansion.

The third and fourth centuries B.C. were notable for growing interregional commerce and diffusion of ceramic types over much of China, a process that culminated in the emergence of classical Chinese civilization around 2000 B.C. (Chang 1986). An important site at Longshan (Lung-shan) in Shandong province (Figure 5) in northeastern China has served as point of reference for the many similarities in ceramics over wide regions of North China and in parts of South China, as well. These similarities emerged increasingly in the course of the fourth millennium B.C., resulting in what has been termed the Longshanoid horizon (Chang 1986:238).[6] Some of its diagnostic features, like tripod vessels, were already present to a very minor extent in the Hemudu culture. Additional features, such as pedestaled bowls as well as tripod vessels, were much more evident in the Majiabang culture and were prominent in the latter's later Songze phase. Stone reaping knives of a kind used to harvest millet in north China began to appear in the Majiabang culture, also (Bellwood 1985:222).

Longshanoid features become more pronounced in the lower Yangzi area, thereafter, in the Liangshu (Liang-chu) culture, successor to the Songze phase of Majiabang with dates of c. 3500-2000 B.C. In Fujian and southwestern Taiwan, Longshanoid features become evident in the latter part of the third millennium B.C. The large number of still unexcavated sites in Fujian that appear to date from this later neolithic period indicate that it was a time of great population growth in which many new settlements were being established (Huang 1989:67).

The earliest Longshanoid culture of northern Fujian is known as Tanshishan (T'an-shih-shan), from a site of that name. The site of Xitou, where early Tanshishan materials appear to overly or mingle with corded-ware deposits, has been dated to c. 2300 B.C. (Wang et al. 1983; Archaeological Institute 1984;158-160; Fujian Provincial

Museum 1984; Huang 1989;67). A portion of the pottery of this period is wheel made. There is also evidence that the practice of tooth extraction was associated with the Tanshishan Culture.

The later geometric pottery is largely wheel made and hard, decorated with "checked, meander, cross-hatched, leaf-vein, circlet, chevron, spiral, 'S' shaped and 'cloud thunder' designs" (Huang 1989:70). Bringing knowledge of bronze, it came into Fujian in the first millennium B.C. during the time of the formation of the Yue state, whose capital was established at Kuaiji (K'uai-chi) in the Lake Tai region of the lower Yangzi in 510 B.C. (Huang 1989:71). The Yue state appears to have been a largely indigenous political development among the pre-Han peoples of the lower Yangzi, and is believed by some traditional Chinese historians to have loosely embraced the various Bai Yue peoples of Zhejiang, Jiangxi, Fujian, and Guangdong. This region corresponds with that of the old corded-ware neolithic, and it continued to be one that shared a number of cultural practices, such as tooth extraction, pile building, and cliff burial, practices that continued until relatively recent times in Taiwan (Huang 1989:76-77). Austronesian speakers, we may presume, also still lived in the region down to its conquest and sinification, beginning about 240 B.C. and ending about A.D. 650 (Huang 1989). We must keep in mind, however, that the interior parts of the region that may have been encompassed by the Yue State is also considered to have been home to Tai-Kadai speakers and perhaps Austro-Asiatic speakers, as well. Differentiation among them in the archaeological record is near to impossible, because they all shared similar cultural traits. They all grew rice, lived in houses built on stilts, made pottery, and raised dogs, pigs, and cattle (Peters 1990).

As for Taiwan during this period, remains of the Dapenkeng Culture and its later Red Cord-Marked Culture phase show little variation wherever they are found. Thereafter, we find the appearance of several, somewhat different Longshanoid cultures in the western coastal regions. Relatively early Longshanoid successors to the Dapenkeng culture have been found at Niuchouzi (Niu-ch'ou-tsu) and Niumatou (Niu-ma-t'ou) in south and central Taiwan respectively. Dating from 2500 to 1500 B.C., these sites exhibit pottery mainly decorated with cord markings, but also with incised designs, circlets, and paint (Huang 1989:68). Pottery types include storage jars, pedestaled bowls, stemmed bowls, and tripods. Axes, adzes, arrow-heads, knives, spear points, and net sinkers comprise the stone tools.

Also in central Taiwan was the Yingpu (Ying-p'u) culture. It was typified by greyish-black pottery with some black, burnished ware, mostly in the form of storage jars, pedestaled bowls, tripod vessels, and lugged jars, decorated with feather, dot, incised, and shell patterns. Axes, adzes, spear points, knives, arrowheads, and net sinkers comprised the stone tools. It has been dated to the first and second millennia B.C. (Huang 1989:69).

Contemporaneous with these cultures was the Yuanshan culture of northern Taiwan, dated from 2500 to the first century B.C. Pottery was predominantly a sandy, reddish-brown ware, and black ware was infrequent. The vessel types included double-handed cooking pots, pedestaled bowls, and double-mouthed jars, decorated with punctations, circlets, and net marks. Stone tools included shouldered axes and stepped adzes. The custom of tooth extraction was evident in burials, as was head hunting (Huang 1989:69).

At Fengbitou (Feng-pi-t'ou) in southwestern Taiwan, the Dapenkeng layer is overlain by a massive settlement of Longshanoid culture, differing from Dapenkeng in fundamental ways. Huang (1988:69) dates it from 1500 to 500 B.C. Known as Taiwan's Fine Red Ware Culture, it was heavily agricultural. Its lithic inventory included hoes, harvesting knives, and arrowheads. Its ceramic assemblage contained painted vessels, highly polished black vessels, and fine-ware red vessels. It included large jars, ring-footed bowls, and tripods (Chang et al. 1969). The artifact inventory at Fengbitou resembles that of Tanshishan and other mainland Longshanoid sites (Chang 1986:238-248). Fengbitou has been interpreted as evidence of a significant seaward expansion from Fujian (Huang 1989:74).

The expansion of Longshanoid cultural technology into Fujian and Taiwan has been variously interpreted as representing replacement or absorption of older Dapenkengian peoples by new immigrants, at the one extreme, and as representing diffusion of cultural traits by trade without significant population movement, at the other extreme. Both processes were most probably going on. Movement of Fujian's Yue (also known as the Min Yue) to Taiwan may well have continued down into China's Three Kingdoms Period (A.D. 220-589), when Fujian was finally brought under Han Chinese rule, as Huang (1989) has observed. He argues that the cultural diversity of Longshanoid sites of Taiwan suggests movement into Taiwan at different times from more than one locality on the coast of southeastern China, but all from within the same cultural region of Yue people, presumably also Austronesian speaking. He notes that early neolithic cultures continued to coexist in interior and eastern Taiwan with the Longshanoid cultures located in the western coastal area. Thus he argues, there was both continuity of older populations as well as colonization by later ones; but, within their variations, they were all culturally and linguistically related.

Kirch (1993) sees the cultures immediately following the Dapenkeng in Taiwan, especially the "fine red ware" assemblage at Fengpitou and the materials recently excavated by Tsang (1992) in the Penghu (Pescadores) Islands as having many parallels with the "early Austronesian assemblages in the Philippines, Sabah, Sulawesi, and Timor." These parallels include a number of pottery vessel forms ("pedestaled feet, bowls and restricted orifice jars with everted rims") and numerous stone. bone, and shell artifacts as well. The Penghu sites date significantly to about 2600 B.C.

Implications for the Spread of Austronesian Languages

Our interpretation of the archaeological record takes Proto-Austronesian origins back to the corded-ware neolithic cultures of the lower Yangzi region. These cultures spread southward up the Yangtzi's southern tributaries from Jiangxi into Guangdong and eastern Guangxi, eastward into the region of Lake Tai and Hangzhou Gulf, and south from there down the Zhejian, Fujian, and Guangdong coast and into Taiwan. This is the region that was later associated with the Bai Yue.

The Austronesian peoples who remained in the Yangzi area were soon caught up in the cultural developments that culminated in classical Chinese civilization, as shown in the Hemudu, Majiabang, and later Longshanoid and Geometric Pottery cultures of that area. The last four millennia B.C. were characterized by increasing commerce and cultural diffusion between the various regions of China. Such commerce was largely by water, following the river systems of China and moving down the many small islands dotting the coastal region of southeast China. It testifies to the emergence of efficient water transportation (Chang 1986:410-411). By 2300 B.C. such commerce was clearly manifested in the many settlements of Fujian and the spread of Longshanoid culture to Taiwan. This growing commerce presumably was an important factor leading to the spread of Austronesian speaking peoples into the Philippines, Indonesia, Malaya, and Melanesia. There were no doubt other important factors, but the coincidence of the southward spread of Austronesians from Fujian and Taiwan with growing commerce and the later formation of the Yue State is remarkable.

Peter Bellwood (1985:223) has suggested that the southward movement of the Proto-Austronesians from Taiwan and Southeast China into Indonesia and the Pacific owed its impetus to the introduction of rice agriculture and resultant population growth. Certainly there was great population growth in mainland China before and during the period in question. But there was still no dearth of available agricultural land.

Contrasting with this is the suggestion that the southward spread of Austronesian speaking peoples was in response to a demand for valued marine and tropical forest products (Goodenough 1982). Such products were increasingly scarce on the Chinese mainland, where climatic change and enormous population growth before, during, and after the Longshanoid period created an expanding market for products that had to be sought from farther and farther away. The already maritime, fishing, and coastal trading people of Fujian were perfectly situated to go abroad, first to southern Taiwan and then farther south in search of these products, for some of which, like camphor, Fujian had itself once been an important source. Evidence of such trade with China goes back to the first millennium B.C. with the discovery of coins from the Qin and Han dynasties at the mouth of the Sarawak River (Wang 1958; Runciman 1960:13).[7] At first, southern Taiwan may have served as a source of these tropical forest products; but when the Philippines, Indonesia, and Malaysia became the major sources, Taiwan became an economic backwater. The main ports of trade had also shifted to the Canton area by the middle of the first millennium B.C. (Wang 1958), though Fujian also remained important. Forest products such as rattan, resins, incense wood, camphor, beeswax, gutta-percha latex, besoar stones, rhinoceros horn, and hornbill ivory and feathers are major exports to China from Borneo to this day (Hoffman 1983).

After commercial outposts were established, locally expanding populations would of necessity have become predominantly agricultural, spreading to island interiors, while at the same time continuing to supply their coastal kin with products for export. In most of insular Southeast Asia, emerging states were based on the coastal trading centers at the mouth of rivers, whose watersheds were organized as trading networks, forest products moving down river and imported, prestige products moving up river. Such inland kingdoms as emerged on Java were excep-tional (Hall 1985). The people of Fujian and Guangdong, following sinification, have continued to be active in the ancient trade, being the principal Chinese ethnic groups now in Singapore, Malaysia, and Indo-nesia. Indeed, Quanzhou, in southern Fujian, was the largest port in the Chinese empire for a time early in the second millennium A.D. (Clark 1991:3).

The possibility that the diaspora of Austronesian peoples was driven by commercial considerations rather than by the search for new agricultural land has implications for where archaeologists should look for further evidence of this diaspora, e.g. the recent work in the Penghu Islands (Tsang 1992), which may well have played an important role as a way station in the trade from the Philippines and Indonesia to China.

Fujian, Taiwan, and Proto-Malayo-Polynesian

If Taiwan continued to receive immigrant groups after the initial neolithic settlement characterized by Dapenkeng, what are we to conclude regarding the role of Taiwan in the southward spread of Austronesian languages into island Southeast Asia and the Pacific? What spread south were languages in the great sub-phylum of Austro-nesian known as Malayo-Polynesian. No languages of this sub-phylum are represented in Taiwan today. All Austronesian languages there belong to other major sub-phyla. It has been inferred that this Malayo-Polynesian phylum of Austronesian had its beginnings in northern Luzon as the earliest southward colony from Taiwan (Bellwood 1985). It may be, however, that its roots should be associated with Fujian as the source of its southward expansion, rather than with Taiwan. From this viewpoint the culture of the Proto-Malayo-Polynesian sub-phylum would have been characterized more by Majiabang and the Longshanoid cultures of Fujian, like the Tanshishan, than by the Dapenkeng neolithic of Taiwan.

If this is so, then it appears that there was an earlier spread of Austronesian speakers into Fujian and Taiwan associated with Dapenkeng and the corded-ware cultures. This was followed by a later spread of Austronesian speakers of Longshanoid culture, who moved into western Taiwan, and by a southward expansion of Proto-Malayo-Polynesian speakers from Fujian, perhaps represented by the distinctive Fengbitou site in southwestern Taiwan, serving as one of the way stations in the developing network of trade between China and insular Southeast Asia. This interpretation fits the historical linguistic evidence that allows us to reconstruct for Proto-Austronesian possibly and for Proto-Malayo-Polynesian certainly a culture that knew the cultivation of both rice and millet and that had a degree of craft sophistication much more like that described for Hemudu and Majiabang than for Dapenkeng (Blust 1976 and chapter 3, this volume).

NOTES

1. The authors are indebted to Dr. Heather Peters for a substantial contribution to this paper in the form of constructive comments and suggested additions to an earlier draft.

2. Cord-marked pottery is found widely in other parts of China. Such pottery, with features roughly similar to those found at these Fujian and Guang-

dong sites, is also found in the northern part of Vietnam and Thailand, dating to the sixth millennium B.C. There it occurs in connection with later phases of the Hoabinhian and Bacsonian Cultures (Mansuy 1924; Colani, 1927; Hig-ham 1989:43-65), whose earlier phases (going back to 10,000 B.C.) were associated with a hunting and gathering subsistence economy. This pottery may be associated with the introduction of rice there. Its connection with Dapen-kengian pottery, other than being part of a broadly distributed general type, is unclear. We may have evidence here of the southward spread into Thailand and inland Vietnam of speakers of Austro-Asiatic languages (see Blust, chapter 7 of this volume).

3. Scholars from mainland China argue that the Bai Yue were speakers of languages in the Tai-Kadai language family (Peters 1990). They interpret the alleged "dispersion" of the Bai Yue in the latter part of the 3rd century B.C. (recorded in the 1st century B.C. text, the *Shi Ji*) as the occasion of the dis-persal of Tai speakers throughout China, following on the conquest and linguistic assimilation of much of the Bai Yue area (but not Fujian) during the Qin (Ch'in) Dynasty. Bai Yue is generally regarded by most scholars as a term used by Northerners for non-Han "barbarians" living in southern regions who spoke a number of different languages (Norman and Lin 1976; Ballard 1981). In any event the non-Sinitic languages that remain represented presently in southern China are all members of three languages families: Austroasiatic, Miao-Yao, and Tai-Kadai. Benedict (1942) has produced considerable evidence for a distant phylogenetic relationship between the Tai-Kadai family and Austronesian in a super-family. He has subsequently argued, more contro-versially, that Miao-Yao languages are also a branch of this super-family, which he named Austro-Tai (Benedict 1975). These more distant proposed relationships of Austronesian languages are discussed by Blust (this volume, chapter 7). The Bai Yue, we must presume, did not speak languages belonging to other than the three families still extant in South China and the Austronesian family, still extant in Taiwan. If other language families were represented among the Bai Yue at the end of the first millennium B.C., they have left no trace and must have had a very limited geographical distribution.

4. Tooth extraction was not peculiar to Majiabang, but was found as far north as the contemporary Dawenkou culture (c. 4500 B.C.), which preceded the Longshan culture in Shandong Province (Chang 1986:162) (Figure 2).

5. Relevant to this discussion is evidence from physical anthropology, which indicates that the Hemudu people with "long heads, low faces, and flat, broad noses" differed from populations in the Yellow River Valley and the Northeast Coast of China, but resembled those from the middle and lower Yangzi Valley and from Southeast China and Taiwan (Hsu and Lindruff 1988:13).

6. The Longshanoid horizon is no longer seen as resulting from a large-scale expansion of Longshanoid people. Recent archaeological data support seeing it as a consequence of intensified interaction among regional cultures, giving rise to the overlapping, similar features found among them (Chang 1989b:94). A modern analogy is the emergence of a globally shared industrial technology and its products among otherwise regionally distinct nations, cultures, and languages.

7. Peters (1983, 1986) discusses at length the trade in exotic products between the Chu state (in Hobei and Hunan) and the deep south of China during the mid first millennium B.C. She proposes that some of these products may have

been imported from insular Southeast Asia. Evidence for this trade was found in the mid 1970s when archaeologists excavated a Qin Dynasty boatyard with the remains of seafaring vessels just outside Guangzhou (Canton). This is the locus of the ancient city of Panyu (Figure 5), probably a port of trade, known from historical sources as early as the Han Dynasty (Wenwu 1977).

APPENDIX: CORDED WARE SITES ON SOUTHEAST COAST OF CHINA

1. XITOU, IN BAISHA, MINHOU, NORTHERN FUJIAN (Fujian Provincial Museum 1984; Wang et al. 1983).

The Neolithic site near Xitou is located on the northern bank of the Min River near its mouth, and it has two cultural layers. The upper layer contains an assemblage of pottery and lithic artifacts similar to those at Tanshishan in northern Fujian and is representative of the culture that immediately succeeded the corded ware cultures of Fujian. The lower layer includes a small amount of gritty potsherds with rows of comb designs and shell-edge tooth patterns. The upper layer culture is regarded by some as intrusive and by others as an indigenous development. This disagreement has a strong bearing on the issue of the fate of the Dapenkengian cultures.

2. KEQIUTOU, PINGTAN ISLAND, FUJIAN (Fujian Provincial Museum 1991).

Pingtan Island is off the Fujian coast, not far from the mouth of the Min River. Several sites have been uncovered here, but Keqiutou is the most important. The lithic artifacts here include worked pebbles, polished adzes, and points with holes at the center. The potsherds were paddled, impressed, incised, dotted, and punctated. The impressed designs were either corded or shell-edged, and the incisions, dots, and punctations were done with molluscan shells. Three radio-carbon dates from Keqiutou place the site at close to 3000 B.C.

3. FUGUODUN, JINMEN ISLAND, FUJIAN (Lin 1973).

This is the first archaeological assemblage of this type found in Fujian, discovered by geologist Lin Chaoqi in 1968. Only a small number of potsherds were collected.They were cord-marked and combed with the edge of molluscan shells, probably those of *Andata granosa*.Three radiocarbon dates place the site within the fifth millen-nium B.C.

4.CHENQIAO, CHAO'AN COUNTY, EASTERN GUANGDONG (Cultural Relics Commission of Guangdong 1961)

The brief report of this site, found in the late 1950s, spoke of potsherds decorated with shell-incised designs.

5. NORTHERN SHAKENG, HAIFENG COUNTY, EASTERN GUANGDONG (Maglioni 1975).

Pottery with combed designs came to light as early as the 1930s in the Haifeng district of eastern Guangdong, investigated by Rafael Maglioni, but the pottery did not receive wide attention until 1970 when his report with photographs was posthumously published.

6. XIANTOULING AND DAHUANGSHA, SHENZHEN, CENTRAL GUANGDONG.

In recent years, because of accelerated economic development in the Pearl Delta region, especially in the city of Shenzhen, many neo-lithic sites have been uncovered, but few if any of these sites have been fully published. On the basis of an illustrated catalogue of some artifacts found in Shenzhen (Chung and Qu 1991), two sites on the seacoast in the eastern end of Shenzhen are particularly noteworthy, i.e., Xiantouling and Dahuangsha. Among the lithic objects, the pecked pebbles at Xiantouling and the grooved (tapa?) beaters at Dahuangsha are strictly Dapenkengian.The surface of many pottery remains is impressed with coarse cord-marks and punctated, incised, and impressed with wavy lines, cross-hatches, parallel strokes, and zoned geometric patterns, many apparently with the edge of molluscan shells. There is no question that these sites contain ceramic components comparable with Fuguodun, Keqiutou, and Bajiacun. The Dahuangsha site has yielded a single radiocarbon date of 5600+200 b.p. (The Museum of Zhuhai City *et al*, 1991), which could place the relevant component into the late fifth or early fourth millennium B.C., contemporary with the Dapenkeng of Taiwan and Fujian.

5. LAPITA AND ITS AFTERMATH: THE AUSTRONESIAN SETTLEMENT OF OCEANIA

PATRICK V. KIRCH
University of California at Berkeley

In *Mr. Bligh's Bad Language*, historian Greg Dening writes that "history is more likely to be born on beaches, marginal spaces in between land and sea." "Beaches," Dening speculates, are landscapes where "everything is relativised a little, turned around, where tradition is as much invented as handed down, where otherness is both a new discovery and a reflection of something old" (1992:177). In the mid-second millennium B.C., the coral sand beaches of the Bismarck Archipelago in western Melanesia became just such landscapes of new discovery and past reflection. On beaches with exotic names such as Talepakemalai, Etakosarai, and Apalo, sea-faring strangers who spoke one or more Austronesian languages encountered indigenous people of the land, descendants of the Pleistocene migrants who had first crossed the water barriers into Sahul or Greater Australia more than 35,000 years earlier.[1] On these tropical beaches between land and sea, a meeting of cultures would transform the face of Melanesia, and within a few short centuries precipitate one of the greatest migratory feats of human history: the conquest of the vast Pacific Ocean and settlement of its myriad islands.

The history (or prehistory) of the discovery and settlement of the Pacific Islands by its indigenous inhabitants is one of the oldest and most enduring intellectual issues of Oceanic anthropology, one that continues to drive current research agendas. The methods and approaches to this issue, however, have changed substantially over the years. Earlier in this century, pioneer ethnographers such as Rivers (1914) and Burrows (1939) attempted historical reconstructions based on regional ethnographic comparisons. Because such comparisons were often unsystematic and lacked direct historical controls, they were rejected by many scholars as "conjectural history" without serious academic merit. Linguistic efforts to address the origins and movements of Pacific peoples has a long and somewhat more respectable tradition, which has been greatly strengthened in recent decades, as reviewed by Blust (this volume). Curiously, the one scholarly discipline which takes as its focus the direct, material evidence of human life— *archaeology*—was the last to be intensively applied to the problems of Pacific prehistory. Archaeological fieldwork in Micronesia, Polynesia, and Melanesia has been increasing rapidly in its tempo over the past two to three decades, with the result that the chronology and sequence of the human conquest of Oceania are finally being tied to a framework of securely-dated archaeological assemblages.

As this archaeological research has progressed from the pioneering excavations of E.W. Gifford in Fiji and New Caledonia some four decades ago to the most recent work in the Bismarck Archipelago, the overarching significance of one major archaeological complex for understanding Oceanic prehistory has become increasingly evident. Marked by a highly distinctive kind of earthenware pottery, this complex bears the name *Lapita,*[2] and is found in beach sites throughout a vast expanse of the southwestern Pacific. The archaeological deposits found in the sand of these beaches provide a record—an historical "text" if you will—of the encounters between Austronesian speaking peoples and the indigenous inhabitants of "Old Melanesia," out of which emerged the roots of Oceanic cultural diversity. It is my aim in this paper to review briefly the significance of the Lapita Cultural Complex for Oceanic culture history, especially with regard to the Austronesian-speaking peoples of this island world.

What is Lapita?

Three and one-half millennia after these cultural encounters commenced, archaeologists have begun to uncover within the coral sands of Talepakemalai, Etakosarai, and other Melanesian beaches, material remains which are providing significant new data for reconstructing Pacific prehistory. Excavations—primarily in coastal beach terrace sites, but also in a few rock shelters and caves—have produced abundant evidence of the Lapita archaeological horizon. It is essential at this point to summarize a few key details of Lapita as an archaeological entity: its main material characteristics, and its distribution in time and space.

Fundamentally, Lapita is defined by a highly distinctive ceramic complex or series (Green 1979a; Kirch and Hunt, eds., 1988; Spriggs, ed. 1990). While the pottery assemblages excavated from Lapita sites vary in details of vessel form and decoration, the similarities between assemblages far outweigh the differences, and the makers of Lapita pottery clearly shared a single cultural tradition. Lapita pottery is earthenware, relatively low-fired without the use of kilns, but incorporating an array of pots, jars, dishes, and bowls, some of the latter supported upon flaring pedestal bases. Much of the pottery, especially the larger storage jars, is undecorated plainware, but between 5-15 percent of most assemblages are marked by a complex, sophisticated, and highly stylized decorative system. The designs were impressed into the ceramic surfaces with a series of finely carved, toothed or dentate stamps, probably made of wood or bamboo. The motifs created through the regular combination of a set of individual stamps or design elements follow a rigorous set of artistic conventions or rules, which we can formally reconstruct. These motifs include anthropomorphic faces (Fig-ure 6), and a variety of geometric designs, some of which appear to be stylized transformations of human faces (Spriggs 1990b). Archaeologists have catalogued about 150 distinct motifs—many of which are represented by several allomorphs— and have mapped the distribution of these motifs among Lapita sites.The extremely widespread distribution of Lapita ceramic motifs provides critical evidence that the occupants of these widely-dispersed communities shared a common culture, including artistic conventions.

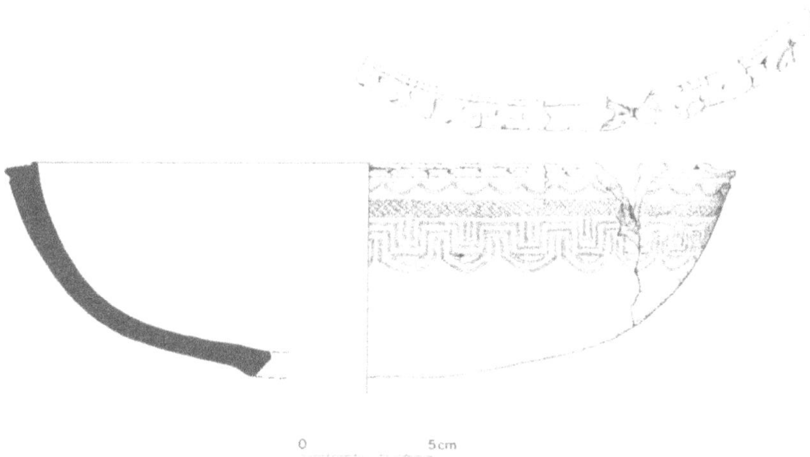

Figure 6. Ceramic bowl, originally supported on a pedestal foot, decorated with classic fine dentate-stamping. Excavated from the Talepakemalai (ECA) site in the Mussau Islands, Papua New Guinea. (Drawing by Margaret Davidson)

But Lapita is more than pots. As Roger Green—one of the pioneers of Lapita archaeology—demonstrated nearly 20 years ago, Lapita constitutes a *cultural complex* of traits, including distinctive settlement patterns, economic subsistence strategies, and non-ceramic material culture. Lapita sites are characteristically situated on beaches, either along the coasts of main islands or frequently on smaller, offshore coral islets (Lepofsky 1988). In these settings at the interface of land and sea, the Lapita people were able to exploit the rich marine resources of the adjacent lagoons and reefs, at the same time that they cleared gardens for tree and root crops inland. Lapita settlements range in size from substantial villages, as represented for example by the extensive Talepakemalai site in the Mussau Islands (Kirch 1988a), down to mid- and small-size hamlets typified by the Nenumbo (RF-2) site in the Reef Islands (Sheppard and Green 1991) and other sites. The architecture of Lapita houses is as yet not well attested, although we know that early settlements in the Bismarck Archipelago included houses elevated on stilts or piles and constructed out over tidal reef flats, while later settlements in the Western Polynesian region seem to have had pole-and-thatch constructions built on beach ridges.

The faunal and botanical remains recovered from Lapita occupations reveal that these people had a broad-spectrum economic base. Anaerobically-preserved nuts and seeds from the Talepakemalai and Arawe sites (Kirch 1989; Gosden 1992) reveal that Lapita gardeners were familiar with most of the key Melanesian tree crops, such as the coconut (*Cocos nucifera*), *Canarium* almond, Vi-apple (*Spondias dulcis*), Tahitian Chestnut (*Inocarpus fagiferus*) and other species. No direct evidence for root crops such as taro or yam has yet been excavated, but these are suggested by the presence of pearl shell peeling knives and scrapers.[3] Faunal remains indicate that Lapita people raised domestic pigs, dogs, and chickens, while also hunting wild birds, and heavily exploiting the rich resources of inshore reefs, lagoons, and the deep sea. Lapita sites are densely packed with fish bones and shellfish from a large number of microhabitats.

Lapita material culture was rich and complex, including woodworking adzes made of stone and shell, culinary implements such as scrapers and peeling knives, and fishing gear such as shell fishhooks (Green 1992; Kirch 1988a). There is as well a wide range of objects usually classified as "ornaments," although these latter may have functioned primarily as exchange valuables (Kirch 1988b), in a manner closely analogous to the famed "shell money" of several ethnographically-attested Melanesian societies. Indeed, exchange at both local and inter-island levels was a key aspect of Lapita, attested archaeologically by the presence of obsidian, chert, exotic pottery, and other material items that can be geochemically "sourced" by archaeologists. Obsidian from the main sources at Talasea (New Britain) and Lou (Admiralty Is.) moved extensively throughout the Bismarck Archipelago, and beyond.

The Lapita Dispersal

Having characterized some key aspects of Lapita, we may move on to the matter of the distributional limits of Lapita in space and time. Geographically, Lapita sites are distributed from the Bismarck Archipelago in the west, through the main Melanesian island arcs (Solomons, Vanuatu, New Caledonia-Loyalties) to Fiji, and beyond to the Polynesian islands of Tonga and Samoa in the east (Figure 7). As the frigate bird flies, this is a straight-line distance of more than 4,000 km. To anyone who has studied Pacific anthropology, that a prehistoric culture should span this particular geographic space is remarkable, for Lapita bridges the classic ethnographic divide between *Melanesia* and *Polynesia.*[4] To earlier generations of ethnologists, the conceptual gulf between Melanesia and Polynesia was vast, yet Lapita archaeology tells us that the varied cultures of these two regions must share a common history.

The temporal dimension of Lapita has been well delimited by more than 150 radiocarbon dates, on samples excavated from sites throughout this geographic region. These dates indicate that the classic Lapita ceramic tradition persisted for about one millennium, beginning ca. 1500 B.C., and ending about 500 B.C. (Kirch and Hunt 1988a, 1988b; Spriggs 1990).[5] The radiocarbon dates also allow us to calibrate approximately the rate of dispersal or movement of Lapita pottery-making groups from west to east. The earliest sites are found in the Bismarck Archipelago at about 3,500 years ago, while the most easterly sites (in Samoa and Tonga) were settled not later than about 3,000 years ago, and perhaps as early as 3,200 years ago. In other words, the dispersal of Lapita over more than 4,000 km was accomplished during a period of between 300 and 500 years. To put this in more directly human terms, if we assume an average of 20 years to a generation, this diaspora took between 15 and 25 human generations to accomplish.

A critical aspect of this eastward Lapita dispersal must be stressed. In his paper in this volume, Jim Allen reviews the significant new evidence that early modern humans were successful in colonizing the larger islands of New Britain, New Ireland, and the Solomons chain about 35,000 years ago (see also Allen 1993). But as far as we can determine, these early populations never pushed beyond the eastern

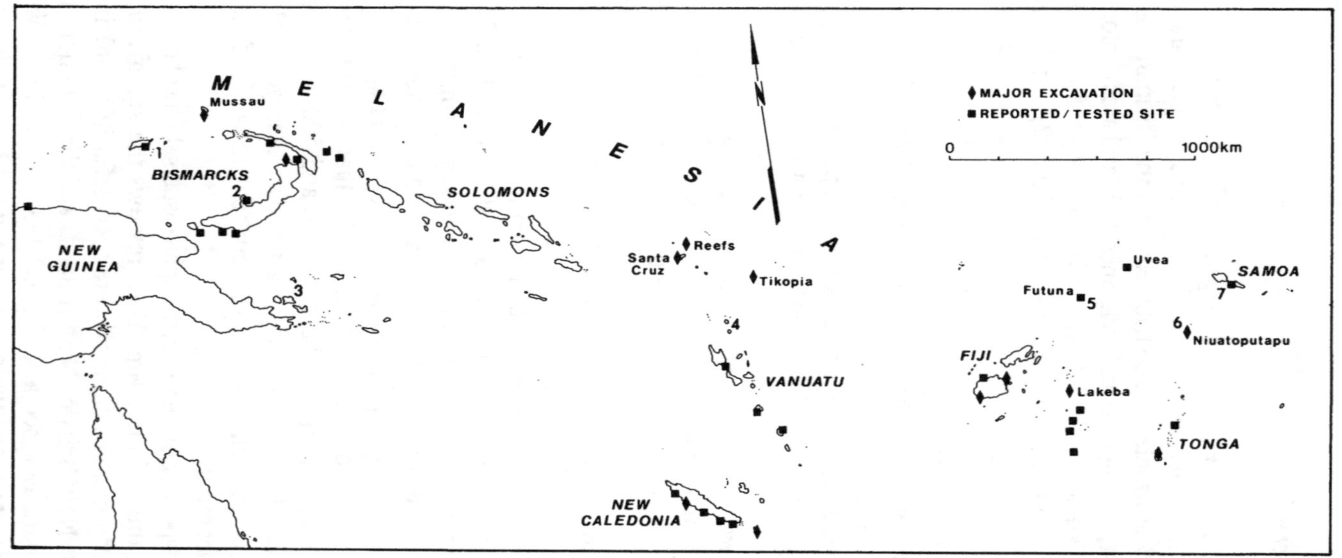

Figure 7. Map of the southwestern Pacific region, showing the locations of known Lapita sites which have been excavated or reported. The numbers refer to obsidian sources, as follows: 1, Admiralty Islands; 2, Willaumez, New Britain; 3, D'Entrecasteaux; 4, Banks Islands; 5, Futuna; 6, Tafahi; and 7, Samoa (Fagaloa).

terminus of the Solomon Islands, where the first major open ocean barrier (some 450 km wide) confronted them. It remained for the Lapita people, in the second millennium B.C., to cross this water gap and to settle the more remote archipelagos of eastern Melanesia and Western Polynesia. Archaeological evidence clearly demonstrates that the Lapita potters were the first humans to beach their canoes on these lands, for the impact of such human settlement on vulnerable and previously unexploited birds and other endemic fauna is unmistakable. In short, it was the bearers of Lapita culture who precipitated the human conquest of remote Oceania.[6]

Lapita and Polynesian Origins

That the first humans to invade the islands of Fiji, Tonga, and Samoa were makers of Lapita pottery has been definitely established (Kirch 1984; Kirch and Green 1987). These archipelagoes lie at the western "gateway" of the vast Polynesian Triangle (which has its apices at Hawai'i, Easter Island, and New Zealand), and it has been long thought by ethnologists, linguists, and archaeologists to be the immediate homeland region in which classic Polynesian culture developed. The historical linguists have shown that the Fijian, Tongan, and Samoan languages all descended from a branch of the Austronesian phylum called Proto-Central Pacific, which probably began to break up as a distinct language community about 3,000 years ago (Geraghty 1983). In this case, the "fit" between archaeology and linguistics seems especially good, and it is entirely reasonable to conclude that the Lapita people who colonized Fiji, Tonga, and Samoa at the close of the second millennium B.C. spoke this Proto-Central Pacific language. Indeed, lexical reconstructions of the Proto-Central Pacific vocabulary are entirely consistent with the archaeological evidence for settlement, agriculture, fishing, and other aspects of the culture.

Moreover, extensive archaeological work in Tonga and Samoa has revealed unbroken cultural sequences linking the later Polynesian cultures of these islands with their Lapita forerunners (Kirch and Green 1987). During the course of the first millennium B.C., we can trace changes in the pottery complex, and in other aspects of material culture, that mark the development of distinctive Polynesian traits. The pottery, for example, undergoes a gradual sequence of technological and stylistic changes over a millennium or more (Sand 1992), ending in the ultimate loss of the ceramic art by about A.D. 300.[7] What is important to stress in the context of this symposium, however, is that an unbroken sequence or chain can be archaeologically and linguistically reconstructed, a sequence that links the modern Polynesian cultures and languages with the ancestral Lapita Cultural Complex.

Let me be clear on one point: I am emphatically *not* saying that the Lapita people were Polynesians. That would be to reinvoke the silly notion that Lapita dispersal represents a "fast train to Polynesia" out of southeast Asia. It is the other way around: Polynesian culture is one development out of certain Lapita groups who voyaged eastwards into the remote Pacific Islands. Another parallel development occurred in eastern Micronesia, where the earliest archaeologically-documented assemblages on islands such as Chuuk (Truk), Pohnpei, and Kosrae include ceramic assemblages that can be linked with late Lapita. What is especially important for understanding Lapita, however, is that the Polynesian evidence unambiguously links Lapita with speakers of Austronesian languages. Keeping this in mind, let us now return to the beaches of the Bismarck Archipelago, and to some aspects of the immediate origins of Lapita.

The Bismarcks, Again: The Immediate Origins of Lapita

In order to assess the immediate origins of Lapita in the Bismarck Archipelago, several points must be emphasized:

(1) throughout this extensive region, Lapita appears suddenly, at about 3,500 years B.P., as a fully-developed archaeological horizon. No preceding developmental stages have been identified.

(2) The earliest Lapita pottery is highly elaborated, with a complex array of vessel forms and a sophisticated design system.[8]

(3) Although some shell working has now been identified from early Holocene assemblages in the Bismarcks, the array of shell tools, fishhooks, and "ornaments" that occur in early Lapita sites is far more diverse than anything preceding it in the region.

(4) The earliest Lapita sites were enmeshed in a highly complex, multi-node, long-distance exchange or trade network, about which I will have more to say shortly.

All of these observations suggest that the Lapita "phenomenon" was something quite new and probably intrusive on the western Melanesian landscape, even though it doubtless incorporated older traditions.

The strongest indication that the appearance of Lapita in the Bismarcks resulted, in part, from some kind of population movement from adjacent parts of island southeast Asia comes from the pottery. While the particular design system that embellishes Lapita vessels seems to be a local Melanesian expression, the Lapita ceramic complex is arguably part of a very widespread ceramic tradition that spread throughout island southeast Asia during the fourth through the second millennia B.C. (Bellwood 1985). This tradition is marked by a large number of attributes—too many to discuss in detail here—but which include aspects of manufacture, vessel forms (including distinctive pedestal-supported bowls), and decorative techniques. Decoration frequently includes both the use of toothed stamps and of red slip. Examples of such southeast Asian ceramic assemblages which closely resemble Lapita include the dentate-stamped Magapit vessels (including pedestal-supported bowls) from northern Luzon in the Philippines (Aoyagi et al. 1985, 1986, 1991), the Kalumpang assemblage from Sulawesi (van Heekeren 1972), and the red-slipped jar assemblage recently excavated by Bellwood and Irwin in Halmahera (Bellwood 1992). Indeed, the multiple similarities between the Halmahera assemblage and the red-slipped Lapita plainware from the EHB and ECA sites in the Mussau Islands, both of which have nearly identical radiocarbon ages, are quite remarkable. Moreover, these southeast Asian sites also contain arrays of shell tools and ornaments, stone and shell adzes, lithic assemblages, and faunal remains highly similar to those found in the earliest Lapita sites.[9]

In sum, the archaeological evidence strongly supports the interpretation advanced by Bellwood (1985) and others, that Lapita should be viewed as a further extension of the process of later Neolithic expansion that rapidly transformed the island southeast Asian world from about 4-2000 B.C. In my view, this picture is wholly consistent with that of linguistics, in which one subgroup of Austronesian-speaking peoples (Proto-Oceanic) penetrated the north coast of New Guinea and Bismarcks region some 3-4,000 years ago (Ross 1988; Pawley and Ross 1993).

Yet, while both the archaeological and linguistic evidence require an interpretation involving the movement of sea-faring, Austronesian-speakers into the Bismarcks in the mid-second millennium B.C., it is also clear that the emergence of the Lapita culture was due to more than this population intrusion alone. As the recent excavations in New Ireland, New Britain, and Buka have shown, western Melanesia had already been settled for more than 30,000 years by the time the Austronesian-speakers appeared on the scene (Allen, this volume). The beaches upon which the Austronesian immigrants landed were not devoid of human tracks. Indeed, western Melanesia was probably already a highly diverse region in terms of the cultures, languages, and genetic makeup of the indigenous inhabitants.

Furthermore, it would be wrong to think that the Non-Austronesian speaking indigenous inhabitants of the Bismarcks in the second millennium B.C. were caught in some kind of Paleolithic cultural time-warp. Golson's excavations at the Kuk site in Highland New Guinea (Golson 1990) have demonstrated that initial experimentation with water-control for intensive horticulture (probably of *Colocasia* taro) had commenced in the early Holocene (ca. 9000 B.P.). Similarly, in the New Guinea lowlands and adjacent islands, we have evidence for tree cropping (of *Canarium* sp.), and for pig husbandry, by the mid-Holocene. Thus it is likely that the Non-Austronesian speaking populations of the Bismarck Archipelago had already developed a horticultural subsistence base prior to Lapita. These indigenous groups were also involved in some long-distance, inter-island exchange, evidenced by the transfer of small quantities of obsidian, beginning as early as 18,000 years BP (Allen 1993; Summerhayes and Allen 1993). Evidence from several sites in the Bismarck and Solomon Islands in the time period of 5,000-3,500 years BP also indicates new technological developments such as edge- ground stone axes, and shell working for such artifacts as arm rings and fishhooks (Spriggs 1993).

Clearly, the emergence of Lapita at about 3,500 years ago in the Bismarcks must have been the result of a complex synergy involving both the indigenous descendants of the Pleistocene colonizers of Sahul, and the immigrant Austronesian-speaking seafarers.[10] Understanding this process requires new kinds of models, those that do not paint Lapita in polarized black-or-white opposites of "fast trains to Polynesia," or of wholly indigenous Melanesian origins in splendid isolation (e.g. Allen and White 1989).

New Models for Melanesia

One such model for the emergence of Lapita in western Melanesia has been proposed by Green (1991b): this is the "Triple-I" model of Intrusion/Innovation/Integration. In Green's words, the Triple-I model

> requires us to establish archaeologically which elements present in the Lapita cultural complex already existed in Near Oceania,...which elements constitute new additions from sources outside that long settled region, and finally which elements are in fact innovations of Lapita itself (1991:298-299).

Let me briefly sketch how such a Triple-I model might help to explain just one aspect of Lapita, namely the highly complex long-distance exchange network. The movement of substantial quantities of materials—pottery, obsidian, chert, metavolcanic adzes, oven stones, and other items—between Lapita communities is well documented archaeologically. In the case of the Mussau Lapita sites excavated between 1985-88, we have demonstrated that pottery was being imported from at least 16 different source localities, as well as large quantities of obsidian from both New Britain and the Manus Islands (Kirch 1988a, 1988b; Kirch et al. 1991). Substantial evidence for craft specialization in the manufacture of shell fishhooks and "ornaments" indicates that the Mussau community was exporting large numbers of finished shell objects, probably in part balancing the inward flow of pottery and obsidian. Of course, exchange in other, perishable kinds of materials (foodstuffs, mats, barkcloth) is not evidenced archaeologically.

The rapid emergence of this highly specialized, multi-node exchange network which linked Lapita communities throughout the Bismarcks, and—within one or two centuries—to communities up to 2,000 km distant in the far eastern Solomon Islands (Sheppard 1993)—can probably only be explained by the kind of Intrusion/Innovation/Integration model just discussed. Intrusion is required to explain the highly mobile, sea transport which depended on a new level of voyaging technology, and to account for the sudden appearance of the elaborate ceramic complex. Innovation is suggested by the Lapita design system, a semiotic device not evidenced in ancestral southeast Asian ceramic traditions.[11] And Integration is clearly reflected in the incorporation of the longstanding obsidian trade into a new system, in which the rate of obsidian movement was increased by an order of magnitude.

In short, the Lapita culture of 3500-3000 BP in the Bismarck Archipelago was presumably the result of complex social, linguistic, and genetic interactions between the Non-Austronesian-speaking inhabitants of the region, and the immigrant Austronesian speakers. However, there is also the matter of whether certain populations and communities that came into contact with each other on the beaches of Manus, Mussau, New Ireland, and New Britain in the mid-second millennium B.C. were in positions of dominance or hegemony. Some scholars would like to shrive us of the idea that technologically superior Austronesians "swept down" on the local Papuans, appropriating nothing more than their obsidian mines (e.g., Allen and White 1989). It is essential to question whether the archaeological records of all the cultural developments that we subsume under the rubric "Lapita" were of Austronesian origin; indeed, we have seen that they were not. But the history of cultural contact teaches us that the relationship between such cultures—the "structure of the conjuncture" as my colleague Marshall Sahlins (1985) puts it—is seldom, if ever, equal. This is not to say that indigenous and dominated populations blithely absorb in totality the culture of immigrant and dominating groups; a far more complex synthesis, a transformation of structures even as some traits of long duration persist (to invoke Braudel's scheme of history), typically marks such episodes of contact. Yet usually in such situations there is also extensive linguistic borrowing or language replacement of the kind that would explain the modern distributional mosaic of Papuan and Austronesian languages in western Melanesia (Pawley and Ross 1993).

I suggest that as seafaring Austronesian speakers ventured into the waters of the Bismarck Sea about 3,500 years ago—perhaps driven, as Goodenough (1982) has speculated, by new opportunities for exploiting interisland trade—the relationships that they established with the indigenous inhabitants of these islands were not equal. I am not necessarily proposing that it was always the Austronesians who were socially, economically, and politically dominant, although the linguistic evidence hints that this may have most frequently been the case.

Scholars of Oceanic folklore have long noted a complex set of myths or legends that revolve around a theme of autochthonous, original "land people" (usually with female symbolic associations) who are invaded from the sea by immigrant "sea folk" (usually male in symbolic orientation). Sahlins (1981) has written of the land-sea dualism inherent in the widespread Oceanic concepts of the "stranger king." Could it be that these myths had their ultimate origin in the socially and politically asymmetric relations that were established and played out on the beaches of Melanesia in the second millennium B.C.? Whether or not such myths have any historical basis, they nonetheless provide important indigenous models for the kind of cultural contact and transformation that most archaeologists now believe resulted in the Lapita cultural complex.

Conclusion

The past decade has truly been an exciting period of discovery in Pacific archaeology, provoking considerable rethinking of our fundamental concepts of Oceanic prehistory. New data excavated from the Pleistocene caves of New Ireland, and from the beach sands of Mussau and New Britain now challenge the very utility of *Melanesia* as a culturally-meaningful concept (Green 1991a). The tripartite division of Oceania into Polynesia, Micronesia, and Melanesia was proposed by the French explorer Dumont D'Urville in 1831. While Polynesia continues to stand up as a meaningful phylogenetic unit for cultural evolutionary studies (Kirch and Green 1987), it is clear that Melanesia has no coherence as other than a geographic space, a region moreover that incorporates tremendous cultural, linguistic, and biological heterogeneity (e.g., Friedlaender 1975). The historical basis for this Melanesian diversity, a story that extends back in time more than 40,000 years, has finally been revealed by modern archaeology, aided by allied studies in historical linguistics and comparative ethnography. Filling in the details of that story, however, is a task which has only just commenced.

NOTES

1. The terms "Sahul" or "Greater Australia" refer to the substantially enlarged continental land mass of New Guinea, Australia, and Tasmania which were joined at various times of lowered sea levels during the Pleistocene (see Allen, this volume).
2. The name Lapita derives from a beach site on the island of New Caledonia, where Prof. E. W. Gifford of the University of California excavated in 1952.
3. Linguistic evidence strongly supports the interpretation of the taro-yam root crop complex being a key component in Lapita agriculture, based on the reconstruction of terms for these plants in the Proto-Oceanic lexicon. French-Wright (1983) has argued on linguistic reconstructions that the Proto-Oceanic speakers had a highly developed horticultural complex based primarily on shifting cultivation.
4. The tripartite division of Oceania into Melanesia, Micronesia, and Polynesia is a nineteenth-century legacy, dating back to the French explorer Dumond d'Urville in 1831.
5. I find no credibility in the recent claim of Spriggs (1990b:19-20) that Lapita in the Bismarck Archipelago has a time depth as great as 1,800 B.C., based as this is on a single questionable radiocarbon date from the inadequately published Kohin Cave site on Manus.
6. The terms Remote Oceania and Near Oceania were defined by Green (1991).
7. The loss of pottery in Polynesia, which also occurred in several parts of Melanesia, is an intriguing matter for which no single compelling explanation exists. Environmental explanations (such as the absence of suitable clays or temper) are unsatisfactory, and a number of complex social factors (such as changing patterns of long-distance exchange) were probably involved.
8. This pottery complex is, in my opinion, wholly unrelated to the Ramu River and other north coast New Guinea ceramics dating to ca. 5-6000 BP

recently reported by Swadling et al. (1988; Swadling et al. 1991), and mentioned by Allen (this volume).

9. For a more extensive review of the Southeast Asian archaeological assemblages most closely related to Lapita, see Kirch (1995).

10. I use the term "seafarers" in conjunction with the Austronesian-speaking populations purposefully, because there is strong linguistic evidence (from reconstructions of Proto-Austronesian lexicon) that the early Austronesians had developed the outrigger-canoe and attendant technology.

11. One quite intriguing hypothesis regarding the apparently "sudden" origins of the sophisticated dentate-stamped decorative system that is the hallmark of Lapita pottery, is that this was a direct transfer of a preexisting art style from one medium—tattooing of the body—to another, namely pots. Tattooing appears to be a very old Austronesian phenomenon, and the technique typically involves the use of a "dentate" or toothed comb to puncture the skin and insert the pigment. Green (1979b) some years ago noted the similarities between ethnographically-documented Polynesian tattooing and the Lapita design system, including many common motifs. Moreover, the high frequency of human face motifs on early Lapita ceramics (Spriggs 1990b) suggests that at least some vessel types might have been symbolic representations of people—living or dead—and that the vessels themselves were then being tattooed. While this remains an untested hypothesis, it would readily explain the very rapid appearance of a highly sophisticated design system.

6. Colonizing an Island World

Ben Finney
University of Hawaii

Introduction

How were the islands strewn across the Pacific colonized? How could stone age peoples have spread out over this great ocean to discover and settle virtually all its inhabitable islands when they had such a seemingly limited seafaring technology: slim canoes hewn with stone adzes, lashed together with coconut fiber line, powered by mat sails, and navigated by naked-eye observations of the stars, the ocean swells, and other cues supplied by nature? These questions are examined here with special reference to Polynesia, that largest cultural province of the Pacific whose many and widely-scattered islands were reached by the longest sea voyages accomplished by stone age navigators.

Before we can begin to answer these questions, however, we must temporarily replace the categories by which we conventionally divide the Pacific island world with ones more appropriate to sketching the direction and sequence of oceanic colonization. Over a century and a half ago the French explorer J. S. C. Dumont d'Urville (1830, 2:614-616) proposed in an address before the Geographical Society of Paris to divide this world into three grand divisions: *Polynésie*, literally the "many islands" within the triangle bounded by Hawai'i, Rapa Nui, and Aotearoa (or, if you prefer, the Sandwich Islands, Easter Island and New Zealand); *Melanésie,* composed of New Guinea and other islands extending east as far as Fiji, and so labeled because of the dark skin of most of its inhabitants; *Micronésie*, located north of New Guinea and east of the Philippines, and so named because the islands there are but tiny specks on the map. Although this convenient categorization has since been employed by generations of geographers, historians, and anthropologists, it creates incommensurate units that obscure the prehistory and resultant cultural mosaic of the Pacific island world. Whereas the individual Polynesian cultures are relatively undifferentiated descendants of a common ancestral one, those of Melanesia are highly diverse because of a long and complex settlement history, and those of Micronesia fall in between these extreme examples of homogeneity and diversity. A better way to comprehend how this cultural

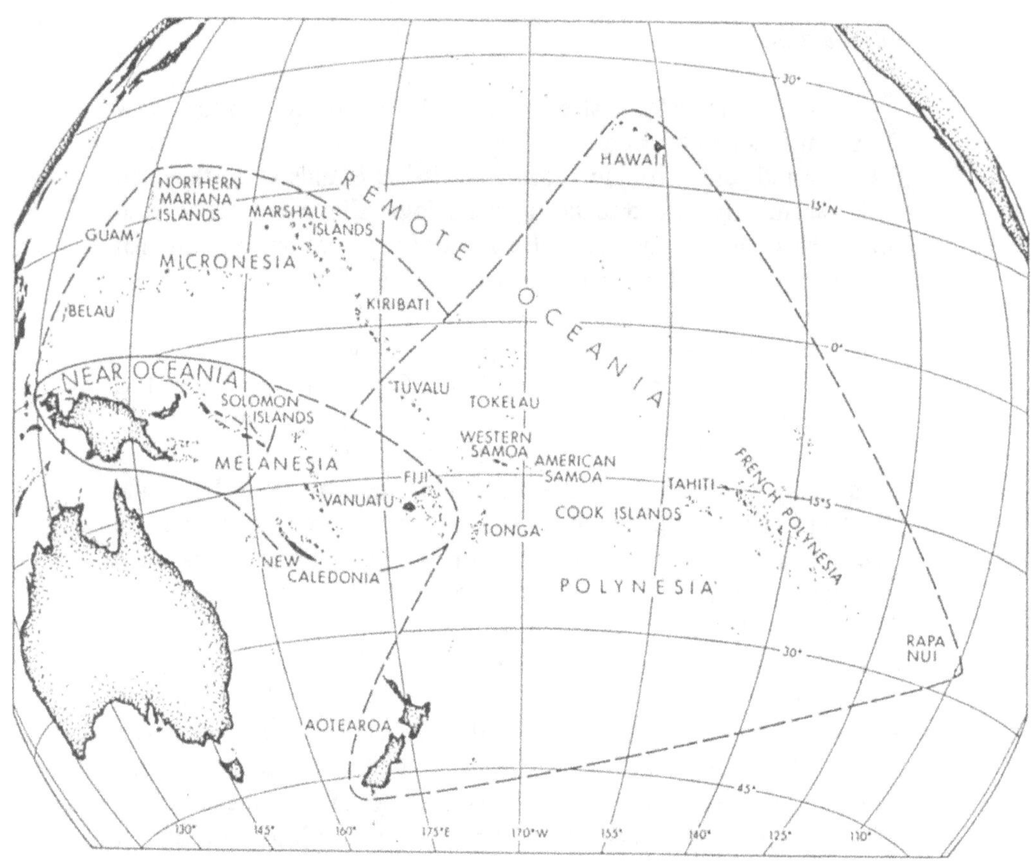

Figure 8. Ways of dividing the Pacific Island world: Near Oceania and Remote Oceania; Melanesia, Micronesia, and Polynesia.

mosaic developed is to employ Roger Green's separation of this island world into only two regions: Near Oceania and Remote Oceania (Pawley and Green 1975). Near Oceania includes New Guinea and adjacent islands to the east at least as far as the Solomons chain. All the islands to the north and east of Near Oceania, that is those of Micronesia, eastern Melanesia, and Polynesia, make up Remote Oceania (Figure 8).

Expansion into these two regions was radically discontinuous. Whereas the settlement of Near Oceania began some 50,000 years ago during the last ice age, the settlement of Remote Oceania did not get started until some 3,500 years ago. As this temporal gap implies, these movements differed greatly in the technology and skills required. During the height of the last glaciation the islands of near Oceania could be reached by hunters and gatherers with only rudimentary craft (such as rafts or dugout canoes) and navigational skills (Allen et al. 1977).[1] So much of the globe's water was then incorporated into the glaciers that the islands of Indonesia as far east as Bali were linked to the mainland to form an extension of what Asia geologists call Sunda, while New Guinea, Australia, and Tasmania, plus their continental shelves, were joined together to form a greater Australia, known as Sahul. Crossing the gap between Sunda and Sahul was further facilitated by the presence of numerous islands that formed intervisible or nearly intervisible stepping stones. In contrast, to move farther out into the ocean to find and colonize the islands of Remote Oceania required sophisticated, deep-sea sailing craft and ways of navigating far out of sight of land. Beyond New Guinea and adjacent archipelagos, the island gaps grow into the hundreds of miles and reach into the thousands of miles at the margins of Polynesia. Furthermore, the colonizers of Remote Oceania had to be more than just blue water sailors. Whereas in the northern, tropical part of Sahul edible plant and animal species were abundant enough to enable hunters and gatherers moving in from the west to survive without radically new adaptations, the islands of Remote Oceania lacked the edible plants needed to sustain sizable permanent populations and therefore had to be settled by farmers skilled at transferring their domesticated plants and animals from one island to another.

The languages spoken by the people of Remote Oceania indicate the source and direction of migration into the ocean. All the peoples of Remote Oceania encountered by European explorers spoke languages belonging to the Austronesian language family. Austronesian speakers are thought to have begun their migration into the Pacific by moving from the Fujian region of southern China to Taiwan at around 4000 B.C., well before Chinese speakers settled there (Blust,this volume; Chang and Goodenough, this volume). From Taiwan some of their descendants moved south to the islands of the Philippines and Indonesia, the Malay Peninsula and the east coast of Viet Nam. Starting around 2000 to 1500 B.C., some descendants of these migrants turned east to move into the Pacific. Those who sailed directly to Belau (Palau) and the Marianas chain at the western edge of Micronesia were apparently the first to reach that part of the Pacific.Those who moved along the north coast of New Guinea and settled among the offshore islands of the Bismarck Archipelago, however, encountered the descendants of the first settlers of Sahul.

Judging from the trail of Lapita pottery and other characteristic artifacts uncovered by archaeologists, as well as from language distributions, it appears that around 1,500 B.C. seafarers speaking Austronesian languages began moving east from the Bismarcks and soon passed the frontier of previous colonization; they alone had the technology and motivation to sail so far out into the ocean. Although we do not know precisely to what extent these Austronesian speakers had mixed biologically and culturally with the original inhabitants of the New Guinea region, it seems likely that they carried into the Pacific some genes from the descendants of the earlier migrants, as well as useful plants and practices they had picked up from them. This migratory movement swept some 2,000 miles eastward through island Melanesia to reach, in as few as two or three centuries, Fiji, Tonga, and Samoa at the edge of Polynesia.[2] A branch of this migration swept northward from eastern Melanesia to Kiribati, the Marshall Islands, and the Caroline Islands to complete the settlement of this region of tiny atolls and a scattering of small high islands that had begun some centuries before when Austronesians had first reached its western edge, presumably sailing directly there from the Philippines (Bellwood 1979, 1989; Green 1979a; Kirch and Hunt 1988a, 1988b; Pawley and Green 1973; Craib 1983).

Starting by at least 500 B.C., canoes headed into the eastern Pacific from Tonga, Samoa, and other adjacent islands of what is now known as West Polynesia. There they found and began colonizing the Cooks, Societies (including Tahiti), Marquesas,Tuamotus and Australs, although not necessarily in that order. These central East Polynesian archipelagos in turn became the source of the migrants who sailed north, southeast, and southwest to colonize Hawai'i, Rapa Nui, and Aotearoa at the extreme points of the Polynesian triangle. Estimates for the settlement of Hawai'i begin in the 200-400 A.D. range, and those for Rapa Nui at around 400 A.D. In contrast, most prehistorians consider that Aotearoa was settled significantly later, sometime in the 800 to 1200 A.D. range (Figure 9).

Well after Austronesian voyagers left the Philippines and eastern Indonesia to begin this colonization of the Pacific, some of their distant cousins from Indonesia reached Madagascar to be the first to occupy that great island where today the official language, Malagasy, testifies to the Austronesian roots of this migration (Dahl 1951). Madagascar was apparently not reached by the same island-to-island expansion across the seas as occurred in the Pacific. No rich profusion of islands extends across the Indian Ocean from Indonesia to Madagascar to entice voyagers deep into the ocean, and those few bits of land found there such as Diego Garcia, Mauritius, and Réunion have not yielded any evidence of early Austronesian colonists. It therefore seems likely that Indonesian traders who had moved along the northern rim of the Indian Ocean and then down the African coast were the first to discover and settle Madagascar.

This spread of Austronesian speakers throughout island and coastal Southeast Asia, to Madagascar, and almost clear across the Pacific made the Austronesian language family the most widespread one in the world—until Western Europeans developed their own seafaring technology and carried Indo-European tongues around the globe. That this dispersion was accomplished by means of canoe voyaging is apparent not only by the traditions of the islanders themselves but also by the nearly congruent distribution of sea-going canoes and that of Austronesian languages (Figure 10). The presence of sea-going canoes but not Austronesian languages in Sri Lanka, the southern tip of India, and to the east coast of Africa facing Madagascar indicates how technology may spread without language adoption.

At the time of European contact three main types of canoes were sailing in the Austronesian world: double-outriggers in which floats were attached to the ends of booms extending from each side of a hull; single-outriggers in which a single float was attached to booms extending from only one side of a hull; and double-canoes composed of two hulls spaced apart and lashed together by means of cross beams (Doran 1981). These compound vessels represent related solutions to the problem of starting with slim canoe hulls and making them into seaworthy vessels capable of carrying sail without capsizing. Whereas Europeans developed stable sailing vessels by broadening the beam of their hulls, and then adding ballast to further counteract the overturning force of the wind, Austronesians made their sailing canoes wide enough to carry sail by adding one or two outrigger floats off one or both

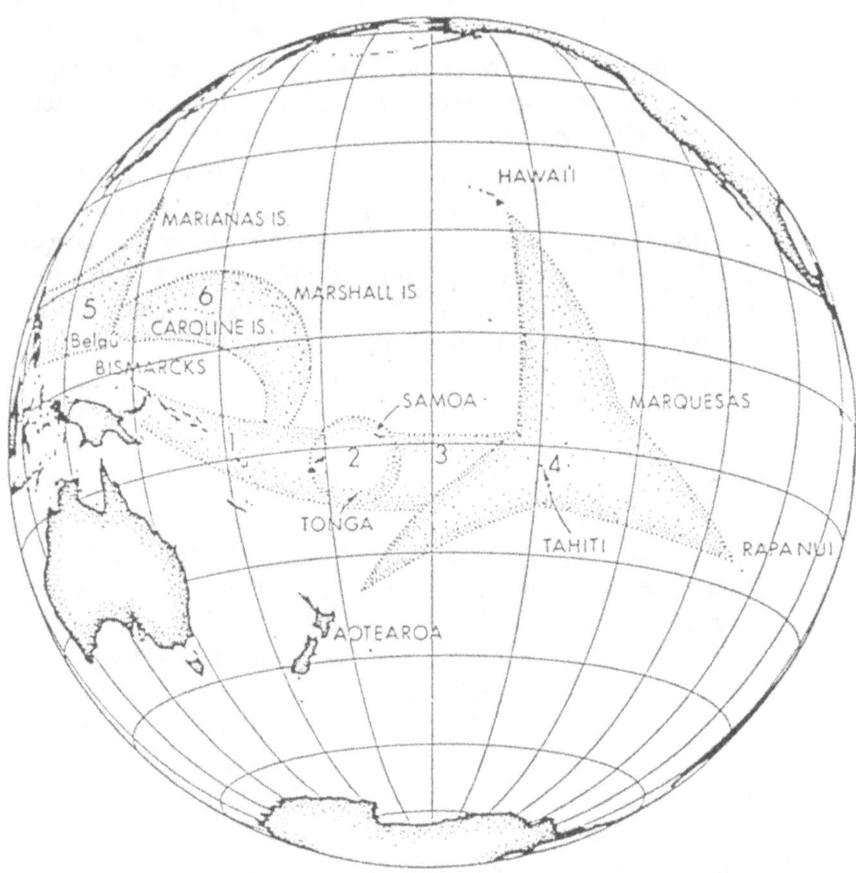

Figure 9. Main Austronesian migrations into the Pacific: 1) from the Bismarcks to the mid-Pacific archipelagos of Fiji, Tonga, and Samoa; 2) the "homeland" of the Polynesians now known as West Polynesia; 3) from West to central East Polynesia; 4) from central East Polynesia to Hawai'i, Rapa Nui, and Aotearoa; 5) from the Philippines to the western edge of Micronesia; 6) from the main migration sequence north to Micronesia and then west across the region.

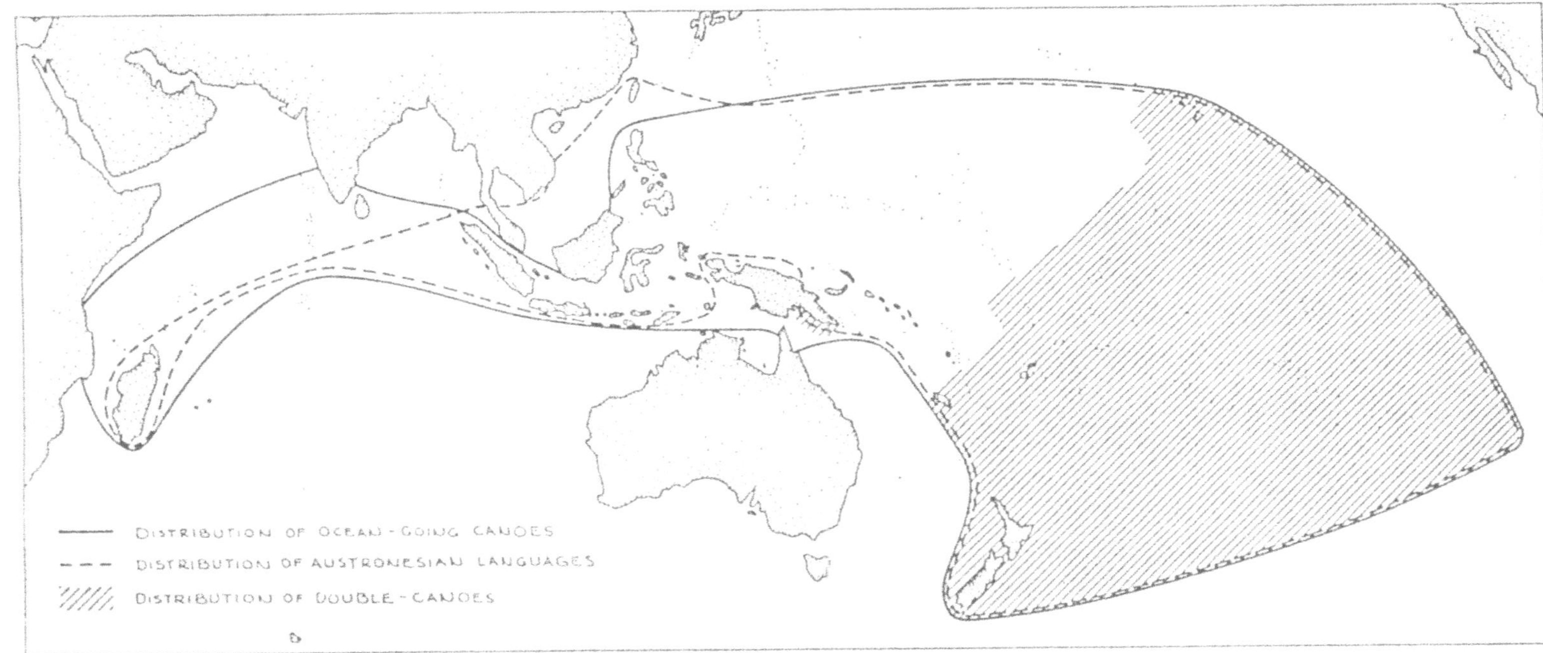

Figure 10. The distribution of ocean-going canoes and Austronesian languages (after Green 1977:224-225; Doran 1973:40-41,46; Haddon and Hornell 1938:85).

sides of the hull, or by joining two hulls together by means of heavy cross beams. Rather than get bogged down in arguments over which type came first, let us simply note that, whereas at the time of European contact the double-outrigger canoe was common to the Philippines and Indonesia and was also employed in Madagascar, the basic outrigger canoe in the Pacific was the single-outrigger. The double-canoe was most commonly employed in eastern Melanesian waters and throughout Polynesia. This distribution, plus the increased stability and carrying capacity provided by linking two hulls, strongly suggests that double-canoes were the primary craft by which Polynesia was colonized. Voyagers expanding into the vast reaches of the Pacific apparently found them to be stable, high-capacity craft, ideal for carrying colon-izing parties of men, women, and children on long voyages, along with the tools, planting material, and domestic animals so necessary to estab-lish a viable subsistence base on the islands they found and settled.

Competing Theories

Most of the interest in Pacific colonization has focused on the Polynesian end of the long migration trail into the ocean—on how stone age peoples could have expanded so far out to sea and settled all the inhabitable islands scattered over an immense area equivalent to the better part of Europe and Asia combined. (The outline of Polynesia, rotated and placed over Europe and Asia, would enclose a Eurasian triangle extending east from France clear across Europe and Russia almost to Kamchatka, then down to Southern India and back to France.) Those first European explorers to enter the Pacific discovered to their surprise that the islands they chanced upon in mid-ocean were already occupied. Particularly since Europeans had only recently developed their own ocean-spanning technology, they wondered how people without ships, the compass, charts, or any other navigational devices could ever have made their way into the middle of this greatest of the world's oceans. Some even refused to consider the possibility that the ancestors of the islanders could have sailed on their own into the Pacific, and speculated that they had been brought there by other earlier European voyagers or had been created in place by God (Finney 1994a:4-6).

Starting, however, with the late eighteenth–century voyages of Captain James Cook, a line of thinking developed that gave credit to the seafaring technology and skills of the islanders, and asserted that they purposefully employed their canoes and ways of navigating to expand into the ocean from the western edge of the Pacific. During his three voyages Cook and his scientists discovered that the people of the

Polynesian triangle all spoke closely related languages which shared a more distant kinship with those of the "East Indias" (Finney 1993a). Cook (1955:154), who admired the canoes, seamanship and navigational skills of the people he met, proposed that their ancestors had moved eastward into the Pacific sailing from island to island until they had found and occupied all the islands of what he called the "same Nation." Later explorers, linguists, and geographers further developed Cook's suggestion. By the nineteenth and early in the twentieth century such dedicated amateur scholars as Abraham Fornander of Hawai'i and S. Percy Smith of New Zealand were embellishing what by then had become the orthodox view of intentional colonization from the west by employing Polynesian oral traditions and far-ranging linguistic comparisons to develop romantic scenarios of Polynesians swiftly migrating en masse from the Asian mainland to the far reaches of Polynesia (Finney 1994a:6-21).

By the mid-twentieth century their claims about rapid migration from India and other even more distant homelands, and their impossibly precise scenarios of dispersion throughout Polynesia, had largely fallen out of favor. Even the more considered views of Polynesian migration by such professional scholars as Peter Buck, the famous part-Maori director of Honolulu's Bishop Museum, came under attack by a number of critics, including, notably, Norwegian adventurer Thor Heyerdahl and New Zealand historian Andrew Sharp. They exploited weak points in the orthodox view of Polynesian migration, including the lack of any credible analyses of how early voyagers could have intentionally sailed canoes all the way from the Asian side of the Pacific into the middle of the ocean and then found and settled all the islands there.

Heyerdahl (1953) rejected the idea of a direct colonization of Polynesia from the west. Primitive voyagers, he claimed, could only sail with wind and current, never against them. Since the winds and currents in the tropical Pacific flow from east to west across the ocean, canoe voyagers could not have crossed the tropical Pacific from west to east because they could not have forced their canoes against what Heyerdahl (1978:332) called the "permanent tradewinds and forceful companion currents." Thus Polynesia must have been settled by voyagers from the Americas who sailed and drifted before the trade winds and accompanying currents. Sharp (1956, 1961, 1963, 1964) took a different tack. He accepted that the Polynesians came from the west, but claimed that their canoes did not sail well enough, and that their non-instrument navigation methods were not sufficiently accurate, for them to have intentionally explored and colonized the Pacific. Sharp maintained that the islands must therefore have been settled accidentally by chance arrivals of drifting canoes that had been blown off course or had strayed through navigational error, or by fortuitous landfalls of canoes bearing desperate exiles fleeing war or famine. Furthermore, he held that the resultant colonies remained isolated from all but their nearby neighbors except for the random arrival of drift or exile canoes.

Although Heyerdahl's contention that Polynesia had been settled from the Americas found little acceptance among prehistorians whose own research showed that the migration had proceeded from the Asian side of the Pacific, Sharp's debunking of what he considered to be the myth of intentional Polynesian colonization was treated more seriously. His theory of random, accidental settlement appealed to many as a realistic correction to what had increasingly come to be regarded as the romantic exaggerations of earlier writers. It also fit in with the then growing rejection by cultural anthropologists and archaeologists alike of the long-dominant culture history paradigm and its focus on the migration of peoples and diffusion of cultural traits in favor of concentrating on reconstructing particular cultures and the processes of adaptation to the environment, evolution, and other processes internal to these cultures (Finney 1994a:255-257).

Those of us who questioned Sharp's assertions about the limitations of Polynesian canoes and navigation and the random, least-moves modeling of Polynesian colonization that it promoted, as well as Heyerdahl's pronouncements about the impossibility of sailing eastward across the Pacific, soon found that we could not conclusively refute them. Long-range voyaging had died out in Polynesia, and written accounts about voyaging penned by early European explorers and visitors were too sketchy to provide the necessary data on canoe sailing and navigation to settle anything. Projected ethnographic studies of how the few surviving traditional navigators to be found in remote corners of Micronesia and Melanesia were able to guide their canoes to distant island landfalls, as well as computer simulations of drift voyages, promised important insights. But, really to understand the role of indigenous technology and skills in voyaging and colonization in Polynesia, we concluded that we had to reconstruct the ancient voyaging canoes, relearn the old ways of navigating, and then test these on the long sea roads of Polynesia.

Experimental Voyaging

This experimental approach got underway in the mid-1960s when David Lewis (1966) navigated his modern catamaran from Tahiti to Aotearoa by quasi-traditional methods to see how it might be possible to sail so far without a compass or other instruments, and my students and I reconstructed and tested a 40-foot long Hawaiian double-canoe to get some idea of its sailing characteristics (Finney 1967). Drawing on lessons from these first experiments, in 1973 a group of us in Hawai'i formed the Polynesian Voyaging Society to reconstruct a 60-foot long voyaging canoe and test her over long routes to provide needed data and insights on traditional canoe sailing and navigation. In 1976 we sailed our double canoe, christened *Hokule'a* after the bright star Arcturus, which transits directly over Hawai'i, from Hawai'i to Tahiti and return. In 1980 this voyage was repeated, and between 1985 and 1987 *Hokule'a* was sailed to Aotearoa and back to Hawai'i, stopping in the Tuamotus, Societies, Cooks, Tonga, and Samoa along the way. In 1992, she was sailed via Tahiti to the Cook Islands to participate in the South Pacific Arts festival held at Rarotonga, and in 1995 was sailed south yet again, this time to take part in a celebration of the voyaging revival among Polynesian peoples that had been inspired by her many voyages. *Hokule'a* and five other recently constructed voyaging canoes from Aotearoa, the Cook Islands and Hawai'i rendezvoused at Tahiti, and then proceeded to the Marquesas Islands, located 750 miles to the north-northeast. From there they sailed together 1,800 miles to Hawai'i in order to commemorate the original discovery of that archipelago. All in all *Hokule'a* has sailed over 60,000 nautical miles of open ocean, and on all but a few of her long crossings she has been navigated without instruments, charts, or other aids.

Hokule'a represents an attempt to re-create a craft that would sail like an archaic voyaging canoe. Unfortunately, we could not follow the experimental archaeology ideal of recreating the artifact to be tested from an archaeologically-recovered example using only traditional materials and tools (Coles 1979, McGrail 1975). No ancient voyaging canoes had been recovered from excavations on land or the sea floor to provide exact models, and we did not have the resources, time, or skills necessary to replicate all the traditional materials, tools, and construction techniques. We therefore developed the design from drawings of voyaging canoes from throughout Polynesia that date from the European exploration era in order to come up with a vessel that incorporated common, presumably archaic, features, and we used some non-traditional materials, and tools to fabricate major components of the craft. *Hokule'a*'s twin hulls, each 19 meters long, are lashed together with cross beams which also support a deck. Two masts are mounted on the deck and rigged with a pair of upward-curving Polynesian sprit sails. Because the hulls were fabricated from layers of cold-molded plywood, and synthetic line and other modern materials were used for some other components, out experiments cannot directly address issues of strength and durability. Since, however, *Hokule'a* follows traditional precedents in terms of her lines, weight (displacing some 12 metric tons fully loaded), and sail plan, we believe that her performance provides data useful for estimating how voyaging canoes sailed.

Judging from *Hokule'a*'s performance, traditional double canoes were seaworthy craft well adapted for long range voyaging.[3] However, they probably did not sail as fast, nor point as close to the wind, as do their modern descendants, racing catamarans. Their relatively narrow stance (a function of the strength of wooden cross beams and coconut fibre lashings) limited sail area and hence speed, and their lack of deep keels or centerboards limited windward ability. Nonetheless, *Hokule'a* can accelerate to at least 10-12 knots when broad reaching across strong winds, and in brisk trades cruises easily in the 6-7 knot range. Furthermore, despite her relatively shallow hulls, she can sail to windward, though not as well as modern high performance craft. Whereas racing yachts may be able to sail to within 45-50 degrees off the wind (calculated by subtracting leeway from the canoe's heading into the true wind), *Hokule'a* cannot sail closer than about 75 degrees off the wind before she begins to lose speed rapidly and increase her leeway. *Hokule'a* is nonetheless well adapted for making long crossings. With the inevitable periods of calms and light winds as well as squalls and storms when sails have to be lowered, on her Pacific cruises she has averaged a little over 4 knots, or around 100 miles a day, and whenever we have had sufficient time to wait for a favorable wind we have been able to sail her exactly where we wanted to go.

The four round-trips *Hokule'a* has made so far between Hawai'i and Tahiti, islands separated by over 2,000 miles of blue water, demonstrate how well such a craft is adapted for sailing long distances across the wind. These voyages also highlight, however, the limits of a double canoe's windward capability. As the meridian of Tahiti lies some 300 miles to the east—to windward with respect to the easterly trade winds—of the Hawaiian chain, *Hokule'a* can be sailed freely from Tahiti to Hawai'i by heading her across and slightly before the trades, the ideal sailing angle for a double canoe. In contrast, to go from Hawai'i to Tahiti she must be sailed close into the wind to make enough easting to reach Tahiti and not be driven west of the island by the easterly flow of the trade winds and accompanying currents. On these crossings we try to reach Tahiti by making one long slant against the wind, resulting in a course that first curves south-southeast across the northeast trades of the Northern Hemisphere, and then curves back toward the south-southwest in the face of the southeast trades of the Southern Hemisphere. On each of the five crossings from Hawai'i to Tahiti *Hokule'a* has gained just enough easting to make it to Tahiti. If, however, we had tried to sail directly to the Marquesas, which is several hundreds of miles farther to the east than Tahiti, we could not have reached this group without laboriously tacking back and forth for much of the way.

How, then, can we maintain that Polynesia was settled from the west by people sailing their canoes east against the direction from whence the trade winds blow? The migration route from Indonesia to Rapa Nui extends over some 120 degrees of longitude—one-third the way around the globe! To tack all that way against the trades would be a most formidable undertaking, even accomplished over many generations by sailing across one inter-island gap at a time. Was Heyerdahl correct when he maintained that the "permanent tradewinds" barred early voyagers from sailing east across the tropical Pacific?

The solution to this apparent dilemma has two parts. First, contra Heyerdahl, the trades do not always blow. They periodically die down and are replaced by spells of westerly winds. Second, the Polynesians and their predecessors were not so foolish as to attempt to tack long distances against the trade winds. Instead, they "sailed smart" by waiting for the inevitable spells of westerlies and then exploited these to probe eastward.

Captain Cook pointed toward this solution in the pages of his journal of his first voyage into the Pacific. When he and his chief scientist, Joseph Banks, began to learn Tahitian they discovered that a number of Tahitian words were practically identical to those found in vocabularies of languages from the "East Indias" (roughly today's Indonesia) which were contained in travel accounts carried on board H.M.S. *Endeavour* (Cook 1955:154; Banks 1962, 1:370-373). They therefore hypothesized that the ancestors of the Tahitians must have come from these islands at the western edge of the Pacific. Yet, however much Cook admired the Tahitians' sailing canoes, he apparently did not think them weatherly enough to have been able to tack all the way against the easterly trade winds from Indonesia to the far reaches of Polynesia. This is a matter of trigonometry. A vessel that can only sail to within about 75 degrees of the wind must tack back and forth over almost four miles of water to make one mile directly into the wind—a figure that rises precipitously when the current flows in the same general direction as the wind, which is usually the case. Thus to sail 500 miles directly against wind and current would require that a canoe be tacked back and forth for well over 2,000 miles; to sail 1,000 miles directly to windward would mean actually covering well over 4,000 miles, and so on (Finney 1985).

Cook, therefore, queried the learned Tupaia, his Tahitian informant, when the latter told him that Tahitians regularly made voyages to islands lying far to the west, and then sailed directly back, eastward, to Tahiti. The English explorer accepted that a canoe could easily run west before the trades, but he apparently thought that to tack back to the east against these winds would so lengthen a voyage, and so subject the canoe to wracking strains of beating into head seas, that long windward crossings would not have been feasible. Tupaia set him straight by explaining that Tahitian sailors did not try to tack long distances against the trades. Whenever they wanted to sail east, he said, they waited for those times when the trades were replaced by spells of westerly winds. The Tahitian's explanation evidently satisfied Cook, who then penned in his journal how it may one day "be prov'd" that the islanders employed these westerly wind shifts to work their way across the ocean from the "East Indias" (Cook 1955:154).

The necessity of waiting for the right winds to make long crossings is manifest in the way we sailed the 12,000 mile voyage which, between 1985 and 1987, took *Hokule'a* from Hawai'i to Aotearoa via the Tuamotus,Tahiti, the rest of the Society group, and the Cook Islands on the outbound leg, and Tonga, Samoa, the Cooks, Tahiti, and the Tuamotu islands on the inbound leg. Theoretically, given the 100 mile a day average of *Hokule'a*, we could have made this voyage in some 120 days, plus perhaps a week at each island group along the way for rest, repairs, and cultural celebrations. Instead, it took us nearly two years—primarily because each leg had to be timed for the right seasonal wind patterns.

Hokule'a sailed from Hawai'i to Tahiti in mid-July of 1985, for example, just before the Northern Hemisphere hurricane season, when tropical storms that often reach hurricane strength cross the Hawai'i-to-Tahiti route as they spin northwestward from their spawning grounds off Mexico. But after arriving at Tahiti in mid-August we could not immediately sail from there to Aotearoa. To do so would have meant sailing southwest out of the trades and into temperate latitudes where, during the Southern Hemisphere winter, cold and often stormy westerly winds periodically sweep across the sea approaches to Aotearoa. Even though *Hokule'a* might have been about to tack laboriously against these winds, we had no desire to endure the weeks and weeks of cold, wet, and miserable sailing that would entail, not to mention the very real prospect of foundering in accompanying heavy seas. Instead, we opted to follow Maori sailing directions, which specified that canoes should depart late in the Southern Hemisphere spring. Accordingly, the crew took their time cruising through the Society Islands, and then through the Cook Islands to Rarotonga, where the canoe was hauled onto shore to wait until mid-November.

Departing then made good sense, both from a traditional and a meteorological point of view. Maori traditions specify a late spring departure, but do not explicitly say why. When we looked at weather charts the reason emerged: starting then, large, slow-moving high pressure systems begin to dominate in the latitudes immediately below the trade wind belt, bringing warm easterly winds favorable for sailing all the way to Aotearoa. We left Rarotonga on 21 November, and, once we had sailed out of the trade wind zone, we were boosted southwestward by favorable easterly winds from three successive high pressure systems. These enabled us to cover the 1,650 miles between Rarotonga and Aotearoa's North Island in just sixteen days of relatively smooth, dry, and comfortable sailing (Figure 11).

After a long layover in Aotearoa, *Hokule'a* was sailed north, first to Tonga and then to Samoa, in order to position the canoe for an attempt to sail directly east from Samoa to Tahiti, following the general direction (but not necessarily the exact route) pioneered by early Polynesian colonists. We had the choice of trying the crossing during the summer, when spells of westerly winds are common, or during the winter, when spells of westerlies caused from passing low pressure troughs only sometimes interrupt the trades. Because dangerous tropical storms periodically develop during the summer months, our Hawaiian navigator, Nainoa Thompson, chose to sail during the winter even though the probability of getting westerly winds then was significantly less. He was gambling that during the winter in question, 1986, westerly winds would interrupt the trades frequently enough to allow *Hokule'a* to be able to reach Tahiti, which lies over 1,200 miles east-southeast of Samoa, almost exactly the mean direction from which the trades blow in that part of the Pacific. Fortunately, Nainoa won his gamble. During the winter months of 1986 one spell of westerly winds after another moved across the seaway between Samoa and Tonga.

In early July 1986 Nainoa and his crew set sail from Ofu island at the eastern end of Samoa, bound for the Cook Islands, where they planned to stop on the way to Tahiti. First, they sailed *Hokule'a* south across the trade winds until a trough emanating from a low pressure zone passing just south of the trade wind zone began to shift the wind in a counter-clockwise direction. The resultant winds blowing successively from the north, northwest, southwest, and south allowed *Hokule'a* to make several hundred miles of easting in three days, after which the southeast trade winds returned and forced the canoe onto a northeasterly path. Enough easting had been gained, however, to enable the canoe to be tacked south to Aitutaki, an island 140 miles due north of Rarotonga. After a month's stay, *Hokule'a* was sailed south to Rarotonga, from where, after an overnight stay, she was put to sea again to take advantage of a northwest wind then blowing. To everyone's surprise, the trough causing the northwesterly winds moved so slowly to the east

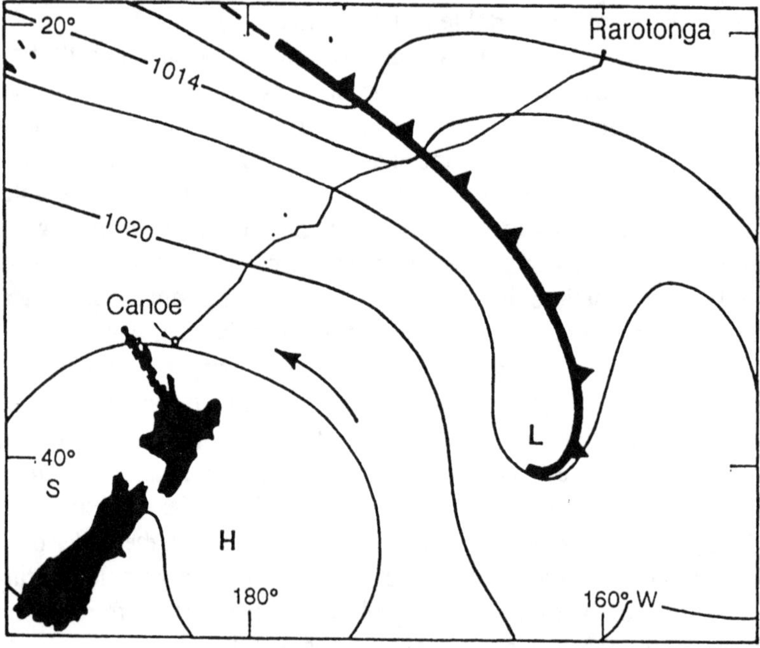

Figure 11. Rarotonga to Aotearoa 7 December 1985: satellite track of *Hokule'a* showing her sailing toward Aotearoa with favorable easterly winds brought by the third high pressure system encountered on the crossing.

that *Hokule'a* remained stuck in the trough for over a week, and the resultant northwesterlies drove her clear past Tahiti and directly towards the Tuamotu Archipelago. Fortunately, before being pushed into that dangerous labyrinth of atolls, the trough finally passed, and the trades returned, allowing *Hokule'a* to turn back to the west toward Tahiti (Figure 12).

Since it was by then too late in the year to be assured of steady, storm-free trades for the final leg back to Hawai'i, *Hokule'a* was once again hauled out of the water to wait until the following April when favorable conditions for the return voyage would be reestablished. Even then, northerly winds brought by an unexpected El Niño condition delayed the departure for home, and fickle winds along the way so slowed the canoe that she did not reach Hawai'i until late May of 1987, almost two years from the date she had sailed for the South Pacific.

As these experiences indicate, canoe performance alone is not the key to understanding Polynesian voyaging. To be sure, *Hokule'a*, may be a lively vessel that easily slips through the seas, making good time when the winds are favorable. But, whenever faced with headwinds, we had to wait, sometimes for months on end, for favorable winds, as it made no sense to try to tack back and forth to a distant upwind target. The crossing from Samoa to Tahiti demolished any notion that the trade winds prevented migration eastward across the Pacific by demonstrating how spells of westerly winds can be used to sail from west to east across Polynesia. Similarly, the crossing from Rarotonga to Aotearoa showed how following the Maori traditions that specify the time of the year appropriate for sailing to Aotearoa put voyagers at sea at just the season when a window of easterly winds will carry a canoe through latitudes dominated by westerly headwinds other times of the year.

During the long voyages of *Hokule'a* we have also been able to gather unique data and insights on how it is possible to navigate without instruments over thousands of miles of open water. We did this by developing, from 1980 onwards, two sets of data: 1) the actual track of *Hokule'a* determined remotely by satellite tracking in which signals from a sealed transponder on board the canoe were picked up by passing satellites which then downloaded the data to NASA and CNES (the French national space agency) for position calculation and retrieval after the voyage; 2) the navigator's dead reckoning calculations of the track phrased in terms of the canoe's changing position in relation to the departure island, intervening islands, and target island as well as a planned reference course, and then verbally recorded on board the canoe twice a day during the voyage. (Not until after each voyage were the satellite and dead reckoning positions charted and compared.)

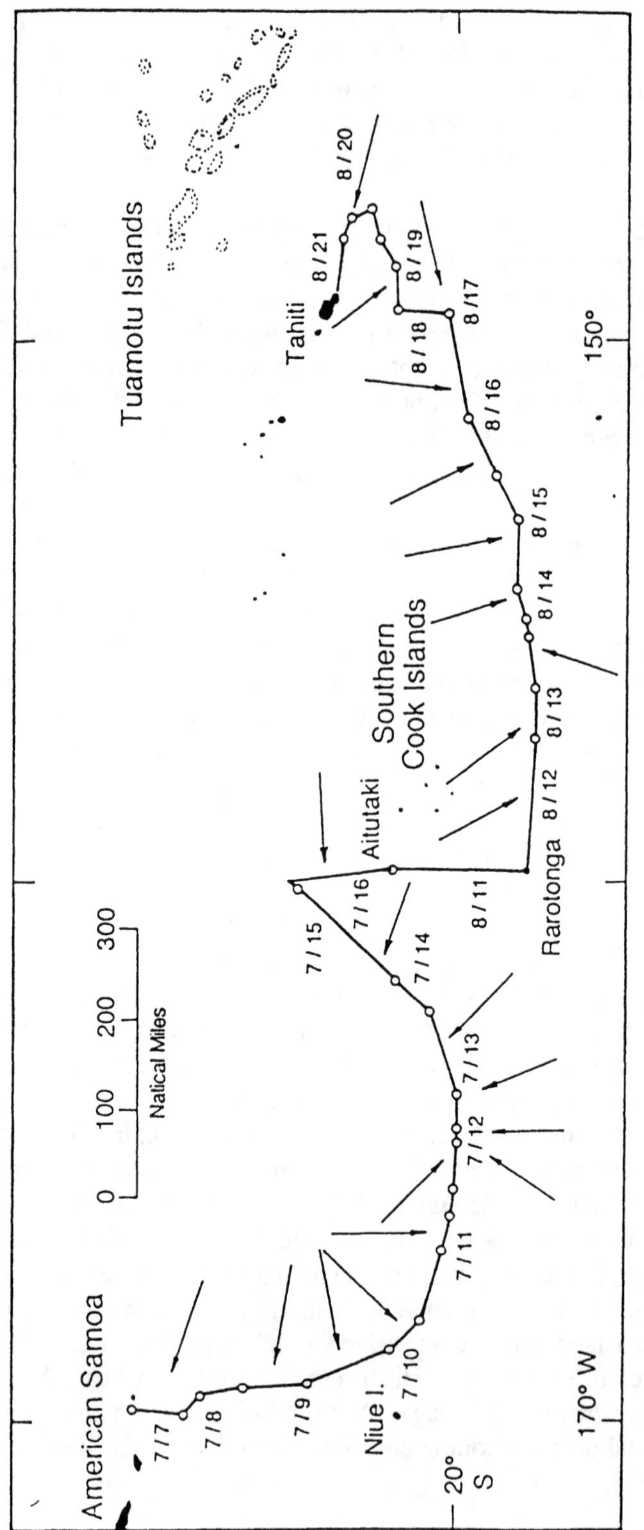

Figure 12. Samoa to Tahiti 1986: satellite track of *Hokule'a* and daily wind directions.

The navigation methods employed by the Polynesians and other Pacific islanders have been extensively documented by Goodenough (1953), Gladwin (1970), Lewis (1972; Thomas (1987), and others. Without going into all the details and variations, these methods may be briefly summarized as follows. At night, navigators oriented on the rising and setting points of key stars and constellations; by day, on the sun when low in the sky (its changing position having been calibrated against the fading star field of the dawn sky). When clouds obscured the stars or sun, and when the sun was too high in the sky to yield a bearing, they oriented on the dominant swells, the direction of which they had previously established in relation to star or sun bearings. During a voyage they kept a running mental calculation of the progress of their canoes in reference to the changing bearing and distances to and from the target and home islands, as well as to known islands off to one side or the other of the course. They compensated for current set and leeway drift across a course by steering on the appropriate star or sun bearing to one side or other of the course, and made course corrections during the voyage as indicated by dead reckoning estimates of the canoe's progress, or as dictated by changing wind and sea conditions. To expand the range at which an island could be detected, they watched for such signs as cloud build-up over high islands, interference in the swell pattern, and the flight of land-nesting birds that daily fly out to sea to fish.

For *Hokule'a*'s first long voyage, that from Hawai'i to Tahiti in 1976, we borrowed the expert services of Mau Piailug, a master navigator from the island of Satawal, one of the atolls in the Caroline Islands of the Federated States of Micronesia where traditional navigation still flourishes. From 1980 onward, *Hokule'a* has either been navigated by Nainoa Thompson, a young Hawaiian who was stimulated to learn non-instrument navigation after seeing Mau in action, or by one of his pupils. Nainoa's methods do include some modern concepts, such as miles and degrees, which he could not expunge from his thinking. Nonetheless, because he navigates in the traditional manner, judging bearing without instruments from the stars, sun, and swells, dead reckons without resort to charts, pen, or paper, and searches for land by looking for the flight of land-nesting birds and other cues supplied by nature, his way of working provides a most informative lens through which to view the strengths and weaknesses of traditional navigation.

Sharp (1956, 1961), echoed by Hilder (1959) and Åkerblom (1968), had set the challenge which our experiments addressed. They had declared that the inaccuracies inherent in judging bearings from the rising and setting points of the stars or sun, particularly when the horizon is hazy, in steering precisely when it is overcast and when the pattern of ocean swells offers only a rough guide, and in estimating the displacement of the canoe to one side or other of the desired course by ocean currents that cannot be directly seen, meant that the non-instrument navigator would be thrown farther and farther off course the longer he sailed. Sharp even went so far as to declare that non-instrument navigation between islands separated by more than 300 miles of ocean was therefore impossible. Yet Nainoa has always been able to bring *Hokule'a* to the intended landfall, whether sailing just a few hundred miles, 1,650 miles from Rarotonga to Aotearoa, or repeatedly back and forth over the thousands of miles of blue water separating Hawai'i and Tahiti. How has it been possible for him to keep *Hokule'a* on course, to maintain an idea of her position as each voyage progressed, and then to bring her to a distant island target when non-instrument navigation contains so many sources for error?

To be sure, Nainoa is an extraordinarily skillful navigator, but two main factors explain why he has been able to apply his skills so successfully on *Hokule'a*'s long voyages. First, oceanic geography is on the navigator's side. Whereas Sharp and other critics biased the discussion by phrasing it in terms of finding a lone island lost in the ocean wastes, in fact most of the islands of Polynesia and elsewhere in the Pacific are found in archipelagos. Whether probing into unknown seas, or sailing to an already known objective, the navigator has *only* to make landfall on any island within a chain of islands. Then, if sailing for a known island, he can reorient himself and head directly for his target. To reach Tahiti, for example, a navigator coming from Hawai'i has only to sight any island in a wide screen of islands formed by the Society chain which extends several hundreds of miles to the west of Tahiti and the northern flank of the Tuamotus which extends even farther to the east of Tahiti. In *Hokule'a*'s five crossings to Tahiti, we have always tried to make landfall on one of the atolls at the western end of the Tuamotus, located just to the north-northeast of Tahiti a day and a half's sail away. Three times the canoe has made landfall on Mataiva, the westernmost island, and once each on Tikehau and Rangiroa, the atolls immediately to the east of Mataiva, a spread only 75 miles wide. From these landfalls, it has been relatively easy to sail directly for Tahiti. Even if *Hokule'a* had made landfall on one of the atolls at either the eastern end of the Tuamotus or the western end of the Societies, she still could have been worked to Tahiti.

Second, misjudgments of bearings or of current flow do not necessarily accumulate in one direction, as Sharp and other critics had assumed. As Lewis (1972:222-223) has stressed, they are more likely to be random, canceling one another out. How such randomness can be self-correcting, particularly on a long voyage, can be seen in the track made by *Hokule'a* on the 1980 crossing from Hawai'i to Tahiti (Figure 13). Right after leaving the doldrums on March 31, *Hokule'a* apparently crossed through one of those swift, narrow current jets that periodically appear near the equator, but which are virtually impossible to notice without a land referent. Nainoa did not detect that the canoe had been quickly set some 90 miles to the west of where he thought it was sailing. With this omission imbedded in his reckoning, as the canoe headed south over the next ten days Nainoa's position estimates paralleled the actual track, but were 90 miles to the east of it. Then, on April 11 Nainoa revised his thinking. Because he reasoned that the slow progress of the canoe below the equator was exposing it to more of the westward-flowing South Equatorial Current than allowed for in his calculations, Nainoa factored in more current set to the west, which, as we discovered later, placed his dead reckoning positions some 90 miles to the west, almost directly on *Hokule'a*'s actual track. Contemporaneous tracking by oceanographers of this current by radio buoys showed, however, that the current was particularly weak then. Nevertheless, Nainoa's overestimate of current strength below the equator in effect canceled out missing the current jet north of the equator, and brought his mental picture of where the canoe was sailing almost directly onto the actual track.

Motivation

Before we can apply these and other findings to reconstructing how generations of seafaring farmers were able to work their way one-third of the way around the globe to colonize virtually all the islands in the middle of the world's greatest ocean, a word about motivation is in order. Goodenough (1982) proposes that the search for trading goods was responsible for the initial Austronesian expansion from South China to Taiwan, then from Taiwan to the Philippines, Indonesia, and New Guinea. Austronesian traders, he hypothesizes, were ever searching for new supplies of such tropical forest products as rattan and camphor (and perhaps also for such coastal marine products as trepang and trochus) to trade back to mainland markets. To gain access to these resources meant that the Austronesians must have entered into relations with the island peoples. Some intermarriage must then have followed, which may explain the recently reported presence of genetic markers among contemporary Polynesian populations that can be traced to the New Guinea region (Gibbons 1994; Hagelberg and Clegg 1993).

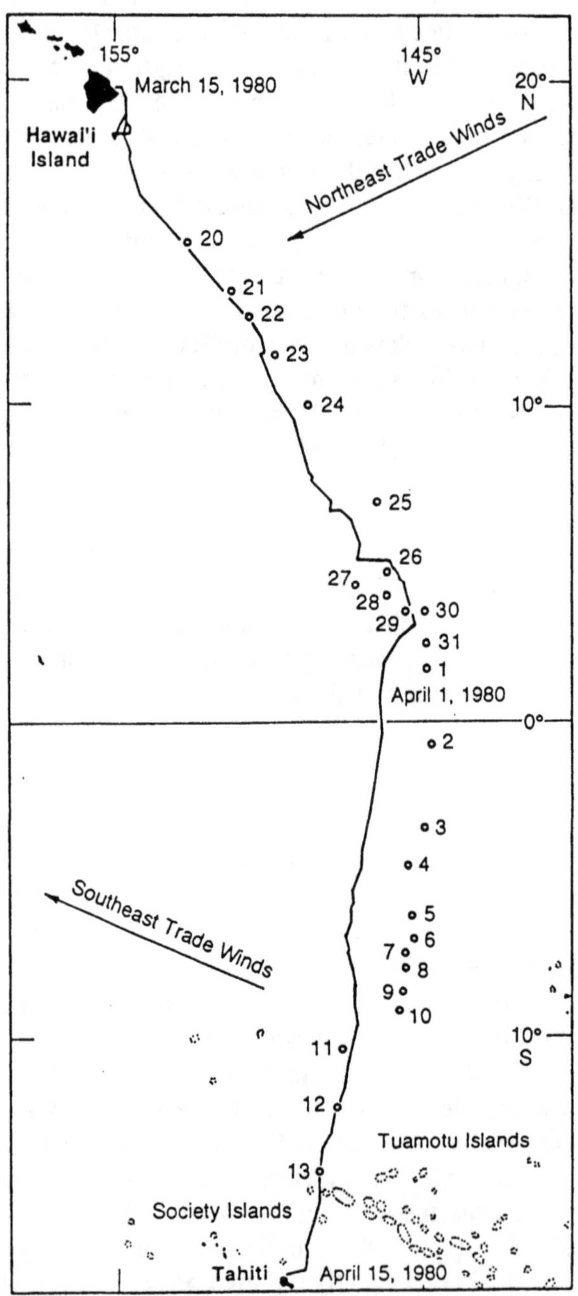

Figure 13. Hawai'i to Tahiti 1980: Satellite track of *Hokule'a* compared to daily dead reckoning positions.

The search for new sources of trade goods does not explain, however, why Austronesians sailed so far into the Pacific, well beyond the frontier of previous settlement and the practical limits of island-continent trade. As they moved farther and farther into the Pacific the Austronesians developed a truly oceanic world view. Their ancestral seafaring experience told them that the sea was filled with islands, and as they moved eastward beyond the Solomons they discovered that the islands they kept finding to windward were uninhabited, for only they could sail so far into the ocean. But they probably were not forced by population pressure to expand so fast and so far. The initial thrust from the Bismarck Archipelago off New Guinea to the mid-Pacific archipelagos of Fiji, Tonga, and Samoa appears to have happened much faster—estimates range from a few to five centuries—than can be accounted for by any model requiring that each island along this 2,000-mile trail become crowded before canoes set out for the next. Similarly, the Polynesians' expansion to such distant outposts as Hawai'i would seem to have happened long before population pressure would have forced people from the initially-colonized central islands to search for new lands.

It is tempting to think of Austronesian voyagers impatiently pressing beyond the known island world for the sheer joy of discovering yet more islands and celebrating the technology that they alone possessed. Or, more sanguinarily, we could take a clue from the disappearance of bird species as people moved across the Pacific and posit that they kept moving so rapidly eastward because as soon as they exhausted the avian resources of one island they moved on to the next in order to have fresh supplies of flightless birds and other easily harvested species. But we should not ignore how highly adaptive Austronesian social structure was for expansion. The characteristic Austronesian stress on primogeniture, particularly in terms of passing leadership to the chief's first-born son, in effect encouraged generations of chiefly younger sons to seek their fortunes on uninhabited islands to be found over the horizon. Younger sons with little hope of succeeding to the chieftainship at home had a more constructive outlet for their ambitions than rebellion or fratricide. They could create chiefdoms of their own by building a voyaging canoe, recruiting followers, and setting sail to find and colonize a new islands.

The Drive toward the Uninhabited East

Whereas the continuous distribution of islands leading eastward across the Pacific obviously invited Austronesians to keep probing farther and farther out to sea by rewarding them with one uninhabited island after another on which to settle, it might seem that the dominance of easterly trade winds across the tropical South Pacific would have inhibited that movement, requiring extraordinary skills in practical meteorology and seamanship to play westerly wind shifts in order to sail to the east. Yet, a good case can be made that the Austronesian sailors turned this unequal alternation of dominant easterly trades and westerly wind shifts to their advantage.

Expanding east against the trade wind direction (but not by tacking against the trades themselves) makes good sailing sense (Finney 1977:1284). Consider first the plight of explorers who had sailed for many days without sighting any land, and were running desperately short of food and water. Because of the dominance of the trades, those who had searched eastward using westerly wind shifts would have had a much better chance of reaching home before their supplies completely ran out than those who had sailed west with the trades. Whereas the latter would have had to gamble on catching the less frequent and briefer spells of westerlies in order to return to their home base in the east, those exploring eastward would have a better chance of exploiting a return of favorable trade winds to take them all the way back to their home base in the west before their supplies ran out. Similarly, with the inevitable return of the trades those explorers who had succeeded in finding an uninhabited island to the east suitable for settlement would have been able to sail back to their home island to spread news of their discovery in order to organize a fully-equipped colonizing expedition.

This alternation between easterlies and westerlies is so pronounced in the western South Pacific from South China Sea eastward through Melanesian waters that the term monsoon is often used in describing it. According to one model, this monsoon pattern arises from the intense heating of the Australian continent during the summer (Steiner 1980; Hessell 1981). During the winter, trade winds blow more or less regularly out of the southeast and across Melanesian waters, northern Australia, and the Indonesian archipelago (Figure 14). With the coming of summer, the increased solar radiation causes a low pressure trough to be formed over northern Australia and to extend eastwards over the Coral Sea, bringing a westerly and northwesterly flow of wind along its northern flank (Figure 15). These summer westerlies periodically extend eastwards beyond the monsoon trough, but become more and more episodic the farther one moves across the Pacific. Figure 16, which depicts mean observed wind flow across the Pacific during January at the height of the summer westerlies season, clearly shows a corridor of westerly winds leading from the Bismarck Archipelago almost to Fiji. Beyond Fiji these winds become much more episodic so that in such a depiction of mean wind flow they only weaken and deflect the arrows to the northeast, rather than reverse them. Nonetheless, even the more sporadic episodes of summer westerlies that cross over into the eastern South Pacific can produce major flows of westerly winds that may last a week or so (Figure 17).

The strong monsoonal pattern in the western South Pacific may help explain why Austronesian pioneers were able to expand so rapidly 2,000 miles from the Bismarcks and across the length of Melanesia to the western edge of Polynesia. The regular appearance of long spells of summer westerlies would have encouraged voyagers to probe to the east, just as the regular alternation of these westerlies with the winter trade winds would have facilitated voyaging back and forth along the migration route, enabling struggling colonies on the frontier of expansion to obtain needed supplies and personnel from longer-settled islands. If, however, the western South Pacific wind pattern is so ideal for eastward expansion, does this necessarily mean that the more episodic nature of the summer westerlies in the eastern South Pacific made it impossible for later voyagers to keep pushing eastward at the same rapid rate? So far the evidence on migration rates seems equivocal. Whereas some prehistorians maintain that the gap between the first occupation of West Polynesia during the period from 1500 to 1000 B.C. and the earliest dates for East Polynesian settlement in the 500 B.C. to 300 A.D. range indicate a marked slowing of the migration rate, if not an actual pause, others claim that, since the earliest sites occupied in East Polynesia have probably not yet been found, there is no reason to posit such a differential in migrational progress.

Whatever the case, the ancestral Polynesians certainly learned how to cope with any problems posed by the less regular appearance of spells of summer westerlies and their shorter duration, for they did succeed in spreading over the eastern Pacific. They also undoubtedly discovered that along the southern fringe of Polynesia brief spells of winter westerlies can also be used to sail to the east. Furthermore, it is likely that they were well acquainted with how those periodic basin-wide disturbances now referred to as El Niño events, or more technically El Niño-Southern Oscillation (ENSO) events, bring long spells of westerlies that can sometimes sweep clear across the eastern South Pacific (Finney 1985).

The exact navigational strategies employed by exploring parties are not known, and, given our prior knowledge of Polynesian geography, we could not really attempt to simulate them on our voyages. Nonetheless, the same basic orientation, dead reckoning, and island finding skills would seem to apply to exploring and colonizing situations

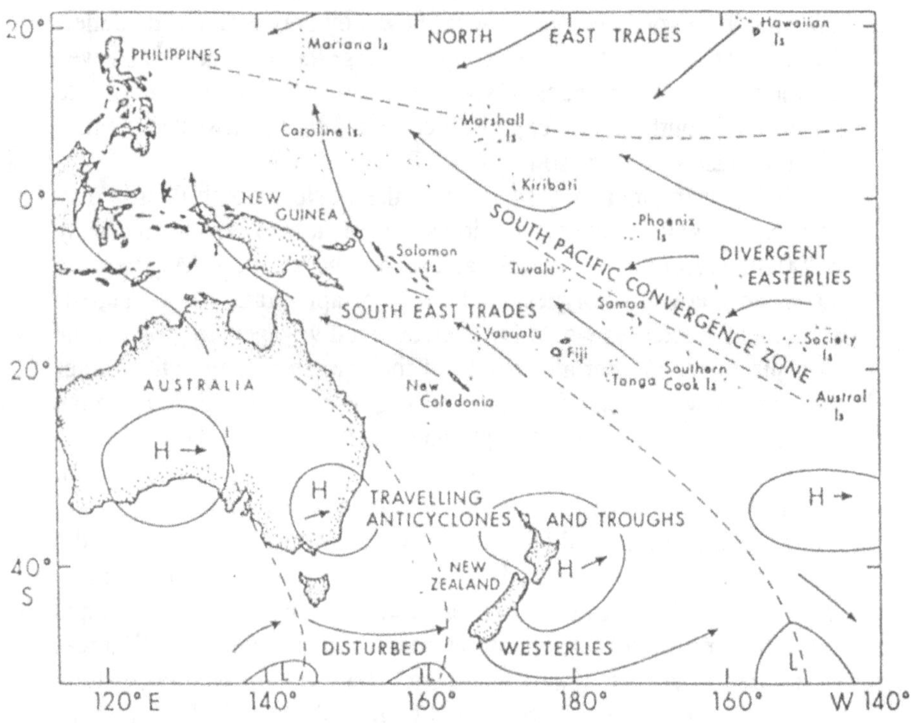

Figure 14. Idealized Southern Hemisphere winter wind circulation in the southwest Pacific (after Steiner 1980:9 and Hessell 1981:43).

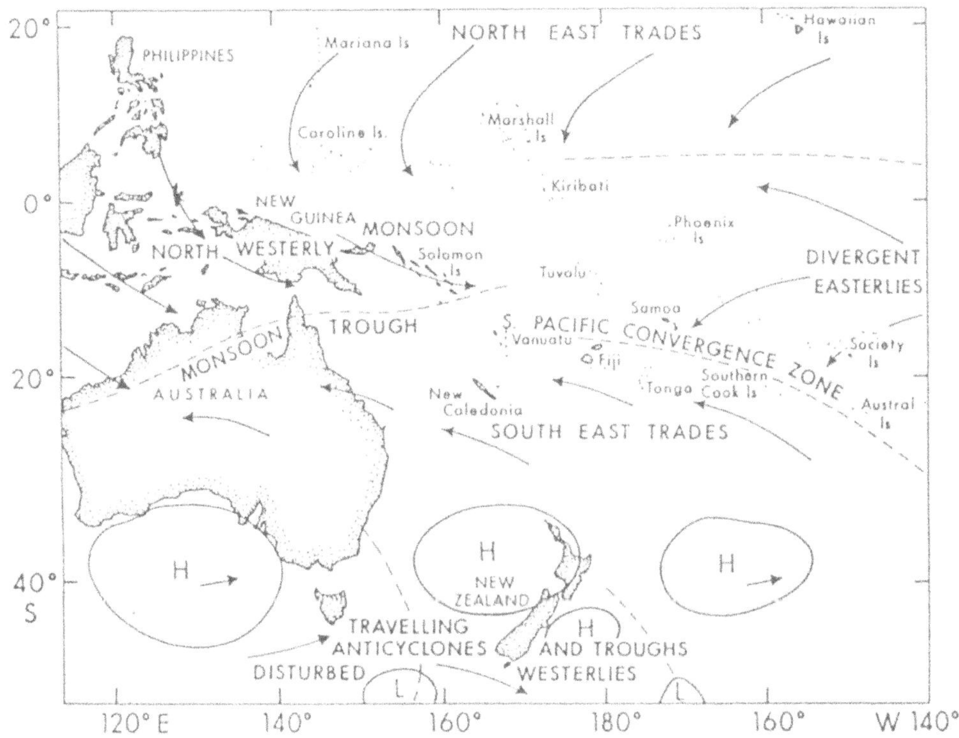

Figure 15. Idealized Southern Hemisphere summer wind circulation in the southwest Pacific (after Steiner 1980:9 and Hessell 1981:42).

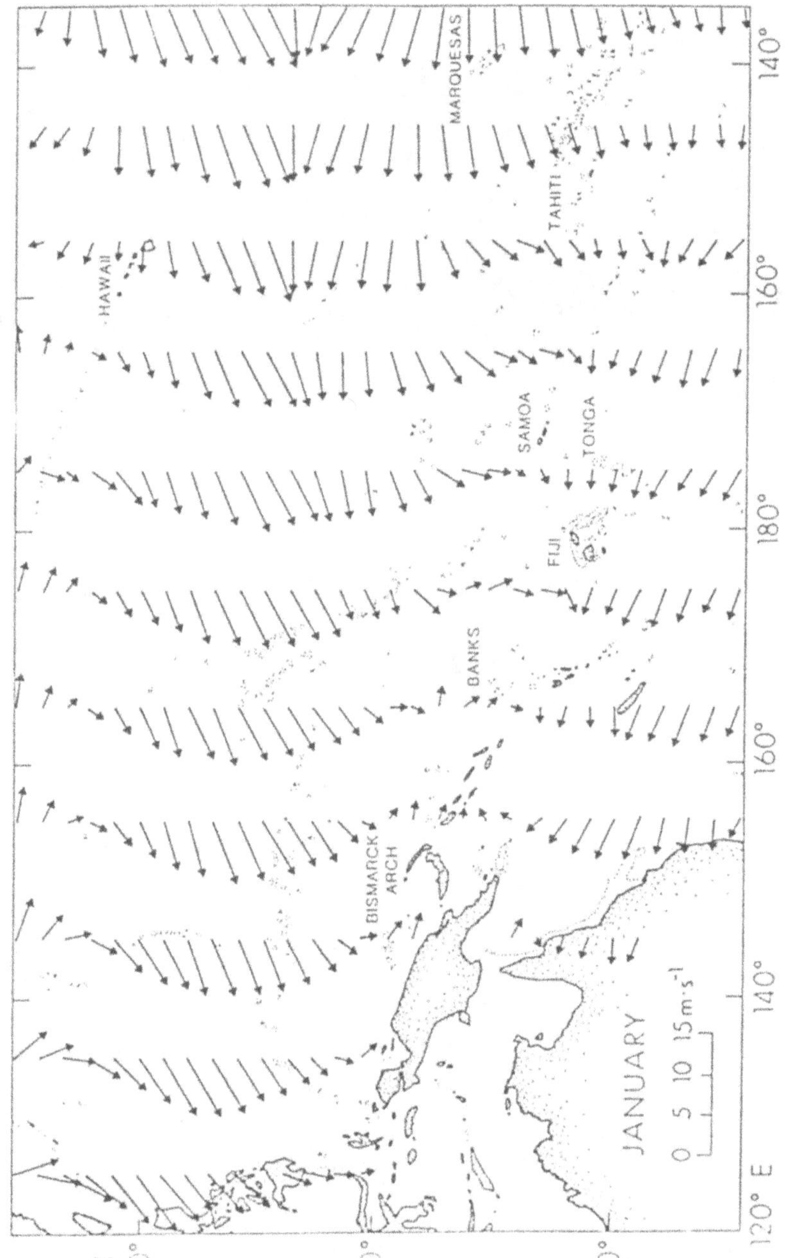

Figure 16. Mean surface wind direction and velocity in the tropical Pacific during January (after Wyrtki and Myers 1975: fig. la). Vector lengths indicate relative wind velocities.

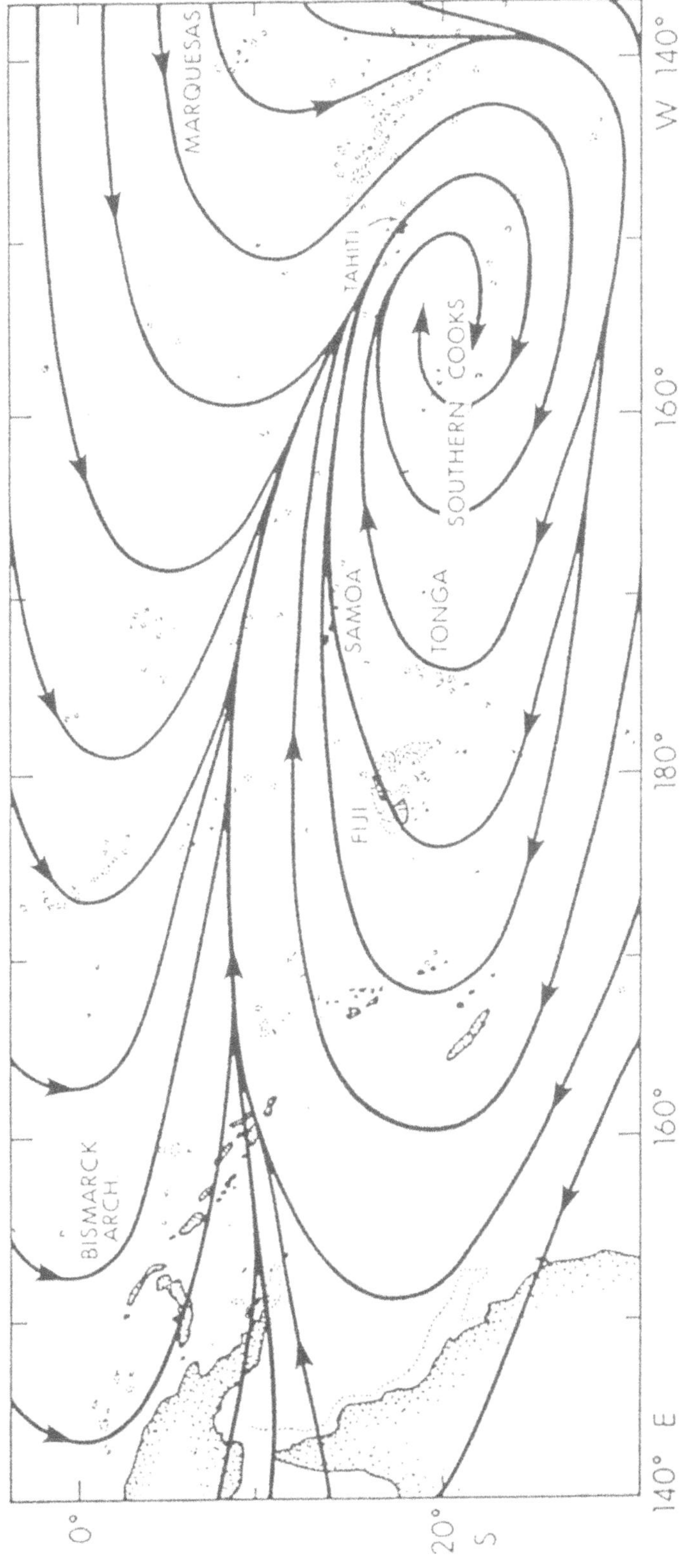

Figure 17. Surface wind streamlines for 16 January 1979 during an episode of summer westerlies.

as to subsequent voyaging between known islands. Orientation by reference to the bearings of celestial bodies and, when necessary, the dominant swell patterns, would allow a navigator to keep a canoe on a desired course, or to keep track of course changes dictated by search strategy or wind shifts. Although we do not know exactly how Polynesians dead reckoned, to judge from a few clues found in ethnographies and explorers' journals as well as from Nainoa's experience it seems likely that a navigator on an exploring canoe would have been able to form a mental picture of the changing position of his canoe in terms of distance (probably phrased in conventional sailing days; Banks, 1962, I:369-370) and bearing (probably phrased in terms of celestial or wind compass points) back to the home island. Once a new island had been found, the navigator would have had a good chance of being able to find his way back home, and then back again to the new discovery.

Lest this sound too casual, remember the basic principle that most Polynesian islands are but parts of archipelagos, and also that land-nesting birds fly out from an island daily to fish. We have found these birds to be most helpful in locating islands before we could directly see them, but our experience is probably just a pale reflection of that enjoyed by pioneering explorers sailing into virgin seas. The paleontological record is clear: species after species of birds disappear from oceanic islands soon after human occupation, and surviving species are typically reduced in number, presumably because of direct predation by humans and those habitual canoe stowaways, the Polynesian rat (*Rattus exulans*), as well as by the disruption of bird habitats by agricultural clearing (Anderson 1989; Steadman 1989). The first explorers to sail within the vicinity of such untouched islands would therefore probably have been greeted by myriads of birds fishing out to sea—perhaps, because of intense competition, as far as thirty, forty, or even fifty miles from each island. This would have enhanced the detection range for a single island, and in the case of an archipelago the overlapping detection ranges of the constituent islands would make a huge zone that would be difficult to miss.

Consider, for example, a canoe approaching at right angles an archipelago made up of a row of seven small atolls separated from one another by some fifty miles of open ocean. Since the tops of the tallest coconut palms on an atoll typically cannot be seen until you are within 10-12 miles, it would certainly be possible to slip through such an archipelago and not directly see an island. However, overlapping circles of fishing birds (as well as changes in swell patterns caused by swells bending around and bouncing off islands, and the greenish reflections cast on the undersides of clouds by broad, shallow atoll lagoons) would have greatly increased an alert crew's chances of detecting when they were crossing through such a group of islands. Approached at its widest extent, for example, the seven islands would form a detectable screen more than 400 miles wide.

We do not know which island group of East Polynesia was first settled. The logic of first settling the islands closest to West Polynesia would suggest that the Cook Islands would have been reached first, with the Societies next, and so on until the more distant groups of central East Polynesia—the Australs, Tuamotus, and Marquesas—had all been occupied. So far, however, there does not seem to have been enough archaeology done to establish any exact sequence of colonization. For example, of the three earliest radiocarbon dates indicating human presence in the area, which arguably range from 500 B.C. to 200 B.C., two come from the Cooks, and one from the Marquesas Islands (Suggs 1961a; Kirch 1986:27; Chicamori 1987; Kirch and Ellison, 1994.

If anything, our sailing experiences and the varieties of westerly winds available could be used to argue against any notion that the East Polynesian region was necessarily settled by a unilineal, archipelago-by-archipelago progression of voyages. Canoes leaving from various points in West Polynesia, and perhaps over a prolonged colonization period, could have made landfalls throughout the region. Even a voyage directly to the Marquesas Islands is not out of the question during a major El Niño when a prolonged spell of westerlies could have carried a canoe straight to this archipelago. Furthermore, there is no reason to assume that the various islands within an archipelago were necessarily settled from only one source—either an island back in West Polynesia or one along the way. It seems likely that at least in some cases canoes from two or more separate sources may have colonized different islands within an archipelago, a theme, for example, in oral traditions from the Cooks and the Marquesas.

The known endpoint of this eastward expansion is the lone island of Rapa Nui, which at a little over 109° East longitude is actually to the east of the meridian running through Salt Lake City, Utah. Rapa Nui lies some 1,100 miles east of the nearest Polynesian outposts—the temporarily settled islands of Pitcairn and Henderson—and some 1,900 miles directly upwind with respect to the southeast trades from major population center of Marquesas Islands. How this lone island measuring only 8 by 15 miles and located so far to the east came to be settled will probably always be a mystery. Two candidate settlement voyages come to mind: from the Marquesas during a massive El Niño such as that of 1982-1983, when westerly winds extended across the eastern South

Pacific; and from Mangareva (or its outlier Pitcairn, located several hundred miles closer to Rapa Nui), or from another island along the southern edge of East Polynesia, by means of spells of winter westerlies such as those that enabled *Hokule'a* to sail from Samoa to Tahiti (Finney 1993b) (Figure 18).

But why would voyagers have headed that way? Were they simply searching for land, any land, to be found beyond the islands of central East Polynesia? Or, were they stimulated to sail specifically toward Rapa Nui after observing that some migratory birds periodically flew toward that direction, and then back from it? Whatever the case, the great profusion of sea birds that daily ranged out from Rapa Nui before humans and their accompanying rats arrived may have provided a significantly broadened radius of discovery for voyagers who sailed anywhere near the island (Van Tilburg, 1994).

The question of whether or not some particularly intrepid voyagers continued on beyond the eastern frontier of Polynesia to reach the coast of the Americas has long been debated. The impetus for such discussion has primarily been the need to explain how the sweet potato, a South American cultigen, reached East Polynesia, where it was being cultivated at the time of European contact (Yen 1974). Strict application of the principle of Occam's Razor that we should always choose the simpler over the more complex explanation would seem to favor a hypothesis of its introduction to Polynesia through a one-way raft trip by South Americans over a more complicated scenario requiring Polynesians to make a long round trip to South America and back. However, given the Polynesian mastery of ocean voyaging, introduction by a round-trip canoe voyage cannot be dismissed simply on grounds of a philosophical principle.

The outbound leg to South America presents the greatest sailing challenge. As tacking directly against the trades 4,000 miles from the Marquesas, or even 2,300 miles from Rapa Nui, seems out of the question, in all likelihood voyagers seeking to sail so far to the east would have done so by exploiting westerly winds. During the age of sail, square riggers bound from Polynesia to South America followed a circuitous route, sailing first south out of the trades and into the higher latitudes, and then turning east to run before the westerlies that prevail there. But to follow this square rigger route would have been most risky for canoe voyagers. Even if a canoe did not break up in the rough seas of the "roaring forties," her crew would have stood a good chance of succumbing from exposure to the cold winds and seas raking over such a low-slung, open vessel. Voyagers from as far away as the

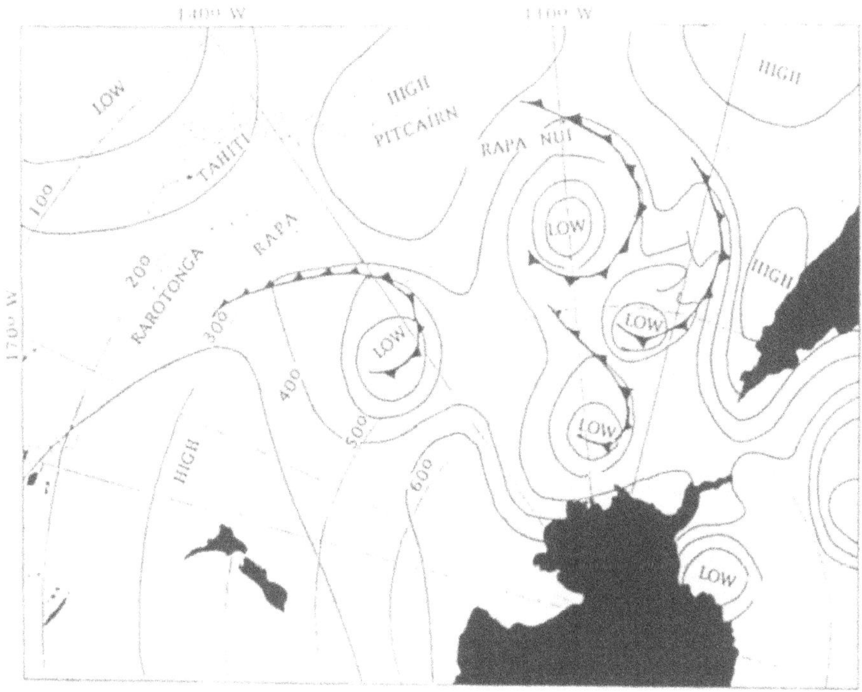

Figure 18. Surface weather patterns for 8 July 1988 showing low pressure troughs extending north into the trade wind belt, bring westerly winds favorable for sailing to Rapa Nui and beyond.

Marquesas might, however, have been able to exploit a massive westerly wind reversal during a major El Niño to sail directly for South America. Alternatively, those starting from Rapa Nui or one of the more southerly islands of central East Polynesia might have been able to work their way to the coast by exploiting a series of episodes of winter westerlies brought about by the successive passage through the trade wind field of low pressure troughs extending north from passing lows (Finney, 1994c).(Figure 19).

For any canoe that reached South America, a return voyage back to Polynesia would seem to have been well within Polynesian nautical capabilities. Once any returning Polynesians cleared the coastal wind belt and the north-flowing Humboldt Current (Peru Current), they would have stood a good chance of running before trade winds all or at least most of the way to East Polynesia—unless they happened to sail during a major El Niño event or strayed too far to the north or south out of the southeast trade wind belt. Using a conservative estimate of an average daily run of 100 miles, a crossing of some 4,000 miles to the Marquesas would take around 40 days. Providing enough food and water could be carried for the trip, and particularly if enough fish and rainwater (or liquid expressed from the flesh of raw fish) could be obtained along the way, such a voyage would be well within survival limits.

North to Hawai'i and Southwest to Aotearoa

Not, apparently, until the central islands of East Polynesia had been settled did voyagers depart from the pattern of eastward expansion and sail out of the tropical South Pacific—north across the equator where they found Hawai'i, and southwest of the tropics and across temperate latitudes to discover the huge continental chunks modern Maori call Aotearoa.

What possessed the discoverers of Hawai'i to sail so far to the north into unfamiliar seas and under stars never seen before? The Marquesas group, located some 1,800 miles southeast by east from Hawai'i, is the leading candidate as the source of the first migrants to colonize Hawai'i primarily because the Hawaiian language is generally considered to be most closely related to Marquesan—specifically, southern Marquesan (Emory 1963; Green 1966; Elbert 1982).[4] If this was the case, were the Marquesan discoverers of Hawai'i enticed northward by observing how each year the plover and other migratory shore birds that cannot rest on water flew off in that direction only to return some months later? Or, had an exploring party heading northwest over the equator spied Polaris

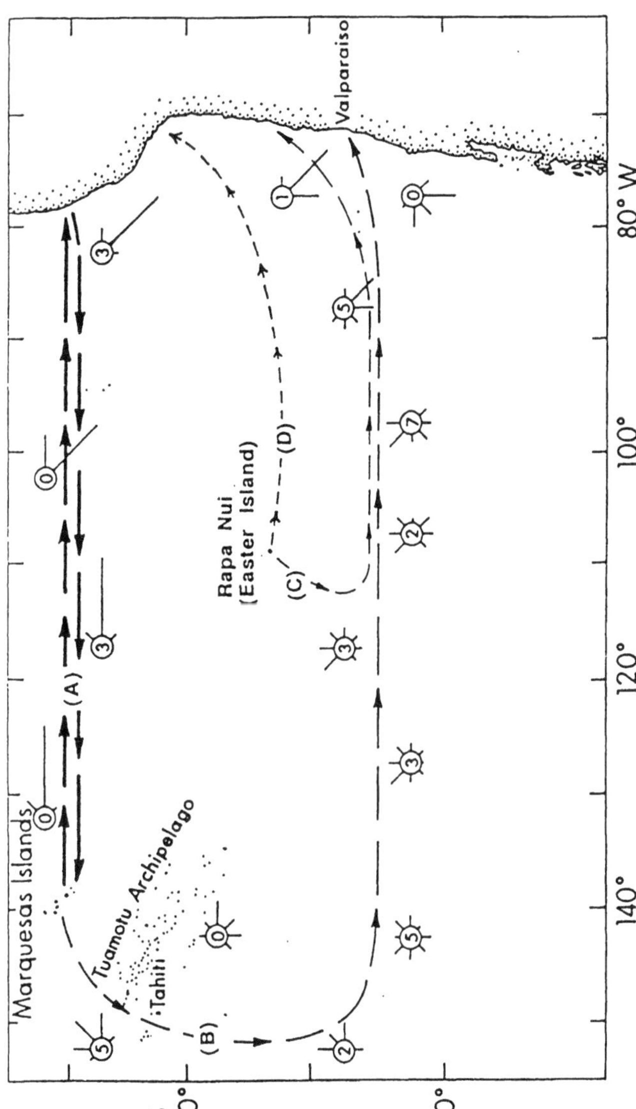

Figure 19. Sailing routes between Polynesia and South America: (A) Peter Buck's hypothesized direct round-trip by sailing canoe from the Marquesas to South America and return; (B) Nineteenth century square-rigger route from the Marquesas using mid-latitude westerlies;(C) proposed sailing canoe route from Rapa Nui using mid-latitude westerlies; (D) proposed sailing canoe route from Rapa Nui using "winter westerlies." Each wind rose indicates the winds that have prevailed in that region according to ship reports. The wind percentages are indicated by the length of the lines drawn along the eight points of the compass; the direction of the wind is toward the circle. The figure in the center of each circle gives the percentage of calms, light airs and variable winds.

just above the northern horizon, and then, entranced by this immobile star that is not visible in the Southern Hemisphere, turned to sail due north directly for it until they chanced upon the Hawaiian islands? Whatever the case, it is clear from both computer simulations or drift voyages and our own experience in sailing between the South and North Pacific that Hawai'i was probably dis-covered by sailors trying to find land, for it takes a conscious and concerted effort to sail across the southeast trades zone, then the doldrum belt, and then into the northeast trades zone to reach Hawai'i from the Marquesas or elsewhere in central East Polynesia.

Hokule'a's voyage from Rarotonga to Aotearoa shows how early Polynesians could have sailed southwest all the way to Aotearoa by exploiting, in the seas south of the trade wind belt, spells of easterly winds revolving around large high pressure zones that begin to dominate these latitudes in the late spring. But, it does not explain why the first discoverers headed that way. Were they sailing along the bearing they had seen taken by migrating land birds, or were they running before easterly winds to see where these would take their canoe? Whatever the case, once voyagers reached Aotearoa the Polynesian realm was extended far to the southwest, making this oceanic triangle the largest portion of the globe by far to be populated by people stemming from a common source and sharing an ancestral culture.

Backwash to the West

When, on his second voyage into the Pacific, Captain Cook sailed from Polynesia west into Melanesian waters and met the islanders there he and his scientists recognized that they had left the realm of his peoples so similar in appearance, language, and customs that they formed a "single Nation," and had entered into a region populated by diverse peoples whose dark skins, various customs, and multitudinous languages so differentiated them from the Polynesians. However, on one island in Vanuatu (the archipelago which Cook named the New Hebrides), they were surprised to encounter people who looked and acted like the islanders to the east and spoke a language they recognized as virtually identical to that of Tonga (Cook 1961:503-504, 529-530, 537, 541). This led Cook to speculate that there might be other such outposts settled from the east scattered throughout the western South Pacific. The English navigator was correct. Some dozen and a half "Polynesian outliers" are found on small islands scattered from Vanuatu west all the way to the atoll of Nukumanu located just north of Bougainville island, and two other atolls, Kapingamarangi and Nukuoro, located farther to the north in seas generally classified as part of Micronesia.

Between these three outliers in the western Pacific and Rapa Nui in the eastern Pacific, Polynesian cultures are spread over some 96 degrees of longitude, more than a quarter of the way around the globe.

These outliers, all small coral or volcanic islands, appear to have been settled late in Polynesian prehistory by a westward, "backwash" movement of canoes from Tonga, Samoa, and other long-settled West Polynesian islands with which they are linguistically affiliated. Since the outliers lie downwind with respect to the trades from West Polynesia, their settlement constitutes the one phase of Polynesian settlement that, according to computer simulated drift voyages, could easily have occurred involuntarily (Ward 1976). This does not rule out the possibility, however, that colonizing groups intentionally sailed to the west in search of a land to raid or conquer, as is suggested by oral traditions from Tikopia and other outliers about marauding Tongans invading their shores (Firth 1961).

Post-Colonization, Inter-Archipelago Voyaging

Once Polynesia had been thoroughly settled, once all the islands had been found and colonized, did long-range voyaging cease? Or did canoes keep sailing back and forth throughout the region, linking islands and archipelagos together in a series of overlapping communication spheres? Judging from the observations made by Cook, Bougainville, and other late eighteenth and early nineteenth century European visitors, we would have to conclude that long-range, two-way voyaging was not at all widespread in Polynesia at that time. The peripheral islands were largely if not totally isolated from the rest of Polynesia; neither the Hawaiians, nor the Rapa Nui, nor the Maori of Aotearoa seem to have been in regular contact with their cousins in the core of Polynesia composed of West Polynesia and central East Polynesia. Even within these central islands, evidence for wide-spread voyaging links at the time of European contact is limited. To be sure, Marquesans may have been raiding the Tuamotu atolls to the south (Quiros 1904, 2:152; Audran 1927), while in turn the Tuamotuans were voyaging to nearby Tahiti and the other Society Islands to obtain stone tools and other high island products (Oliver, 1974, 1:214), just as the atoll-dwellers of Pukapuka in the Northern Cooks were similarly sailing to Samoa to obtain their high island products (Beaglehole and Beaglehole 1938:352). But these and most other documented routes from this period were between adjacent archipelagos and were within or just slightly above Sharp's 300 mile limit. Only from Tonga is there clear evidence of major long-distance voyaging. In late prehistoric times, and continuing into the contact period, the Tongans were sailing their large and fast double canoes throughout West Polynesia and far into Melanesian waters to the west (Dillon 1829:112; Kirch 1984:237-242).

Yet oral traditions from throughout Polynesia are filled with references about canoes sailing to distant islands for a variety of purposes. These voyaging traditions include, for example, tales about the rovings around Polynesia of the Samoan chief Karika (Williams 1838:64, 165-169; 1876:23-28; Crocombe and Crocombe 1968:140-142), about chiefs and priests making long voyages back and forth between Hawai'i and "Kahiki" (arguably the island of Tahiti) (Emerson 1893; Finney 1991), about periodic pilgrimages made by islanders from as far away as Aotearoa and Rotuma to the great Tahitian temple of Taputapuatea on the island of Ra'iatea (Henry 1928:121-127), and about Marquesas voyages made to Rarotonga to obtain supplies of precious red feathers (Von Den Steinen 1988:11-31). If we accept these and other such tales as indicative of a period when Polynesians were sailing freely throughout the region, then it follows that at the time of European contact voyaging must have been, with the exception of Tonga and perhaps a few other islands, in a state of decline. This, of course, is exactly the thesis promulgated by such late nineteenth and early twentieth century writers as Abraham Fornander (1969) and S. Percy Smith (1898).

Andrew Sharp treated their notion of a golden age of voyaging with contempt. His logic was simple. If intentional voyaging was not wide-spread when Cook and the other navigators saw the Polynesians, then it never was. Tales about such voyaging were myths that had nothing to do with reality. To Sharp, contact period Polynesians were not intentionally undertaking long voyages because they, like their ancestors had been "accidentally" deposited on an island by the vagaries of wind and current, they and their descendants had been essentially stuck there, able to travel back and forth only to nearby islands no more than 300 miles away.

Yet our experimental voyages, as well as the documented maritime adventures of the Tongans, certainly demonstrate that Polynesian canoes, seamanship, and ways of navigating were up to the task of making long, navigated voyages. This suggests that although such tales as those cited above may not be literal history, they could indicate that there was a period following initial settlement when canoes ranged widely over much of Polynesia. If so, what might have motivated such voyaging activity?

Sheer necessity must have played some role. A number of archaeologists have recently begun to posit that the ability to sail back and forth between a newly settled island and the home island would have given a struggling colony an edge for survival in that planting materials, tools and healthy, marriageable youths could be obtained through such continuing links (Kirch 1988b; Hunt 1989). Furthermore, it seems clear that atoll societies such as those in the Tuamotus and Northern Cooks needed to keep in contact with high islands in order to obtain stone tools and other high islands products not available on islands composed only of coral and sand. But such utilitarian reasoning cannot explain all voyaging, whether documented in the historical record or featured in legend.

The Tongans, for example, voyaged much farther and wider than any trade imperatives. In fact, during the late prehistoric period extending into post contact times they seem to have been reinventing Polynesian voyaging on an imperial model, establishing exchange links and military-political overlordship with islands throughout the Lau group of Fiji and as far away as Rotuma well to the north of Fiji, as well as venturing far into Melanesian waters on raiding voyages. As for the voyages featured in oral traditions around Polynesia, some were said to have been made for such eminently practical reasons as to fetch breadfruit, sweet potato or some other cultigen needed by a struggling colonial outpost. Many voyaging legends, however, tell about chiefs, priests, and other high-ranking people sailing the seas to visit far off lands for a variety of reasons that might be called "adventurous" to make a pilgrimage to a sacred center, to bring new religious ideas and institutions to a "backward" island, to wreak revenge on a mortal enemy, to marry a fabled beauty, to seek red feathers and other prestigious items, and so on. Judging from the nature of Polynesian culture, as well as Mary Helms's intriguing analysis of the importance of such motivations for travel in the ancient world (Helms 1988), voyaging for such "adventurous" purposes cannot be dismissed as so much wishful thinking on the part of story tellers, particularly since, as will be discussed in the next section, the events in some of these tales may be reflected in the archaeological record.

If, however, long range voyaging was once so useful and fulfilling, why would it have declined? In a few cases environmental degradation may have been at work. For example, once the Rapa Nui had denuded their island of trees they were left with only scraps of wood out of which they could build vessels no larger than the tiny fishing canoes seen by the first Europeans to visit their lonely island. But this reasoning cannot be applied to such islands as Hawai'i, Tahiti, Samoa, and Aotearoa, where at contact times there were still ample timber supplies for building large canoes.

Why would Polynesians living on such well-timbered high islands ever have given up such an exciting activity as overseas voyaging? One explanation that came to mind as we labored to build *Hokule'a*, and then to sail her over legendary sea routes, hinges upon the economists' concept of "opportunity cost." Building, sailing, and maintaining a large voyaging canoe is costly, whether measured in dollars or in months of labor, trees sacrificed to make the hulls and other components, and fathoms of coconut fiber line to lash these together and make the rigging. Early in the evolution of Polynesian societies it must have been judged worthwhile to invest so much labor and material resources in voyaging. Once, however, the islands had enough people, once the resultant populations had grown and matured, competing activities evidently came to be considered as more exciting or pressing. At the time of contact, for example, the leaders of the mature chiefdoms of Hawai'i and Tahiti were not concentrating their energy and resources on mounting overseas expeditions, but rather on intensifying agricultural production, expanding their chiefdom's boundaries at the expense of others, promoting their favored gods, and other local endeavors.

Discussion

One of the first direct attacks against least-moves modeling of Polynesian migration and the assumption of the relative if not absolute isolation of an island or group after settlement was mounted in 1970. At a meeting on Polynesian prehistory held in Fiji, linguist Bruce Biggs (1972) decried what he called the "simplistic view of Polynesian settlement" that was then popular. In particular, he admonished archaeologists not to be misled by the spare, family-tree diagrams linguists employ to portray the relationships between Polynesian languages. These should be taken as models of language relationships, he said, and not as diagrams indicating a unilineal series of migrations and branchings without any backtracking along the way or voyaging back and forth between the nodes and end points of the branches. Biggs argued that neither the logic of language classification, nor the empirical record in Polynesia of language borrowing and replacement supported such a view. Accordingly he called upon his archaeological colleagues to develop a theory of "multiple intra-Polynesian migration and settlement" to account for the complex reality of Polynesian colonization and subsequent inter-island relations.

Our experimental demonstration of how a double-canoe and non-instrument navigation methods can be used to make long, navigated voyages throughout Polynesia has helped to stimulate the emergence of such a theory. Critical elements toward it have been appearing in such publications as Roger Green's writings about adaptational steps in Pacific colonization (Green 1975;1987), Patrick Kirch's (1986) rethinking of central East Polynesia as constituting a regional homeland of intercommunicating cultures, William Keegan and Jared Diamond's (1987) analysis of Polynesian colonization in global biogeographical perspective, and most recently, in the work of Geoffrey Irwin and his colleagues joining computer simulations of intentional voyaging with the latest archaeological finds to model the colonization of the Pacific (Irwin 1992; Irwin et al. 1990).

In addition to our experiments, the discoveries made by the archaeologists themselves in their excavations have been critical to this reemergence of voyaging as central to Polynesian prehistory. Those made on islands spread from the Bismarck Archipelago to the western edge of Polynesia have demonstrated how rapidly island after island along this two thousand mile migration route was discovered and colonized, and also that the resultant colonies were able to maintain contact with each other over great distances (Green 1979a; Kirch and Hunt 1988a).[5] Within Polynesia proper, evidence found in early sites indicating that colonists brought their plants and animals with them, and in later sites indicating that stone adzes and other items were exchanged widely among islands and archipelagos, has provided a broader perspective on the process of oceanic colonization and regional development (Suggs 1961b, Yen 1973; Davidson 1974; Bellwood 1978). Even excavations conducted on Polynesian outliers in Melanesia have contributed by showing how legends of settlement and cultural intrusion can be supported by hard evidence (Garanger 1972a, 1972b; Kirch and Yen 1984).

Determining the extent of inter-island and inter-archipelago links is now becoming one of the most exciting fields in Pacific Island archaeology. For example, four recent Ph.D. dissertations—Walter (1990) on the Cook Islands, Rolett (in press) on the Marquesas, Weisler (1993) on Samoa, the Cook Islands, and Mangareva and its outliers, and Hunt (1989) on a Lapita culture in the Bismarcks—have focused on the analysis of archaeological evidence for the transport of pottery, stone tools, volcanic glass, and other artifacts and materials that can be traced to their geological source. In particular, much attention is currently being directed toward sourcing adze blades and other tools made from basalt. Studies of the distribution of Samoan adzes in the central South Pacific have already demonstrated that adzes found within a wide circle of islands formed by the Tuvalu, Tokelau, Cooks, Tonga, and Fiji archipelagos can be traced to or near the famous quarry of Tatagamatau on the island of Tutuila, American Samoa (Best et al.

1992). Researchers are now working to sample all known sources of tool-grade basalt around Polynesia in order to develop a data base with which to source adzes and other basalt tools found in excavations and documented collections from throughout the region.

Following the lead of Garanger and of Kirch and Yen in the outliers, several prehistorians working in Polynesia proper are reviving the notion that oral traditions about migration and voyaging might actually reflect real events and processes and not simply be myths composed for functional, structural, or symbolic purposes, as Piddington (1956), Orbell (1985), and others have claimed over the last several decades. Some are even proposing that such once-anathematized migration scenarios drawn from tradition as the arrival in Aotearoa of a number of migratory canoes during the same period (Anderson 1991:790), the settlement of islands from multiple sources (Law 1994), and the impact of new migrants on an already established Hawaiian population, may be reflected in the archaeological record (Spriggs 1988; Dye 1989; Cachola-Abad 1993).

Yet however heartening it is to see that our research has helped make prehistorians consider seriously the role of voyaging, a few words of caution are in order about the application of the results of our experiments to modeling oceanic colonization.

First, the route-specific nature of our findings about two-way voyaging should not be overlooked. Repeatedly sailing *Hokule'a* between Hawai'i and Tahiti does not mean that earlier voyagers could have so successful sailed back and forth between all other pairs of distantly spaced islands. Whereas the Hawaiian archipelago and the Societies-Northern Tuamotus spread of islands form wide targets, and the alignment of Hawai'i and Tahiti across the trades are conducive for voyaging back and forth, conditions for sailing between some other sets of islands are less favorable. For example, Rapa Nui's position 1,100 to 1,900 miles to windward (with respect to the trades) of the nearest islands to the west, and its lack of surrounding islands to provide an expanded target for navigators, would have greatly challenged any would-be, two-way voyagers. Although sailing west before the trades to large, archipelagic targets would not have been difficult, the exact timing of westerly wind shifts required to sail back to Rapa Nui and smallness of this lone target would have greatly tested any voyagers wanting to return to this tiny, isolated outpost—particularly after the island's bird populations, and hence its detectability, had been reduced (Finney 1993b).

The conditions that made it difficult to sail repeatedly to Rapa Nui did not apply, however, to the archipelagos to the west—the Australs, Tuamotus, Marquesas, Societies, and Cooks—which were all within sailing and navigational range of each other. If, as currently is being investigated, during the early centuries of occupation people traveled widely among these archipelagos, differentiation between the islands and groups may have been delayed as people shared artifacts, ideas, and linguistic innovations. The uniqueness of Rapa Nui, as marked by the great elaboration of the huge stone statues and other features of their culture, may therefore be a function of isolation from regional cultural developments shared among populations in these central archipelagos and not because Rapa Nui was settled significantly earlier than other East Polynesian islands, or directly from West Polynesia or even more exotic sources (Pawley and Green 1984:123; Langdon and Tryon 1983; Biggs 1972:134-152).

Second, there is a temptation to presume too much planning and order in the process of oceanic colonization. Just because voyaging experiments indicate how well adapted the canoes and methods of navigation were for two-way voyaging, and computer simulations demonstrate how voyagers could have employed this capability for rapid and efficient expansion, it does not necessarily follow that all the islands were discovered and settled through a series of planned voyages of exploration, followed by returns to the home islands and then the sending out of fully equipped colonizing expeditions. Judging from numerous legends as well as some eye-witness tales reported by early European visitors (for example, Porter [1822:54-55] on the Marquesas), it seems likely that one-way ventures, combining exploration and colonization in a single voyage, and accidental discoveries, whereby an uninhabited island was found when sailing for a purpose other than discovery, played important roles in this oceanic expansion. Consider, for example the saga of the twin atolls of Manihiki and Rakahanga in the Northern Cooks as recorded from the elders by Peter Buck (1932). A man named Huku chanced upon the atolls while fishing in seas far to the north of his own island, but kept his discovery secret when he returned to his home island, believed to be Rarotonga. Some years later Huku's son-in-law was defeated in war and forced to flee with his wife, Huku's daughter. Using directions from her father, the couple sailed to Manihiki-Rakahanga and founded the first settlement there.

Third, although *Hokule'a*'s record of sailing around Polynesia without major mishaps might seem to indicate that long-distance canoe travel was a safe, even routine activity, our experiences and those of other experimental voyagers, as well as historical reports of canoe disasters, suggest that some losses were inevitable. When *Hokule'a* sails on long voyages away from Hawai'i, she is followed by a yacht and carries safety gear dictated by Coast Guard regulations as well as by the experience of two accidents that occurred while sailing unescorted in the rough seas between the islands of the Hawaiian chain: a swamp-ing, and a capsize. Both times the canoe was recovered and all the crew saved, except for one crewman who disappeared after the capsize while attempting to summon help by paddling a surfboard to land. Had these accidents happened while sailing alone in heavy weather, the craft and everyone on board would probably have been lost.

Two reconstructed canoes built after *Hokule'a* have been lost at sea in attempts to make long crossings. The double-canoe *Spirit of Nukuhiva* broke up when cross beams connecting her hulls failed during squally weather while sailing from the Marquesas to Hawai'i (Finney 1994a:298-299), and the *Taratai II*, an outrigger canoe modeled along Micronesian lines, broke up when her outrigger support beams gave way during an attempt to sail from Tonga to Tahiti (Siers 1978). Fortunately, the survivors from the *Spirit of Nukuhiva* were rescued by an escorting yacht and those from *Taratai II* by a small ship that just happened by several days after the accident. Otherwise these modern voyagers would have suffered the fate that must have befallen more than a few canoes that broke up at sea during the colonization of the Pacific, and subsequent inter-island voyaging.

Early European visitors to Polynesia recorded a number of harrowing tales of misadventures at sea. For example, in 1826 Captain Beechey of *H.M.S. Blossom* chanced upon the forty survivors of some 150 people who had set out from Ana'a atoll in the Tuamotus in three double canoes to sail to Tahiti, several hundreds of miles to the east. When they were within a half-day's sail of Tahiti the trade winds died and a spell of violent northwesterly winds erupted forcing the canoes to the southeast. When the westerlies subsided and the trades returned, they tried to sail for Tahiti once more. Again, however, upon nearing Tahiti they were struck by northwesterlies which this time drove them into the southeastern Tuamotus, wrecking the single surviving canoe on the uninhabited atoll of Ahunui where Beechey found the shattered vessel and her forlorn passengers. At the time they were attempting to rebuild the canoe and lay in stores to sail back to Ana'a, although it is not recorded whether or not they ever reached there (Beechey 1831, 1:220-237).

Perhaps the only systematic attempt to compile a record of lost canoes was conducted in the Marshall Islands of Micronesia at the turn of the last century by a seasoned mariner who signed his report "Captain Winkler of the German Navy" (Winkler 1901:507-508). The Marshal-lese, who at that time were still sailing widely in their swift outrigger canoes, could recall the loss over previous generations of many single canoes, as well as five instances when all or most of the canoes in large fleets had set sail but were never seen again. For example, one of Winkler's informants told him how, in "about 1830, a flotilla of over 100 canoes set out on a voyage. It was destroyed, and only one boat, with the chief's daughter, Ligibberik, on board, drove on an island in the ocean; the others were never heard from again." Although the round figure of one hundred may not be exact, this tale of mass disaster, and four other cases of the loss of all or most of the canoes of a fleet (from tropical cyclones?) that his informants told him had occurred over the previous century, cannot be ignored.

To my knowledge, no similar survey was ever attempted (or at least published) for any Polynesian group. Although Polynesian voyaging tales primarily chronicle the adventures of successful seafarers, some do mention those, such as Hawai'i's Lonoikamakahiki, who set sail for overseas but were never heard from again. Probably many of those who disappeared actually reached land, but chose not to return or were unable to do so. Some, however, must never have made it to another shore. In *Vikings of the Sunrise*, Peter Buck's lyrical if now largely ignored treatment of Polynesian migration and culture, this Maori scholar recognizes that although the vast majority of those who braved the seas reached land, over the centuries many were lost at sea when their canoes broke up, or, as the following passage relates, when they failed to find land (Buck 1938:96):

> Others there must have been, as daring and trusting in their star, whose course led them into empty seas. Such unlucky ones sleep beneath the barren sea roads they so vainly followed. If the sea ever gives up its dead, what a parade of Polynesian mariners will rise from the depths when the call of the shell trumpet summons them to the last muster roll! Their numbers will bear witness to the courage of those who dared but failed to reach the land which was not there. For them no human songs were sung, but the sea croons a requiem in a language they understand.

Obviously, however, such losses did not stop pioneering Austronesian sailors and their Micronesian and Polynesian successors from expanding over the Pacific. Neither did it prevent them, during certain periods, from voyaging widely back and forth between already settled islands and archipelagos, as their traditions celebrate and archaeological work is beginning to confirm. Their world was oceanic. The sea was not a barrier but a broad, multi-directional highway, over which they sailed to find new homes, obtain scarce resources, visit friends and relatives, pick a fight, make pilgrimages to sacred temples, and accomplish various other purposes.

NOTES

1. Chappell (1993) suggests that evidence of widespread fires in pollen cores may indicate a human presence in Australia as early as 140,000 years ago.
2. Nautical miles and knots (nautical miles per hour) are used throughout this essay. One nautical mile equals 1.15 statute (land) miles, and 1.85 kilometers.
3. The sailing performance of *Hokule'a* and the accomplishments of her non-instrument navigators are documented in Baybayan et al. (1987), Finney (1977, 1979a, 1979b, 1993, 1994a, 1994b), Finney et al. (1986), and Finney et al. (1989), Kyselka (1989), and Lewis (1977).
4. Alternatively, it could be argued that the Hawaiian language seems so Marquesan not because Marquesans were necessarily the first to settle Hawai'i, but because of the many canoes that reached Hawai'i most came from the Marquesas.
5. In addition to evidence of widespread exchange along the Lapita route eastward into the Pacific, recent discoveries in Indonesian archaeological sites of obsidian from the Bismarcks indicate that exchange links were also maintained with islands to the west of the Bismarcks (Bellwood and Koon 1989).

7. BEYOND THE AUSTRONESIAN HOMELAND: THE AUSTRIC HYPOTHESIS AND ITS IMPLICATIONS FOR ARCHAEOLOGY

Robert Blust

University of Hawaii

Introduction.

When it comes to questions of distant genetic relationship in linguistics I must confess that I have always come down very decidedly on the side of skepticism. To some extent this orientation may be a prejudice instilled by training, a point made repeatedly by outraged long-rangers such as Harold Fleming (the flamboyant and somewhat self-persecuted editor of *Mother Tongue)*. I was taught as a student that the only reliable basis for demonstrating the common origin of languages is the complete elimination of chance and borrowing as plausible explanations for observed similarity. I was also taught that the best evidence that can be marshaled for this purpose is lexical, since the generally arbitrary linking of sound and meaning in the lexicon can be seen as a mass of *independent* historical events not likely to be duplicated by convergent development, and in the case of basic vocabulary not likely to be acquired by contact.

The enduring basis of my skepticism, however, has been empirical, not ideological. Despite a general agnosticism toward all claims of distant genetic relationship in linguistics I have consistently maintained a lively respect for observation, and in particular for observations that appear anomalous in the light of prevailing theory. The problem that I have had with such theories quite simply is the quality of the arguments offered in support of them. Those that I am in a position to judge professionally, that is, those theories which involve the Austronesian (AN) languages, in general have a rather dismal history of misrepresenting the data, or at the very least of stretching meanings beyond the limits of credibility, of bizarre leaps of faith based on nothing better than random similarities, or of wild distortions of the Comparative Method intended to manufacture sound correspondences where none in fact exist. And, of course, these theories have attempted to link AN with almost everything under the sun, from Indo-European (Humboldt 1836-39, Bopp 1840, Brandstetter 1937), to Austroasiatic (Schmidt 1906), to Semitic (Macdonald 1907), to Japanese (van Hinloopen Labberton 1924, Kawamoto 1977 et seq., Benedict 1990), to Tai-Kadai (Benedict 1942, 1975, 1990), to Chinese (Sagart 1993, 1994), to various South American Indian languages (Rivet 1925, 1926), and to Beothuk of Newfoundland (Campbell 1892), among others perhaps best left unmentioned.

Probably the most sophisticated and certainly the most influential of these proposals in recent decades has been the Austro-Tai hypothesis of Paul Benedict.[1] Benedict (1942) presented enough evidence to support what might be described as a tantalizing argument for distant genetic relationship. One of the charms of this publication is its elegant restraint: a suggestive set of lexical similarities is presented and some tentative conclusions drawn. Where reconstructions are cited they are Austronesian (called "Indonesian") forms drawn from Dempwolff (1938), or less commonly, ancestral Tai reconstructions based on Benedict's own research. No attempt is made to reconstruct Proto-Austro-Tai, and near the end of his article Benedict maintains (597) that "most of the important lexical correspondences have been uncovered." The general tone of the paper is, I believe, accurately reflected by the following quotation (599), which refers to Thai, Kadai and "Indonesian" as established linguistic stocks:

> If we accept the view that these three linguistic stocks are genetically related, we must place the center of their dispersion somewhere in the South China area, the present home of the Kadai tribes, as well as the early home of the Thai peoples. On the basis of this distribution we can conclude, with a high degree of probability, that the proto-IN-speaking peoples migrated from the South China coast, perhaps via the island of Hainan, to Formosa on the north, the Philippines on the east, and Annam, Borneo, Java, Sumatra, and the Malay Peninsula on the south. The Cham and Malay linguistic areas, in southern Annam and the Malay Peninsula, respectively, surely are to be regarded as Indonesian enclaves on the Asiatic mainland, not as possible points of departure for the Indonesian migrations.

Following a lapse of a quarter of a century during which he practiced psychiatry for a living but continued to pursue linguistics as an absorbing avocation, Benedict returned to Austro-Tai with a vengeance in a series of publications which appeared in 1966 and 1967. The results of this work were brought together and supplemented in

Benedict (1975). What perhaps first strikes the reader who compares Benedict's 1975 book with his 1942 article is the remarkable difference in his approach to method in the two publications. Gone is the restraint of the early 1940s and in its place are discussions in a mode that might be called "argument by hyperbole." The following quotation, in which Benedict describes his return to the Austro-Tai question after a quarter of a century, is illustrative (1975: 2-3):

> His goals were extremely modest: to strengthen a point here or there, to come up with a few lexical correspondences previously not noted. He was totally unprepared for the mass of material which he uncovered, partly with the aid of new key factors which will be described. After all, he had already announced in the original paper his belief that "most of the important lexical correspondences have been uncovered," and he had seen no reason, over the years, for changing this view. What is more, his colleagues appear to have believed him, since virtually no new comparative material has been brought forward to this time. It would appear that this unfortunate statement, which surely must be ranked with the most egregious overstatements of our times, contributed to a veritable standstill in this field.

To anyone seriously interested in the question of distant genetic relationship in Southeast Asia Benedict's "new key factors" turn out to be a major disappointment. Far from being metaphorical keys to unlock a previously unknown treasure trove of language history, these new procedures of reconstruction amount to an abandonment of the constraints that gave the Comparative Method its historical successes not only in the Indo-European field, but also in the Austronesian field as established by Dempwolff (1934-38). In fact Benedict's methods afford so much latitude to the imagination that almost any two language families could be "related" through the application of a similar approach to different data, and indeed, in his later work he extends the original hypothesis to include the Miao-Yao (now called Hmong-Mien) languages of eastern China. We need only consider his reconstruction for 'dog', in which PAN *asu (reflected with an unexplained initial /w/ in a handful of Formosan languages), Proto-Thai *hma, and Proto-Miao-Yao *klu are derived from PAT *[wa]kləwm[a]. There is no evidence of any kind for recurrent sound correspondences between these forms. But then, strictly speaking, the method does not require recurrent sound correspondences, since 1.bracketed elements can be included or omitted at one's convenience, 2. many PAT consonant clusters are unique, and 3. although Benedict pays lip service to the Comparative Method by including a table of so-called "Austro-Thai sound correspondences" (p. 155), these often fail to agree with the actual correspondences which the diligent reader can independently extract from the proposed cognate sets. Finally, even when the correspondences listed in Benedict's table do agree with those that emerge from a study of the supporting evidence, they frequently show unexplained splits, as where PAN *b corresponds unpredictably to PTK *p, *b or *v in initial position, and to *b, *v and *w medially (Benedict 1975: 155).

What Benedict has done in this sample reconstruction (and many others like it) does not differ essentially from a proposal to combine say, English 'dog' and Tagalog *asó* in a reconstructed Proto-English-Tagalog *dogasu, the first three segments having been lost in Tagalog, and the last three in English. To most scholars this is the very model of methodological madness. To Benedict in the years since his return to this field in the mid 1960s, something very similar to it has been the key to what he regards as progress in understanding the linguistic prehistory of Southeast Asia.

Apart from his methodological idiosyncracies, Benedict is an extraordinary scholar, probably unmatched in the history of the field for the breadth and detail of his knowledge of Southeast Asian linguistics. Moreover, the Austro-Tai hypothesis is not in itself implausible. It is generally agreed that both the Austronesian and Tai-Kadai language families have probable homelands in southern China. But in attempting to inflate what initially was a controlled and carefully argued proposal with hundreds of fanciful etymologies, Benedict has damaged his credibility, and tainted the discussion of what could very well be a valid genetic relationship.

There is another proposal regarding the distant genetic relationship of languages in Southeast Asia which has a more venerable pedigree than Austro-Tai, and it is one that Benedict has consciously rejected in print (1976, 1993). I am referring to the Austric hypothesis, first formulated explicitly by the Austrian ethnologist and linguist Wilhelm Schmidt in his book *Die Mon-Khmer Völker* 1906). Schmidt's book advanced two theses: 1) that the Munda languages of Eastern India and the Mon-Khmer languages of mainland Southeast Asia constitute a single language family to which he gave the name "Austroasiatic" (AA) and 2) that the Malayo-Polynesian languages, rechristened "Austronesian," are related to Austroasiatic in a superfamily that he called "Austric." The first of these theses is now well established, and the existence of an AA language family is not in doubt. The second thesis has had a more checkered history. Although it was initially accepted by such influential Austronesianists as Kern and Brandstetter, it was ignored by Otto Dempwolff, whose work laid the foundations for the comparative phonology of the Austronesian languages, and until fairly recently it has received only limited attention.

Schmidt's evidence for Austric consists of several formally similar affixes, and of a set of 215 appended lexical comparisons. The morphological evidence is particularly interesting, and at first sight compelling. The major syntactic relationships of many of the AN languages of Taiwan, the Philippines, western Indonesia, and a few other languages outside these areas such as Malagasy and Chamorro are expressed through an elaborate system of verbal affixes which generally work in conjunction with a smaller set of particles preposed to the noun phrase. These affixes include a variety of prefixes, the infixes *-um- and *-in-, and suffixes *-a, *-an, *-en and *-I. In some of the languages of the Philippines the infix *-um- (which typically marks inchoative and meteorological verbs, along with some other types of intransitives) and *-in- (which marks completive aspect, and is often used to form deverbal nominals) co-occur as *-inum- or *-umin-. Schmidt noted that Khmer, and to a lesser extent some other AA languages have infixes -m-, -n-, and that the double infix -mn- is found in Khmer and Nicobarese. He maintained further that the meanings of the infixes in the two families, though different, could plausibly be regarded as related.

Given the rarity of infixes in natural languages generally these agreements, down to specific details of co-occurrence, can hardly fail to be impressive. However, as Schmidt himself pointed out, in some AA languages almost any sonorous consonant may be infixed, including m, n, ñ, ŋ, l, and r. The striking superficial resemblance between the AN and AA infixes thus loses much of its force when the facts are viewed in a fuller comparative context.

Schmidt's lexical comparisons, although sometimes quite striking, fail to exhibit systematic phonological correspondences. Where the formal similarity is greatest he sometimes permits the meaning to vary considerably, as with Malay *lumut,* Tagalog *lúmot,* Mota *lumuta* 'moss', next to Khmer *lemuot* 'sticky, viscous, slippery'. Where the meaning is close or identical, the phonetic agreement — although still not based on recurrent sound correspondences— need not be close, as with Malay *ñamuk,* Munda *gamit* 'mosquito'. In a few cases Schmidt appears to have identified true cognates, but these are best explained as loans, as with the well-known AN form seen in Malay *danau*, Jarai *dənaw*next to *dönau* 'lake' in the Mon-Khmer language Bahnar, which borders Jarai on the north, and shows other evidence of borrowing from Jarai or other members of the Chamic branch of AN to which Jarai belongs.

Austric resurrected.

In short, throughout most of this century Schmidt's Austric hypothesis has been regarded as interesting, but inconclusive. Until quite recently this was my own assessment of the matter. However, my view of the Austric hypothesis has begun to change during the past year or two as a result of work by Lawrence A. Reid of the University of Hawaii (most notably Reid 1994b). Reid's background is principally in AN linguistics, and within this field his major area of concentration has been on the languages of the northern Philippines, with particular reference to morphological reconstruction and change. His interest in Austric was initially piqued by an unpublished description of Nancowry, an AA language spoken in the geographically isolated Nicobar Islands of the Andaman Sea. Perhaps in part because of their isolation the languages of the Nicobars have not experienced certain phonological mergers which are typical of mainland Mon-Khmer, where networks of contact and mutual influence have tended to create widely shared areal features. One of these changes is the centralization of penultimate vowels in what are called the 'presyllables' of 'sesquisyllabic' word forms. As a result of this change the vowel of an earlier infix which had the shape *-VC- became nondistinctive in the great majority of mainland Mon-Khmer languages, or dropped out entirely. This is not true, however, of Nicobarese, and the forms of the Nicobarese infixes corresponding to mainland Mon-Khmer -m- and -n- turn out to be -um- and -in-. This point may at first seem small, but in fact the preservation of earlier vowel contrasts in these two infixes is highly significant, as it greatly reduces the likelihood that the M-K and AN infixes resemble one another through chance. In general the Nancowry infix -um- has a causative function, although Reid argues that it sometimes marks inceptive verb forms, as in AN languages. Nancowry -in- and -an- are allomorphs of a noun-deriving infix which has functions that clearly overlap those of the similar infix *-in- in AN languages.

In addition, it had long been known that a causative prefix *pa- is widespread in AA as well as in AN languages. While this agreement is striking, it could conceivably be the result of a convergent innovation. What Reid has done in my view is to eliminate convincingly this alternative. In AN languages reflexes both of *pa- and of *ka causative are widespread. Moreover, in a number of disparate languages these affixes are combined as *paka-. Reid points out that not only Nicobarese, but also a number of mainland M-K languages including Mon, Khmer, Semai and Katu, have reflexes of a causative prefix *ka-, and that Katu combines the two as *paka-* to form double causatives. These are only some of the more striking pieces of morphological evidence that Reid has found in support of Schmidt's Austric hypothesis. He carefully considers both chance and borrowing as possible explanations, and finds neither of these alternatives convincing. At this point I must say that my general skepticism about such proposals crumbled rapidly. Here at last was a claim about the external relationships of the AN languages that appeared to meet the same demands made of established language families: that chance and borrowing be convincingly eliminated as alternative explanations of observed similarity before advancing a hypothesis of genetic relationship.

The archaeological implications of Austric.

No matter how much one may try to prepare for them in advance, I suspect that fundamental changes of belief are always abrupt. The evidence needed to bring about a change of conviction reaches a certain critical mass, and one is pushed over the brink. It is a somewhat dizzying experience to suddenly see the world in a different perspective than the one made familiar through long habituation. But, as I said earlier, the issues at stake in such claims are ultimately empirical, not ideological, and it therefore struck me almost immediately that while the Austric hypothesis may help to explain what would otherwise appear to be very surprising similarities between unrelated languages, it also raises some very fundamental questions. The first of these concerns cognate vocabulary. If AA and AN are genetically related, why have scholars had so little success in demonstrating recurrent sound correspondences between them? I suppose that my answer to this question must be as follows: in the absence of any empirically supported argument to the contrary, I am willing to believe that a core of key grammatical morphemes could survive long enough for virtually all of the vocabulary of a proto-language to be lost through attrition. It is certainly not inherently implausible that lexical evidence could fall away over the millennia while a core of grammatically central affixes survives, albeit with evolving differences of function, and in fact there are known cases that suggest the same. One or more of the AN affixes *-um-, *-in-, *pa-, *ka-, *paka-, *-a and *-an, for example, are attested with the same or different functions in languages which sometimes share less than 10 percent of their basic vocabulary.[2]

The second question, in my view, is at least as interesting and challenging as the question of genetic relationship itself. If there was an Austric proto-language, where was it spoken? Reid does not address this issue at all, but it clearly is the question of greatest importance to the archaeologist.

The determination of linguistic homelands is ultimately based on the subgrouping of the languages compared, even when the evidence used relates to such lexical domains as terms for flora and fauna (Blust 1984/85). The basic principle for inferring probable centers of dispersal was first clearly enunciated by Sapir (1916), and formalized by Dyen (1956) under the name "principle of least moves." Briefly, it holds that the area of greatest diversity is the most likely center of origin, where "diversity" is understood in terms of the number of primary subgroups, not number of languages. Based on this principle, and on temporal extrapolations from radiocarbon dates which must be associated with ancestral AN-speaking communities in the central Pacific, I have maintained in a number of publications since the mid-1970s that PAN probably was spoken on or near the island of Taiwan in the period 6000-7000 BP. As it turns out, the radiocarbon profile for Neolithic cultures in island Southeast Asia fully supports this inference.[3]

Where, then, was the AA homeland? Diffloth (p.c.) has suggested, that it was in the Burma-Yunnan border region, perhaps in the middle Salween basin (Figure 5). There is almost universal agreement that the first split within AA separated the Munda languages of central and eastern India on the one hand from the M-K languages of mainland SEA on the other, and the Burma-Yunnan border region is roughly midway between these two geographical areas. In another publication (Blust 1994), I suggest that AA has the longest record of settlement in mainland SEA south of China, well antedating the expansion of Tibeto-Burman, Tai-Kadai, Austronesian and Hmong-Mien languages into this area, and I propose there that PAA was spoken in the Assam-Burma border region by 6000 BP or earlier. Discussions with Munda and Mon-Khmer specialists have since persuaded me that PAA probably was spoken as much as a millennium earlier than PAN.

If PAN was spoken in Taiwan by 6000-6500 BP, and PAA was spoken in upper Burma by perhaps 7500 BP, the question of an Austric homeland becomes highly intriguing, since about 1,200 lineal miles of rugged mountainous terrain plus the 100-mile wide Formosa Strait separate upper Burma from Taiwan. Is there any empirically motivated manner in which we can deal with such a problem? I would argue that there is, and that the soundest way to proceed is by small steps from the known to the unknown, making use of whatever linguistic and archaeo-logical evidence is available, and then where necessary extrapolating beyond the available evidence through adherence to principles of simplicity. For convenience I will divide my argument into a series of steps intended to bridge what I will call the "upper Burma-Taiwan gap."

STEP 1: From island to mainland. If we first consider the AN homeland, there is a natural direction in which research is likely to lead us. We know that in other parts of the world islands have been settled relatively late, and from adjacent continents.[4] Since the AN languages of Taiwan show considerably greater internal diversity than those of the Philippines a south-to-north movement from the Philippines to Taiwan does not appear to be warranted by the linguistic evidence. East of Taiwan is the open Pacific, and to the north only the Ryukyus and Japan. Even without considering the archaeological evidence, then, there seems to be no reasonable alternative to inferring an AN movement into Taiwan from the adjacent mainland of China. In past publications I have stated that the AN homeland appears to have been on or near the island of Taiwan, thereby leaving open the possibility that PAN was spoken (or at least also spoken) on the adjacent Fujian coast (Figure 5).

There is a somewhat hair-splitting theoretical issue here as to when the AN-speaking tradition became PAN, and I have heard my position criticized on the grounds that since AN languages are not historically attested on the coast of Southeast China, it is gratuitous to include this area as a possible AN homeland. I personally consider this observation to be of little importance for the issue at hand, and for convenience will refer to the linguistic tradition which gave rise to PAN as 'Austronesian' even though technically the term 'preAustronesian' might be more exact. If Taiwan was settled from the Fujian coast, it would be extremely unlikely:

1. for there to have been no settlement on the intervening Pescadores Islands, and

2. for AN-speakers to settle the Pescadores Islands and Taiwan while leaving no related groups on the mainland.

I know of no historical migration which shows such a pattern, and to follow up on my suggestion that we work from the known to the unknown, I would suggest that history must be considered our best guide to prehistory.

The archaeological record is, of course, fully supportive of these views. Neolithic cultures appear on Taiwan rather suddenly a little before 6000 BP. This is at least half a millennium before the earliest Neolithic cultures reported to date in the Philippines, but approximately two millennia after the earliest Neolithic cultures reported from central and southern China. The first step in bridging the 1,300 mile gap between upper Burma and Taiwan is thus to trace the AN lineage back to the Fujian coast. In all probability during the late fifth millennium BC, AN-speaking peoples were sailing along this coast, hunting, fishing, growing rice, millet, and sugarcane, producing pottery, weaving, and building villages of substantial pile dwellings both on the mainland and on the adjacent Pescadores Islands and Taiwan. The devil's advocate must find an alternative hypothesis capable of explaining both the linguistic reconstructions which support these inferences (at least for Taiwan), and the archaeological relationships between the Lungshanoid cultures of Taiwan and those of the adjacent mainland which have been noted repeatedly at least since 1969 by K.C. Chang.

STEP 2. From the Fujian coast to the mouth of the Yangzi. The Fujian coast is a narrow strip between the mountains and the sea with many small offshore islands, a region which during recorded Chinese history has tended to isolate the populations which settled it from the rest of China, and to encourage their migration into various parts of Southeast Asia. If the first step needed to bridge the upper Burma-Taiwan gap is to track AN speakers back to the Fujian coast, the second step must be to track them from the Fujian coast to some other region in which the same type of archaeological culture is attested with an appropriately earlier chronology.

It is at this point that we reach a methodological impasse. Although reconstructed vocabulary may tell us a good deal about the kind of material culture a prehistoric society possessed, material artefacts do not tell us what language their makers used. In the SE Solomons, Vanuatu, Micronesia, Fiji, or Polynesia, where there is no evidence of any kind for a pre-AN population, we can safely infer that the bearers of the archaeological cultures were ancestral to the attested indigenous populations, and hence were AN-speaking. But in continental areas with a much longer history of human settlement, the matter is more complicated. The evidence of linguistic subgrouping can help us to place the AN homeland on Taiwan and the AA homeland in upper Burma. To some extent, given an independently dated baseline, the internal structure of a linguistic family tree can even provide approximate dates for the dispersal of proto-languages. What the Comparative Method of linguistics cannot provide, however, is a motivated basis for correlating proto-languages with archaeological cultures. To track the pre-PAN migration to Taiwan further back than the Fujian coast the linguist must rely on the ability of archaeologists to establish likely historical connections between archaeological cultures.

Having stated these qualifications on the power of linguistic inferences, I must add immediately that if the Austric hypothesis is valid there is no escape from the problem of bridging what I have called the "upper Burma-Taiwan gap," a problem that probably would never arise in a purely archaeological context. In principle the problem of deter-mining the Austric homeland is no different from that of determining the AN or AA homelands. In fact, the AN languages are almost continuously distributed through island SE Asia and the Pacific, and although there is a geographical gap between the Munda and Mon-Khmer branches of AA, it is relatively small (about 400 miles from the Palaung of central Burma to the isolated Mon-Khmer-speaking Khasi of the middle Brahmaputra River in Assam, and a similar distance to Mundari and other Munda groups of Bihar in northeast India). By contrast, the gap between the inferred homelands of AA and AN is over three times this distance, a fact that complicates the problem of determining a center of dispersal in at least two ways:

1) a greater distance between coordinate subgroups implies either that intermediate connecting links have been lost, or that at least one subgroup has migrated a considerable distance from the area of origin

2) the greater the geographical distance between coordinate subgroups the larger the number of possible migration routes that must be considered to bridge the gap.

Historically the mountains just inland from the Fujian coast have effectively blocked migration to or from the west. This leaves only two plausible routes of prehistoric population movement to the Fujian coast: northward from the region of Hong Kong or southward from the region of the Yangzi. Here once again comparative linguistics may be of use. Although the archaeological evidence for early rice in Taiwan is still somewhat limited and controversial, the linguistic evidence is not just clear, but abundantly clear, that rice was grown by speakers of PAN, and hence was present in Taiwan by 6000-6500 BP. Since the only earlier dates for rice in China or Southeast Asia are found north rather than south of the Fujian coast (T.T. Chang 1984/85, Bellwood 1985, Yan 1990), our efforts to retrace the steps of the AN migration from its Austric origins compel us to look northward toward the mouth of the Yangzi River rather than southward toward Hong Kong and Hainan Island. This inference is further strengthened by the clear linguistic evidence (PAN *beCeŋ 'millet sp'., probably foxtail millet *zawa 'millet sp.') that millet was also cultivated by speakers of PAN, since this cultigen was first domesticated in the Yellow River Valley about 8000 BP, and could only have reached Taiwan from the north.

I need not belabor the point here that the 7,000 year old material culture of Hemudu (Figure 5), located some 60 miles south of the mouth of the Yangzi in what is now northern Zhejiang Province is closely similar to the 6,000 year old culture inferred for PAN on

Taiwan in Blust (1976). In some ways Hemudu reveals direct physical evidence for more of the details inferred by linguistic comparison than any early site yet excavated in Taiwan, and it is clear that in reaching inferences about material culture from the archaeological record alone we must always factor in the accidents of preservation. Bellwood (1985, 1991) states emphatically that of all known mainland archaeological sites Hemudu is perhaps the best candidate in terms both of its material culture and its chronology for an ancestral line leading to the AN colonization of Taiwan. Of course, we know nothing of the language spoken 7,000 years ago at Hemudu, but if this language was not AN, other languages in the area almost certainly were. PAN did not arise spontaneously. Like modern languages, it developed from ancestral forms which were spoken by real human populations in a definite time and place. Since there is no linguistic evidence of any kind that it developed in island Southeast Asia, we are left only with the mainland of China as a likely place of origin.

STEP 3. From Hemudu to the Lower and Middle Yangzi. According to K.C. Chang (1986: 208), the Hemudu culture, first recognized in excavations carried out in the 1970s, is "known from some two dozen sites along the southern coastal plains of the Hang-chou Bay, from Hsiao-shan to Ning-po and on out to the Chou-shan Archipelago." A glance at the map will show that this location is no closer than Taiwan to upper Burma. What, then, have we gained in our search for the Austric homeland? As Bellwood (1985), Chang (1986), and others have made clear, Hemudu was only one of various Neolithic cultures that evidently pioneered the domestication of rice in the lower and middle Yangzi basin in the period 8000-8500 BP. Like North American Pueblo or Plains cultures, these Middle and Lower Yangzi cultures may have been linguistically diverse. Whether or not this was the case, chronology, location and inferred cultural type all lend strong support to the argument that PAN, spoken on Taiwan by 6500 BP, arose from one of these rice-growing mainland cultures.

If pre-PAN speakers were at least among those peoples cultivating rice in the lower and middle reaches of the Yangzi River by 8000-8500 BP are we brought any closer to reconciling the AA and AN homelands in time and space? Chang (1986: 221) maps the distribution of rice-growing Neolithic cultures in the middle Yangzi. Most of these sites cluster around Lake Dongting, about midway between Wuhan and Yichang, but the westernmost known sites extend to more than 80 miles west of Yichang, or to within about 750 lineal miles from the Yunnan upper Burma border region. The earliest known Neolithic cultures in the Yangzi basin that are likely to have been ancestral to the Hemudu culture of 7000 BP are thus only slightly downriver from the halfway point between upper Burma and Taiwan. It is clear that by proceeding in small and reasonably controlled steps we have begun to bridge the "upper Burma-Taiwan gap."

Chang (1977:142) points out that the Neolithic cultures of the lower Yangzi plains appear abruptly, with little indication of possible precedents. He suggests that this region was perhaps too marshy for habitation, or was even submerged prior to the rise of the first rice-growing cultures in the fifth millennium BC, and speculates that these cultures came in either from the Yellow River Valley to the north, or from the Fujian coast to the south. There is, of course, a third possibility: that they came downriver from the middle Yangzi, where for generations they would have adapted to conditions of periodic flooding and life on the water before ever reaching the coast. In the most recent edition of his book, *The Archaeology of Ancient China*, Chang (1986: 224) adopts this view, but in a somewhat different form from what I believe is needed to best reconcile the homelands of the AA and AN languages.

By the 1980s a number of middle Yangzi sites had been recorded with clear evidence of rice dating to as much as 8000 BP (Chang 1986). Because the earliest available radiocarbon dates for the *westernmost* sites were relatively late, Chang concluded that the Daxi culture of the middle Yangzi originated in the region of Lake Dongting, and spread out from there to both west and east. More recently Yan (1990) has presented a series of even earlier radiocarbon dates for the Pengtoushan Culture on the northwest shores of Lake Dongting clustering in the period 7800-8500 BP.

As first pointed out by Sapir (1968), the favored alternative for the homeland of a language family is one that is central in relation to the distribution of primary subgroups. In the case of AN the boundary between primary branches falls between Taiwan and the northern Philippines. There are no intervening nonmember languages, and for all practical purposes, the distribution of AN languages can be considered continuous. As noted earlier, although there are geographical gaps within AA, distributional evidence suggests a primary center of dispersal in the upper Burma-Yunnan border region. A consistent application of the same principle would lead us to posit an Austric homeland in the middle Yangzi (midway between the AA homeland in the middle Salween basin, and the AN homeland on Taiwan). To the extent that we are able to correlate archaeological cultures with one another and with attested language families, then, such an inference would be remarkably consistent with current archaeological knowledge. However, I believe there are important reasons to question it.

Having come this far on the basis of both linguistic and archaeological evidence, we are perhaps justified in a simple extrapolation: if the cultural tradition leading to the AN settlement of Taiwan was present on that island and the adjacent mainland by 6500 BP, probably was present at Hemudu or similar sites near the mouth of the Yangzi River half a millennium earlier, and was present in the middle Yangzi basin by 8000 to 8500 BP, it would appear that the long-term direction of migration was from the upper Yangzi to the coast and thence south to Taiwan. But to date there is no archaeological support for a derivation of middle Yangzi cultures from the upper Yangzi.

Even with modern technology, the Yangzi is a formidable opponent to upriver traffic. Its currents are strong and clearly favor one-way travel. This is particularly true in those stretches where the river runs through narrow steep-sided gorges, and there is little margin for overland travel, let alone cultivation.[5] The region of the Three Gorges begins not far beyond Yichang, and for speakers of Proto-AA to have reached the middle Salween by 5500 BC would have required an improbable migration from the middle Yangzi; against powerful currents and away from areas in which natural food resources evidently were more abundant. Travel between the upper and middle Yangzi, did not, of course, need to be by river. Given the mountainous terrain which surrounds the upper and middle Yangzi basins, however, there were clear advantages to traveling in the relatively sheltered and far better provisioned river valley. Moreover, if the wild progenitor of *Oryza sativa* is native to the Himalayan foothills, its domesticated descendants must have reached the middle Yangzi via human intervention, thereby implying that it was grown at an earlier date in areas further to the west (T.T. Chang 1984/85: Fig. 1). It thus appears likely that evidence for rice cultivation predating that at Pengtoushan ultimately will be found much further up the Yangzi basin, although probably on a smaller scale.

A conjectural history of the Austric dispersal.

I will now present a conjectural history of the Austric dispersal, a reconstruction which admittedly is speculative, but which at the same time is capable of archaeological testing. In so doing, I will attempt to justify some critical features of my proposal with ethnographic support from present day societies and with ethnohistorical parallels from other areas. Following this, I will consider and reply to certain theoretical objections, and in a concluding section I will return briefly to the question of Austro-Tai.

For a span of nearly 200 miles in northwestern Yunnan near the borders of Burma, Tibet and Sichuan, the Salween, Mekong, and Yangzi rivers run roughly parallel, separated for much of this distance by watersheds no more than 30 miles in width (Figure 5) . In the millennia immediately following the Pleistocene-Holocene transition this region of montane valleys presented a range of environments with cooler uplands and warmer lowlands, as it does today. It also presented abundant game and wild plant resources, which varied with altitude, as it does today. Apart from possible mean annual temperature differences, perhaps the major difference was the far greater abundance of large game animals and probably of wild food plants during this period than during the present. Game animals that almost certainly would have been available to hunters of this period and location would have included elephant, wild cattle, rhinoceros, panda, bear, various types of deer, wild pig, pangolin, monkey, hedgehog, and hare. The tiger would have been a dangerous adversary on the hunt. I have been unable to obtain much information regarding wild food plants that might have been available in the upper Yangzi region early in the Holocene, but T.T.Chang (1984/85: 69) argues that Asian rice *(Oryza sativa)* "evolved during the Neothermal period (about 15,000-10,000 BP) through early-maturing annual forms along the foothills on both flanks of the Himalaya range." If so, wild rice presumably was one of the important food plants available to populations of the region. Archaeologically the area that I have in mind is a virtual *tabula rasa*. What I propose for archaeological testing is that the food resources of this region were sufficient to support sedentary populations that lived in permanent villages of well-made timber houses by 9000 BP. Whether agriculture and domestication of any animal other than the dog had actually begun is a moot point, my only claim is that resources were sufficient to support permanent villages, and that rice almost certainly was consumed, if not cultivated by the population. There should be archaeological evidence, then, for at least woodworking tools, if not also agricultural tools. Even wild rice must be reaped, and rice cannot be cooked without boiling. Reaping knives and pottery thus presumably were also in use by Proto-Austric speakers.[6]

The region that I have in mind is defined by the area in which the Salween, Mekong and Yangzi rivers run parallel at their narrowest watershed. I would not, however, want this definition to be taken too literally. To account most parsimoniously for the attested distribution of daughter languages, the Austric homeland need only have been an area in which these rivers were easily accessible, and could have included much of northwestern Yunnan from the southern end of Lake Erh (Erh Hai) to the great bend of the Yangzi where the river turns sharply eastward. From this general region around 9000 BP, the ancestral line leading to AN entered the Yangzi basin, following the river ever eastward toward the coast. By 7000-7500 BP, PAA had separated into western (Munda) and eastern (Mon-Khmer) dialect areas; speakers of western dialects, probably following the Brahmaputra basin, entered eastern India, while speakers of eastern dialects gradually spread southward down the Salween and Mekong Rivers into mainland Southeast Asia.[7]

Once in the Yangzi basin the settlers almost certainly would have made extensive use of bamboo rafts for basic transport of persons and goods, much as the local Chinese population has within the recent past. Not only is bamboo extremely buoyant, but it is the most readily available and easily prepared material for watercraft intended to carry more than one or two persons. Wild rice would have been available, presumably in abundance, on the rich, if narrow, alluvial flood plains periodically inundated by the rising and falling river. In addition to these plant resources there would have been an abundance of fish, including carp, and the large Yangzi sturgeon, which today swims upriver as far as Yibin in south-central Sichuan on its annual cycle of reproduction. Virtually all of the game animals previously mentioned would have been available in the valley, as well as a variety of ducks and other wildfowl, river otters, turtles, dolphins, and flying squirrels. Hemp plants are abundant on the hillsides today, and could have furnished fibers for loom weaving, archaeologically attested at Hemudu around 5000 BC.

The Yangzi has a tremendous water volume, and for this reason the current is often swift and the river subject to dramatic changes of height. Such environmental conditions would have had two important consequences: first, pile dwellings would develop as a natural adaptation to flooding; second, the direction of migration would have been continuously downstream, at least on the main branch of the Yangzi itself.

If rice was not domesticated prior to entering the Yangzi Valley, it would have been harvested wild along the river margins generation after generation until gradually the conditions governing its growth and yield were brought more completely under human control.[8] If pigs were not domesticated prior to entering the valley, once plant food was readily available to humans on a surplus basis, wild pigs could have been brought under control through deliberate feeding. A comparison of this type of migration to the one (or ones) that led to the peopling of the New World may prove instructive: if the populations in both cases began essentially as foragers, riverine hunter-gatherers almost certainly would be steered toward agriculture much earlier than hunter-gatherers in the open plains or savannas.

Such a hypothesis raises some important new questions, but it also appears to provide satisfying answers to some preexisting ones. I will first consider the new questions.

Bellwood (p. c.) questions the plausibility of an AN movement from the upper Burma-Yunnan frontier into the Yangzi basin, since the proposed Austric homeland is not a known center of population dispersal. His views on this matter are colored by a belief that agriculture was the dynamic which powered the AN diaspora from Taiwan over island SEA and the Pacific, and that determinable human migrations in general have been motivated by agricultural innovation, population increase and migration in search of new land (Bellwood 1994).

I believe that there is much merit in the position Bellwood represents, but I also feel that he has taken this position too far. On a small spatial and temporal scale, for example, his model applies well to Sutlive's (1978) description of the Iban migrations over the past two centuries, where the restless search for new hunting and agricultural lands evidently was a major factor in territorial expansion. In the case of the Malagasy migration from southeast Borneo, however, agricultural expansion is a very unlikely factor, since the need for new agricultural lands could have been satisfied much closer to home. Further afield, but perhaps more spectacularly, the apparently quite rapid expansion of Athapaskan-speaking peoples from a homeland in central Alaska southward over more than 40 degrees of latitude to southern Texas and northern Mexico shows quite clearly that some important determinable migrations had nothing to do with agricultural expansion.

The objection that the upper Burma-Yunnan border region is not a known center of agricultural innovation is, moreover, meaningless until the archaeological picture of Yunnan becomes far more complete. Within the ethnographic present the region of Lake Erh (Erh Hai) and the Dali plain in northwestern Yunnan have been home to the Tibeto-Burman speaking Minchia or Bai ethnic group (Fitzgerald (1941). According to Lebar, Hickey and Musgrave (1964: 10), the Minchia have a history of indigenous rice cultivation long antedating the arrival of the Chinese among them during the Yuan dynasty (thirteenth-fourteenth century), a history which may well reflect traditions which were present in the area at the time of their arrival.[9] Finally, whatever reservations might be expressed about this region in relation to the Austric homeland circa 7000 BC must be expressed equally in relation to the Austroasiatic homeland circa 5500 BC.

The initial impetus for entering the upper Yangzi valley could well have been a combination of such factors as 1. its relatively sheltered topography and mild climate, and 2. its relative abundance of wild game, and particularly wild plant resources. Whatever the reasons, it is clear that, once there, populations could have grown rapidly as a result of abundant and reliable food resources available both from the river and from its periodically inundated flood plains.

Austro-Tai revisited.

The preceding conjectural history is motivated entirely by a need to reconcile the homeland of PAA with that of PAN, and it makes no claims as to whether there were other linguistically distinct groups in the Yangzi basin during the period in question. Indeed, we have little idea of what other languages might have been spoken in southern China or Southeast Asia during the seventh millennium BC. We do know, however, that the Tai-Kadai family is widely distributed in this region, and evidently has a long history in situ. Having confessed my conversion to the Austric hypothesis I must now return briefly to Austro-Tai.

Reid (1984/85) quite correctly criticizes Benedict for an approach to linguistic reconstruction that does little to discriminate between resemblances produced by common origin and resemblances produced by chance. At the same time he points to a number of striking recurrent lexical similarities shared by Tai-Kadai and AN languages. In each case these involve the correspondence of an entire Tai-Kadai monosyllable with the *last* syllable of a reconstructed AN disyllable. Although I do not accept all of his proposed etymologies, I concur with Reid in seeing this as the only acceptable type of match in comparing AN with T-K forms.[10]

Thurgood (1988) posits a primary split between 1.Gelao, and 2. the rest of Tai-Kadai. In a later publication (Thurgood 1994) he posits a similar split between Gelao and Lati on the one hand, and the rest of Tai-Kadai on the other. Gelao and Lati remain among the least known of all Tai-Kadai languages, and based on recent Chinese publications Thurgood (p. c.) has suggested that 'Gelao' may be a cover term for a number of undescribed or poorly described languages that comprise more than one primary branch of Tai-Kadai. Whatever conclusion is eventually reached regarding the subgrouping of these languages, the maps in Lebar, Hickey and Musgrave(1964) and Edmondson and Solnit

(1988) make it clear that the Gelao languages are scattered about the upper course of the Wu River in the west-central region of China's Guizhou Province, while Lati is spoken in the border region of Yunnan and Vietnam. Thurgood (1994) divides the remaining Tai-Kadai languages into two coordinate groups: 1. Hlai. (Hainan Island), and Laqua or Laha (Yunnan-Vietnam border region), and 2. Lakkia (Guangxi Province), Kam-Sui (primarily Guizhou Province), Be (Hainan) and Tai (Yunnan, Guangxi, and Guangdong Provinces in China, Laos, Thailand, eastern Burma). Thurgood's subgrouping of Tai-Kadai thus points clearly to the region of the upper Wu River in Guizhou as the primary center of dispersal of this group, with a likely secondary center of dispersal in southern Yunnan or the coastal areas of mainland China facing Hainan Island.

The Wu or Fu-ling River (Figure 5) which joins the main stream at the city of Fu-ling, some 50-60 miles downriver from Chongqing, is the major southern tributary of the middle Yangzi. A nineteenth century British traveler in the area (Bishop 1899: 501) described it at the confluence with the Yangzi as "a clear stream, about 200 yards broad, and navigable for 200 miles." She added that although it is navigable, the Wu River is known for its whirlpools and reefs, which presented a hazard to the Chinese watercraft she observed on it. Since movement southward on the Wu would have been against the current and hence difficult by boat, it seems a priori likely that a population that migrated into this tributary—even if it maintained a riverine orientation— would have become more oriented to overland travel than one which remained on the main branch of the Yangzi and continued to follow it ever further downstream.

If the Austric superfamily includes AA as one branch, and T-K and AN as the other, we must ask the same question about the Austro-Tai homeland that we have been forced to ask about the Austric homeland. The choice of the upper Wu or Fu-ling River as the homeland of Tai-Kadai peoples follows from the internal subgrouping of the Tai-Kadai languages themselves. If a cultural and linguistic tradition which was ancestral to PAN on Taiwan and to PTK in the upper Wu Valley of Guizhou was present in the middle Yangzi Valley by 6500 BC, we can at last replace the rather vague statements by Benedict (1942) about AN and T-K origins "somewhere in the South China area." Under the interpretation adopted here, PAT was spoken by bearers of the rice-growing middle Yangzi cultures of 6000 BC, the split between AN and T-K occurring when one segment of the population chose to move southward up the Wu Valley, while the other remained on the main river, which it continued to follow downstream over the generations until it reached the sea.

As an aside it might be useful to note that in the general ethnographic literature pile dwellings appear to have been innovated almost exclusively in areas subject to flooding or tidal bores (Murdock 1967, column 81). The widespread use of pile dwellings among both AN and T-K peoples in environments in which they are sometimes no longer physically motivated suggests that both language groups derive from an ancestral riverine culture which had a practical concern with the danger of sudden changes in water level.

Thurgood himself does not believe that the linguistic evidence supports a genetic relationship between T-K and AN; however, he does believe (15-16) that "considerable contact occurred before the Austronesians left the mainland, as at least some of the obvious borrowings were replaced in Western Malayo-Polynesian before Austronesian languages returned to the mainland." Thurgood's reservations regarding the linguistic evidence for an Austro-Tai unity are based on irregularities in the tonal correspondences of T-K languages, irregularities which suggest that the words in question were borrowed after tonal distinctions had already arisen in the T-K languages. A number of the forms that he cites, however, belong to basic vocabulary, and hence presumably would be resistant to borrowing. Whether one adopts a hypothesis of genetic relationship or of borrowing to explain the similarities between AN and T-K, the Wu Valley of Guizhou should provide archaeological evidence of a southern extension of rice-growing, middle Yangzi cultures beginning perhaps as early as 6000 BC and continuing for millennia into the modern Gelao-speaking peoples of the region.

Conclusion.

Just as the AN languages, with their extraordinarily wide dispersal over some 72 degrees of latitude and more than 206 degrees of longitude, can be traced back with considerable confidence to a homeland on the island of Taiwan, so can the Austric languages as a whole be traced back to a homeland in the general region where the Salween, Mekong and Yangzi Rivers run parallel on the Burma-Yunnan frontier. The dispersal of AN, T-K, and Austric language groups appears to have followed riverine courses: AN down the Yangzi to its mouth and thence down the Fujian coast to Taiwan; T-K down the Yangzi to the Wu, or Fu-Ling River, and thence southward, probably reaching the coast of Guangdong and Hainan Island by 3000 BC; Munda probably down the Brahmaputra Valley into Assam and

Bangladesh, whence they gradually spread westward, and Mon-Khmer down the Salween and Mekong Valleys into mainland Southeast Asia. The subsequent spread of Tibeto-Burman-speaking peoples down the Irrawaddy and Salween Valleys would have separated Khasi on the west from the rest of Mon-Khmer, and displaced or absorbed many earlier M-K groups in the region of the Salween. Similarly, some pre-AN speakers probably spread down the coast of southern China past Taiwan as far as the Gulf of Tonkin, where they may have encountered Tai-Kadai speakers migrating southward from the upper Wu Valley. In time the southward spread of Han Chinese led to the sinicization of all AN-speaking populations that remained on the mainland, whether in the Yangzi valley or in coastal areas from the mouth of the Yangzi to the Gulf of Tonkin (a process that continues today in Taiwan).

In conclusion, without in the least intending to be disparaging, I think it is fair to say that, because of differences in the type of material used, comparative linguistics can sometimes, so to speak, fly where archaeology can only crawl. In other words, it is capable of generating archaeologically testable hypotheses far more rapidly than they can be confirmed or discarded. I look forward eagerly to the results of archaeological testing of the ideas put forward here, but recognize that it may be some time before definitive results emerge. In the meanwhile we must not forget that language and material culture are simply different aspects of what to the native participant must be considered a "way of life," and as a reflection of this fact I would hope that linguists and archaeologists alike come increasingly to realize the benefits of interdisciplinary cooperation in our common attempt to understand the history of our species as a cultural animal.

ACKNOWLEDGMENT

Peter Bellwood, Paul Benedict, George W. Grace, Charles F.W. Higham, Lawrence A. Reid and Graham Thurgood read and commented on an earlier version of the present manuscript. None of them necessarily accepts its arguments or conclusions. In addition, I am indebted to Joyce White for useful criticism based on an oral presentation of the paper, and for time-saving information on references to the archaeological literature on early rice.

NOTES

1. The spelling "Tai" normally refers to the entire group of Daic languages, which includes Zhuang, Saek, Lao, Siamese and Shan, among others, while "Thai" is used distinctively for Siamese. In practice, however, the two spellings often have the same referent (witness Benedict 1975 "Austro-Thai" but Benedict 1990 "Austro-Tai"). I generally adhere to the Tai = Daic, Thai = Siamese distinction, but allow spellings to vary with the source cited.

2. Examples include Cebuano and Roviana, both of which reflect *-in- marker of deverbal nouns', *pa- 'causative', *-a '3sg. object', and *-an 'locative', yet share only 14/200 items on the modified form of the Swadesh 200-item lexicostatistical test-list reported in Blust (1981), or 7 percent of their basic vocabulary. Cebuano and Roviana probably have been separated no longer than 5000 years; as will be seen, the separation of AA and AN almost certainly took place by at least 8500 BP.

3. See Blust (1976: 29ff), where a separation time of 6000 BP for Atayalic from all other AN languages is accepted; Blust (1977: 2), where a subgrouping which implies a Formosan homeland is proposed; and Blust (1980: 13) and (1984/85: 54), where time-depths of 7000 and 6500 BP respectively are suggested for Proto-Austronesian. These estimates were originally made in ignorance of the 6300 BP radiocarbon date for Ta-p'en-keng which is the earliest known evidence of the Neolithic on Taiwan, and were based on extrapolations from a date of 5000 BP for the break-up of Proto-Oceanic made by Pawley and Green (1973: 53, fn. 1). Although a date closer to 4000 BP for the latter event now appears to be archaeologically better-supported, a date of 6000-6500 BP for the break-up of Proto-Austronesian would seem to be quite reasonable.

4. To somewhat belabor the obvious, we can cite Greenland, Iceland, the British Isles, all of the Mediterranean Islands, the Canaries, Zanzibar, Madagascar, Sri Langka, Japan, the Queen Charlotte Islands, Newfoundland, the Greater and Lesser Antilles, and Tierra del Fuego, among many others. The hominid line evolved in continental areas, and in general island environments were among the last to be reached, although the continental "island" of Sahul Land was settled very early (Allen, this volume).

5. For a graphic and highly readable personal account of the difficulties of traveling up the Yangzi by Chinese junk in the winter (low-water) season, see Bishop (1899). Most river travel in the period 8000-8500 BP almost certainly would have been by bamboo raft for the transport of goods and of families, since timber for large canoes is not available in the middle and upper Yangzi basins, while groves of large bamboo are plentiful all along the river.

6. Lawrence Reid (personal com.) has reminded me that in the Philippines

(as elsewhere in Southeast Asia) one traditional method of cooking rice was by boiling in bamboo tubes. It is thus possible that early sites may be found with abundant evidence for rice, but without pottery. The sedentary exploitation of wild resources over lengthy time periods is, of course, not ethnographically unparalleled. The entire Northwest Coast culture area in the Pacific Northwest of North America, with its permanent villages of large timber houses and its distinctive lineage-connected totem poles, rested economically on the consumption of fish (principally salmon, which could be preserved by smoking), marine mammals, and wild plant resources, entirely without the benefit of agriculture.

7. On a far smaller scale we can see such a pattern of radiating dispersal along river valleys in the prehistoric migration of the Kayan, who crossed the watershed from the basins of the Kahayan and Mahakam Rivers in east Borneo, and entered the upper reaches of such rivers as the Kapuas, Rejang and Baram, whence they spread over a considerable distance to the west and south by following the diverging river valleys toward the coast. Photographic accounts of the Yangzi such as that of Wong (1989), and personal narrative, such as that of Bishop (1899), show that the river basin exhibits dramatic topographic changes over relatively short distances. The Yangzi begins to diverge sharply from the Salween and Mekong at the town of Shigu, in northwestern Yunnan, where it turns abruptly north and flows through the spectacular 'Tiger Leaping Gorge', with steep mountain slopes rising nearly 10,000 feet on both sides. It is obvious that such a point of entry would be improbable. On the Yongling Plain less than 40 linear miles to the east, however, the mountain slopes rising from the river are much less precipitous, and reportedly are terraced for small hillside rice farms by the modern Tibeto-Burman speaking Naxi and Lisu of the region, while less than 200 sailing miles further down the river the hillsides are extensively terraced for wet rice by the Tibeto-Burman speaking Yi or Lolo (Lebar, Hickey and Musgrave 1964, Wong 1989).

8. Under this interpretation wet rice under natural conditions would have preceded swidden cultivation. As a linguist my remarks on the transition from harvesting a basically wild form of *Oryza* to sustained cultivation are, of course, largely impressionistic. However, White (1995) reaches a very similar conclusion with regard to the development of early rice agriculture in northeast Thailand: "The essence of agricultural development in this region was not from shifting cultivation to permanent fields, or technologically simpler to techno-logically advanced, or polyculture to monoculture, rather I suspect it was from haphazard, opportunistic, and diffuse to systematic, integrated and focused." As the centerpiece of her theory of agricultural evolution, White notes that environments of permanent inundation do not provide the optimal conditions for high rice yields or short growing cycles. Rather, these conditions exist in areas of fluctuating water levels, where wild strains of *Oryza* tended to develop accelerated growing cycles and increased

yields, presumably as an adaptive reaction to environmental stress.

9. Lebar, Hickey and Musgrave (1964), citing Fitzgerald (1941: 21-22), claim that the Minchia "have been rice farmers in the area at least as far back as the seventh and eighth centuries A.D., when Tali was a capital in the kingdom of Nanchao." Fitzgerald himself only states that "The Min Chia lack any tradition of immigration to their present home, and it may be regarded as certain that they have practiced their present mode of life for at least seven centuries." In either case it appears that rice cultivation has some antiquity in the region of the Dali plain. Chang (1977: 454) suggests that, "civilization apparently came to Yunnan during the latter part of the Eastern Chou period, simultaneously with irrigated farming and the use of iron implements." However, on the next page he notes the discovery, in 1957, of a habitation site near Lake Erh that "is a pile village, built along the Hai-Wei River, half on the bank, the other half submerged. Remains of agricultural implements and grains of rice, wheat, and millet were found, together with a large number of mollusk shells, animal bones, and fishhooks." A piece of wood from the site yielded a calibrated radiocarbon date of 1480-1170 BC. I suspect that far earlier dates for rice ultimately will be found in this area.

10. I also recognize some additional comparisons, as PMP *sakit 'pain, sickness': KAM /kit^9/ 'pain', and PAN *Sema: KAM /ma^2/ 'tongue' (where the numerals mark tone classes).

REFERENCES

ABBREVIATIONS:

AA: *American Anthropologist.*
ALCC: *Archaeology of the Lapita Cultural Complex.- A Critical Review.* Thomas Burke Memorial Washington State Museum Research Report No. 5. Seattle: Thomas Burke Museum.
AO: *AO.*
AP. *AP.*
ASTA: *Anthropological Studies of the Taiwani Area. - Accomplishments and Prospects. Taipei.-* Department of Anthropology, National Taiwan University.
BMP: Bishop Museum Bulletin. Honolulu: Bernice P. Bishop Museum.
JPS: *JPS.*
JSAS: *JSAS.*
OL: *Oceanic linguistics.*
OLSP: Oceanic Linguistics Special Publication. Honolulu: University of Hawaii Press.
OPP: Occasional Papers in Prehistory. Department of Prehistory, Research School of Pacific Studies, Australian National University.
PLP: *Poterie Lapita et Peuplement, Actes du Colloque LAPITA* Noumea: ORSTROM.
YUPA: Yale University Publications in Anthropology. New Haven: Department of Anthropology, Yale University.

ÅKERBLOM, KJELL. 1968. Astronomy and Navigation in Polynesia and Melanesia. Monograph Series, No. 14. Stockholm: Ethnografiska Museet.

ALLEN, J. 1984. Pots and Poor Princes: A Multidimensional Approach to the Role of Pottery Trading in Coastal Papua *in* S.E. van Leuuw and A.C. Pritchard, eds., *The Many Dimensions of Pottery*, pp. 409-63. Amsterdam: University of Amsterdam.

—. 1991 The Chronology of Colonization in New Zealand. *Antiquity* 65:767-795

—. 1993. Notions of the Pleistocene in Greater Australia. *In* M. A.Smith, M. Spriggs, and B. Fankhauser, eds., *Sahul in Review: Pleisto- cene Archaeology in Australia, New Guinea and Island Melanesia*, pp. 139-51. OPP, No. 24.

—. 1994 Radiocarbon Determination, Luminescence Dating and Aus- tralian Archaeology. *Antiquity* 68:339-343.

—, Jack Golson, and Rhys Jones. 1977. *Sunda and Sahul*: Prehistoric Studies in Southeast Asia, Melanesia and Australia. New York: Academic Press.

— and C. GOSDEN (eds) 1991. *Report of the Lapita Homeland Project*. Canberra: OPP, No. 20.

— and C. GOSDEN. In press. Spheres of Interaction and Integration: Modeling the Culture History of the Bismarck Archipelago. *In* J. Davidson, G. Irwin and A. Pawley (eds) *Pacific culture history: essays in honour of Roger Green*.

—, C. GOSDEN AND J.P. WHITE. 1989. Human Pleistocene Adaptations in the Tropical Island Pacific: Recent Evidence from New Ireland, a Greater Australian Outlier. *Antiquity* 63(240): 548-61.

— AND J. P. WHITE. 1989. The Lapita Homeland: some new data and an interpretation. *JPS* 98:129-146.

ANDERSON, ATHOLL. 1989. Prodigious Birds: Moas and Moa Hunting in Prehistoric New Zealand. Cambridge: Cambridge University Press.

—, 1991. The Chronology of Colonization in New Zealand. *Antiquity* 65:767-795.

AOYAGI, Y., M. L. AGUILERA, JR., H. OGAWA, AND K. TANAKA. 1986. The shell middens in the lower reaches of the Cagayan River. *JSAS* 4:45-89.

—, M. L. AGUILERA, JR., H. OGAWA, AND K. TANAKA. 1991. Excavations at Lal-lo shell middens (3). *JSAS* 9:49-137.

— and K. TANAKA. 1985. Some problems of the shell mound potteries found in the lower reaches of Cagayan River, Northern Luzon, Philippines. *JSAS* 3:81-129.

AUDRAN, R. P. HERVÉ. 1927. Les Hiva. *Bulletin de la Société des Etudes Océaniennes* 22:317-8.

BAYBAYAN, CHAD, BEN FINNEY, BERNARD KILONSKY, AND NAINOA THOMPSON. 1987. Voyage to Aotearoa. *JPS* 96:161-200.

BALEAN, C. E. 1989. Caves as Refuge Sites: an Analysis of Shell Material from Buang Merabak, New Ireland. Unpublished B.A. Honours thesis, Department of Prehistory and Anthropology, Australian National University.

BALLARD, W. L. 1981. Aspects of the Linguistic History of South China. *AP* 24(2):163-185.

BANKS, JOSEPH. 1962. *The Endeavour Journal of Joseph Banks 1768-1771*. John C. Beaglehole, ed. 2 vols. Sydney: Angus and Robertson.

BEAGLEHOLE, ERNEST, AND PEARL BEAGLEHOLE. 1938. Ethnology of Pukapuka. BMB, No. 150.

BEECHEY, FREDERICK WILLIAM. 1831. *Narrative of a Voyage to the Pacific and Beering's Strait to Co-operate with Polar Expeditions*. 2 vols. London: Henry Colburn and Richard Bentley.

BELLWOOD, PETER. 1978. Archaeological Research in the Cook Islands. *Pacific Anthropological Records*, No. 27. Honolulu: Department of Anthropology, Bernice P. Bishop Museum.

—.1979. *Man's Conquest of the Pacific*. New York: Oxford University Press.

—. 1980. The Peopling of the Pacific. *Scientific American* 243 (5):174-185.

—. 1985. *Prehistory of the Indo-Malaysian Archipelago*. New York: Academic Press.

—. 1989. The Colonization of the Pacific; Some Current Hypotheses. In *The Colonization of the Pacific: A Genetic Trail*. Adrian V.S. Hill and Susan W. Searjeantson, eds. Pp 1-59. Oxford: Clarendon Press.

—. 1991.The Austronesian Dispersal and the origin of Languages. *Scientific American* 265(1):88-93.

— . 1992a. New Dates for Prehistoric Asian Rice. *AP* 31(2):161-170.

—. 1992b. New discoveries in southeast Asia relevant for Melanesian (especially Lapita) prehistory. *In* J. C. Galipaud, ed., *PLP*, pp. 49-66.

— . 1993. Cultural and Biological Differentiation in Peninsular Malaysia. *AP* 8:37-59.

— . 1994. An Archaeologist's View of Language Macrofamily Relationships. *OL* 33:391-406.

— . and P. KOON. 1989. "Lapita colonists leave boats unburned!" The question of Lapita links with southeast Asia. *Antiquity* 63:613-22.

BENEDICT, PAUL K. 1942. Thai, Kadai, and Indonesian: A New Alignment in Southeast Asia. *AA* 44:576-601.

—. 1975. *Austro-Tai Language and Culture*. New Haven, CT: HRAF Press.

—. 1976. Shorto: In Defense of Austric-Comment. *Computational Analyses of Asian & African Languages* 6:105-108.

—. 1990. *Japanese/Austro-Tai*. Linguistica Extranea, Studia 20.Ann Arbor: Karoma Publishers.

—. 1993. Austric: An'Extinct' Proto-language. In J. H. C. S.Davidson (ed.), *Austroasiatic Languages: Essays in Honour of H. L. Shorto*, pp. 7-1 1. Collected Papers in Oriental and African Studies.London: School of Oriental and African Studies, University of London.

BEST, SIMON, PETER SHEPPARD, ROGER GREEN AND ROBIN PARKER. 1991. Necromancing the Stone: Archaeologists and adzes in Samoa. *Journal of the Polynesian Society* 101:45-85.

BIGGS, BRUCE G. 1972. Implications of Linguistic Subgrouping with Special Reference to Polynesia. In *Studies in Oceanic Culture History*, Vol. 3, Roger C. Green and Marion Kelly eds. Pp. 143-152. Pacific Anthro pological Records, No. 13. Honolulu: Department of Anthropology, Bernice P. Bishop Museum.

BIRDSELL, J. B. 1977. The recalibration of a paradigm for the first peopling of Greater Australia. *In* J. Allen, J. Golson and R. Jones (eds) *Sunda and Sahul, Prehistoric Studies in Southeast Asia, Melanesia and Australia*, pp. 113-67. London: Academic Press.

BISHOP, J.F. (ISABELLA L. BIRD). 1899. *The Yangtse Valley and Beyond: An Account of Journeys in China, Chiefly in the province of Sze Chuan and Among the Man-Tze of the Somo Territory*. London: John Murray.

BLUST, ROBERT. 1976. Austronesian culture history: some linguistic inferences and their relations to the archaeological record. *World Archaeology* 8(1):19-43.

—. 1977. The Proto-Austronesian pronouns and Austronesian subgrouping: a preliminary report. Working Papers in Linguistics 9(2): 1-15. Honolulu: Department of Linguistics, University of Hawaii.

—. 1980. Austronesian etymologies. OL 19(1-2): I-181.

—. 1981. Variation in retention rate among Austronesian languages. Paper presented at the Third International Conference on Austronesian Linguistics, Den Pasar, Bali, January 1-11, 1981. Ms., 83pp.

—. 1984/85. The Austronesian homeland: a linguistic perspective. AP 26: 45-67.

—. 1994. The Austronesian Settlement of Mainland Southeast Asia. *In* K.L. Adams and T.J. Hudak (eds.), *Papers from the Second Annual Meeting of the Southeast Asian Linguistics Society—1992*, pp. 25-83. Tempe, AZ: Program for Southeast Asian Studies, Arizona State University.

BUCK, PETER H. 1932. Ethnology of Manihiki-Rakahanga. *BMB*, No. 99. Honolulu; Bernice P. Bishop Museum.

—.1938. *Vikings of the Sunrise*. Philadelphia: Lippincott.

BULMER S.1975. Settlement and economy in prehistoric Papua New Guinea: a review of the archaeological evidence. *Journal de la Société des Océanistes* 31:7-75.

BURROWS, E. G. 1939. *Western Polynesia: A Study of Cultural Differentiation*. Etnologiska Studier 7.

CACHOLA-ABAD, C. K. 1993.Evaluating the Orthodox Dual settlement Model for the Hawaiian Islands: An Analysis of Artifact Distributions and Hawaiian Oral Traditions. In *The Evolution and Organization of Prehistoric Social Systems in Polynesia*. Michael Graves and Roger Green, eds. Pp. 13-32. Auckland: New Zealand Archaeological Association.

CAMPBELL, JOHN. 1892. Remarks on George Patterson, 'Beothick Vocabularies'. *Transactions of the Royal Society of Canada, Section II*, pp. 26-30.

CASS. 1984. *Xin Zhongguo de Kaoqu Faxian he Yanjiu (Archaeological Excavation and Researches in New China)*. Beijing: Wenwu Press

CHANG, KWANG-CHIH. 1970. Prehistoric Archaeology of Taiwan. *Asian Perspectives* 13:59-77.

—. 1986. *The Archaeology of Ancient China*, 4th edition. New Haven: Yale University Press.

—. 1989a. Xin Shiqi Shidai de Taiwan Haixia (The Neolithic of the Taiwan Strait). *Kaogu* 6:542-550, 569.

—. 1989b. Taiwan Archaeology in Pacific Perspective. In *Anthropological Studies of xthe Taiwan Area*, edited by Kwan-Chi Chang, Kuang-chou Li, Arthur P. Wolf, and Alexander Chien-chung Yin, pp. 87-98. Taipei: Department of Anthropology, National Taiwan

University.

— , *et alii*. 1969. *Fengpitou, Tapenkeng, and the Prehistory of Taiwan*. YUPA, No. 73.

CHAPPELL, JOHN. 1993. Late Pleistocene coasts and human migrations in the Austral region. *In* M. Spriggs, D. E. Yen, W. Ambrose, R. Jones, A. Thorne and A. Andrews (eds) *A Community of Culture: The People and Prehistory of the Pacific*, pp. 43-8. Canberra: Department of Prehistory, Research School of Pacific Studies, Australian National University.

CHIKAMORI, MASASHI. 1987. Archaeology on Pukapuka Atoll. *Man and Culture in Oceania* 3:105-119.

CHOWNING, ANN. 1976. Austronesian Languages: New Britain. In *New Guinea Area Languages and Language Study*, vol 2: *Austronesian Languages*, edited by S. A. Wurm, pp. 365-386.Pacific Linguistics C-39. Canberra: Australian National University.

CLARK, HUGH R. 1991. *Community, Trade, and Networks: Southern Fujian Province from the Third to Thirteenth Century*. Cambridge: Cambridge University Press.

COLANI, MADELEINE. 1927. L'age de la pierre dans la province de Hoa Binh. *Memoires du Service Geologique de l'Indochine* 8:1.

COLES, JOHN M. 1979. *Experimental Archaeology*. New York: Academic Press.

COOK, JAMES. 1955. *The Voyage of the Endeavour, 1768-1771*. John C. Beaglehole, ed. Cambridge: Hakluyt Society.

—. 1961. *The Voyage of the Resolution and Adventure, 1772-1775*. John C. Beaglehole, ed. Cambridge: Hakluyt Society.

CRAIB, J. L. 1983.Micronesian Prehistory; an Archaeological Overview. *Science* 219:922-927

CROCOMBE, RONALD G., AND MARJORIE CROCOMBE. 1968. *The Works of Ta'unga*. Canberra: Australian National University Press.

CULTURAL RELICS COMMISSION OF GUANGDONG. 1961. Shellmound sites in Chao'an, Guangdong. *Kaogu* 11:577-584.

DAHL, O. C. 1951. *Malagache et Maanyan*. Oslo.

DAVIDSON, JANET. 1974. Cultural Replacement on Small Islands: New evidence from Polynesian Outliers. *Mankind* 9:273-277.

DEMPWOLFF, OTTO. 1934-38. Vergleichende Lautlehre des austronesischen Wortschatzes. Zeitschrift für Eingeborenen-Sprachen. I. Induktiver Aufbau einer indonesischen Ursprache, Supplement 15 (1934), 2. Deduktive Anwendung des Urindonesischen auf austronesische Einzelsprachen, Supplement 17 (1937). 3. Austronesisches Wörterverzeichnis, Supplement 19 (1938). Berlin: Reimer.

DENING, G.1992. *Mr. Bligh's Bad Language*. Cambridge: Cambridge University Press.

DILLON, PETER. 1829. *Narrative of a Voyage in the South Seas...to Ascertain the Actual Fate of the La Perouse Expedition*. London: Hurst, Chance & Co.

DORAN, EDWIN, JR. 1973. *Nao, Junk and Vaka: Boats and Culture History*. College Station, Texas: Texas A&M University.

—. 1981. *Wangka: Austronesian Canoe Origins*. College Station, Texas: Texas A&M University Press.

DUMONT-D'URVILLE, JULES-SÉBASTIEN-CÉSAR. 1830. *Voyage de laCorvette L'Astrolabe...Pendant les annéees 1826, 1827, 1828, 1829*. 5 Vols. Paris: J. Tastu.

DYE, TOM. 1989. Tales of Two Cultures: Traditional Historical and Archaeological Interpretations of Hawaiian Prehistory. Honolulu: Bishop Museum Occasional Papers 29:3-22.

DYEN, ISIDORE. 1956. Language distribution and migrations theory. Language 32: 611-26.

EDMONDSON, JEROLD A. and David B. Solnit, eds. 1988. Comparative Kadai: linguistic studies beyond Tai. The Summer Institute of linguistics and The University of Texas at Arlington.

ELBERT, SAMUEL H.1982. Lexical Diffusion in Polynesian and the Marquesas-Hawaiian Relationship. *JPS* 91:499-517.

EMERSON, NATHANIEL B.1983.The Long Voyages of the Ancient Hawaiians. *Papers of the Hawaiian Historian Society*, No. 5. Honolulu: Hawaiian Historical Society.

EMORY, KENNETH P. 1963. East Polynesian Relationships: Settlement Pattern and Time Involved as Indicated by Vocabulary Agreements. *Journal of the Polynesian Society* 72:78-100.

FINNEY, BEN. 1967. New Perspectives on Polynesian Voyaging. In *Polynesian Culture History: Essays in Honor of Kenneth P. Emory*. Genevieve A. Highland, Roland W. Force, Alan Howard, Marion Kelly and Yosihiko Sinoto, eds. Pp. 141-166. Honolulu: Bernice P. Bishop Museum Press.

—. 1977. Voyaging Canoes and the Settlement of Polynesia. *Science* 196:1277-1285.

—. 1979a. Voyaging. In *The Prehistory of Polynesia*. Jesse Jennings, ed., pp. 323-351. Cambridge: Harvard University Press.

—. 1979b. *Hokule'a, the Way to Tahiti*. New York: Dodd, Mead.

—. 1985. Anomalous Westerlies, El Niño, and the Colonization of Polynesia. *AA* 87:9-26.

—. 1991. Myth, Experiment and the Re-invention of Polynesian Voyaging. *AA* 92:383-404.

—. 1993a. James Cook and the European Discovery of Polynesia. In *From Maps to Metaphors*. Robin Fisher and Hugh Johnston, eds.

—. 1993b. Voyaging and Isolation in Rapa Nui Prehistory. *Rapa Nui Journal* 7:1-6.

—. 1994a. *Voyage of Rediscovery: A Cultural Odyssey Through Polynesia*. Berkeley: University of California Press.

—. 1994b. Experimental Voyaging and Maori Settlement. In *The Origins of the First New Zealanders*. Douglas Sutton, ed. Pp. 52-76. Auckland: Auckland University Press.

—. 1994c. *Polynesian Voyagers to the New World. Man and Culture in Oceania.*

—, BERNARD J. KILONSKY, STEPHEN SOMSEN, AND EDWARD D. STROUP

—. 1986. Re-Learning a Vanishing Art. *Journal of the Polynesian Society* 95: 41-90.

— . PAUL FROST, RICHARD RHODES, AND NAINOA THOMPSON.1989. Wait for the West Wind. *JPS* 98:261-302.

FIRTH, RAYMOND. 1961. The History and Traditions of Tikopia. *Polynesian Society Memoir*, No. 33. Wellington: The Polynesian Society.

FITZGERALD, C.P. 1941. The tower of five glories: a study of the Min Chia of Ta li, Yunnan. London: The Cresset Press.

FOLEY, WILLIAM A. 1986. *The Papuan Languages of New Guinea*. Cambridge: Cambridge University press.

FORNANDER, ABRAHAM. 1969. An Account of the Polynesian Race: its Origin and Migrations. 3 vols. Rutland, Vermont: Tuttle (Reprint of works by the same title published in 1878, 1880, and 1885, London: Trübner.)

FREDRICKSEN, C., M. SPRIGGS and W. AMBROSE. 1993. Pamwak rock-shelter: a Pleistocene site on Manus Island, Papua New Guinea. *In* M. A. Smith, M. Spriggs and B. Fankhauser (eds) *Sahul in Review*. OPP No. 24, pp. 144-52.

FRENCH-WRIGHT, R. 1983. Proto-Oceanic Horticultural Practices. Unpublished M. A. Thesis, University of Auckland, New Zealand.

FRIEDLANDER, J. S. 1875. *Patterns of Human Variation. The Demography, Genetics, and Phenetics of Bougainville Islanders*. Cambridge: Harvard University Press.

FUJIAN PROVINCIAL MUSEUM. 1984. Report of the Second Season of Excavations of the Xitou Site in Minhou. *Kaogu Xuebao* 4:459-500.

—. 1991. Brier Report of the Excavation of the Keqiutou Site in Pingtan, Fujian. *Kaoqu* 199(7):587-599.

GARANGER, JOSÉ. 1972a. Mythes et Archéologie en Océanie. *La Recherche* 3(21):233-242.

—.1972b. Archaéologie des Nouvelles Hebrides; Contribution à la Connaissance des lles du Centre. Publications de la Société des Océanistes, No. 30. Paris: Société des Océanistes.

GERAGHTY, PAUL A. 1983. *The History of the Fijian Languages* . Oceanic Linguistics Special Publication No. 19. Honolulu: University of Hawaii Press.

GILL, WILLIAM WYATT. 1876. *Myths and Songs from the South Pacific*. London: King.

GIBBONS, ANN. 1994. Genes Point to a New Identity for Pacific Pioneers. *Science* 263:32-33.

GLADWIN, THOMAS. 1970. *East is a Big Bird*. Cambridge: Harvard University Press.

GLOVER, I. 1986. *Archaeology in Eastern Timor, 1966-67.* Terra Aus tralis 11. Canberra: Department of Prehistory, Research School of Pacific

Studies, Australian National University.

GOLSON, J. 1990. Kuk and the development of agriculture in New Guinea: Retrospection and introspection. *In* D. E. Yen and J. M. J. Mummery, eds., *Pacific Production Systems: Approaches to Economic Prehistory*, pp. 139-47. *Occasional Papers in Prehistory* No. 18. Canberra: Department of Prehistory, Australian National University

—. 1991. The New Guinea Highlands on the eve of agriculture. In P. Bellwood (ed.) *Indo-Pacific Prehistory 1990*, pp. 82-91. Bulletin of the Indo-Pacific Prehistory Association 11.

GOODENOUGH, WARD H. 1953. *Native Astronomy in the Central Carolines*. Museum Monographs. Philadelphia: The University Museum, University of Pennsylvania.

—. 1961. Migrations Implied by Relationships of New Britain Dialects to Central Pacific Languages. *Journal of the Polynesian Society* 70:112- 126.

—. 1970. Native Astronomy in the Central Caroline Islands. Museum Monographs, Philadelphia: The University Museum, University of Pennsylvania.

—.1982. Ban Chang in World Ethnological Perspective. In *Ban Chang: Discovery of a Lost Bronze Age* by Joyce C. White, pp. 52-53. Philadelphia: The University Museum, University of Pennsylvania.

— . 1992. A Lapita smoke screen? In J-C. Galipaud (ed.) Poterie, Lapita et Peuplement. pp. 27-47. Noumea: ORSTOM.

GORECKI, P., M. MABIN AND J. CAMPBELL. 1991. Archaeology and geomorphology of the Vanimo coast, Papua New Guinea: preliminary results. *AO* 26:119-122.

—, M. MABIN, AND J. CAMPBELL. 1991. Archaeology and Geomorph ology of the Vanimo Coast, Papua New Guinea: Prliminary Results. *AO* 26: 119-122.

GOSDEN, C. 1992. Production systems and the colonization of the Western Pacific. *World Archaeology* 24:55-69.

— and N. ROBERTSON. 1991. Models for Matenkupkum: interpreting a late Pleistocene site from southern New Ireland, Papua New Guinea. *In* J. Allen and C. Gosden (eds) *Report of the Lapita Homeland Project*. Occasional Papers 20, pp. 20-45. Canberra: Department of Prehistory, Research School of Pacific Studies, Australian National University.

GREEN ROGER C. 1966. Linguistic Subgrouping within Polynesia: the Implications for Prehistoric Settlement. *JPS* 75:6-38

—. 1975. Adaptation and Change in Maori Culture. In *Biogeography and Ecology in New Zealand*. G. Kuschel, ed. Pp. 591-641. The Hague: W. Junk.

—. 1977. Professor Roger Green. In *Taratai, A Pacific Adventure*. James Siers, ed. Pp. 220-239.

—. 1979a . Lapita. In J. Jennings, ed., *The Prehistory of Polynesia*, pp. 27-60. Cambridge: Harvard University Press.

—. 1979b. Early Lapita art from Polynesia and Island Melanesia: Continuities in ceramic, barkcloth, and tattoo decorations. In S. Mead, ed., *Exploring the Visual Art of Oceania*, pp. 13-31. Honolulu: University of Hawaii Press.

—. 1987. Peopling of the Pacific: a Series of adaptive Steps, or Punctuated Evolution. Paper presented at Section H, 57th Annual Meeting of Australian and New Zealand Association for the Advancement of Science, August 24, 1987.

—. 1991a Near and Remote Oceania: Disestablishing "Melanesia" in culture history. *In* A. Pawley, ed., *Man and a Half: Essays in Pacific Anthropology and Ethnobiology in Honour of Ralph Bulmer*, pp. 491-502. Auckland: The Polynesian Society.

—. 1991b. The Lapita Cultural Complex: current evidence and proposed models. *Bulletin of the Indo-Pacific Prehistory Association* 11:295-305.

—. 1992. Definitions of the Lapita cultural complex and its non-ceramic component. *In* J.-C. Galipaud, ed., *Poterie Lapita et Peuplement, Actes du Colloque LAPITA*, pp. 7-20. Noumea: ORSTOM.

GROUBE, L. 1971. Tonga, Lapita pottery, and Polynesian origins. *Journal of the Polynesian Society* 80:278-316.

HADDON, A. C., AND JAMES HORNELL. 1938. *Canoes of Oceania, Volume 3: Definition of Terms, General Survey, and Conclusions*. Honolulu: Bernice P. Bishop Museum Press.

HAGELBERG, E., AND J. D. CLEGG. 1993. Genetic Polymorphisms in Prehistoric Pacific Islanders. Determined by Analysis of Ancient Bone DNA. Proceedings of the Royal Society of London. Series B, 252: 163-170.

HALL, KENNETH R. 1985. *Maritime Trade and State Development in Early Southeast Asia*. Honolulu: University of Hawaii Press.

HELMS, MARY W. 1988. *Ulysses' Sail*. Princeton, New Jersey: Princeton University Press.

HENRY, TEUIRA. 1928. Ancient Tahiti. *BMB*, No. 48. Honolulu: Bernice P. Bishop Museum.

HESSELL, J. W. D.1981. Climatology of the South-west Pacific Islands. 2. Climatological Statistics. In Pacific Islands Water Resources. W. R. Dale, ed. Pp. 35-43 South Pacific Technical Inventory, No. 2. Wellington, Department of Scientific and Industrial Research.

HEYERDAHL, THOR. 1953. *American Indians in the Pacific*. Chicago: Rand McNally.

—. 1978. *Early Man and the Ocean*. London: Allen and Unwin.

HIGHAM, CHARLES. 1989. *The Archaeology of Mainland South-east Asia*. Cambridge: Cambridge University Press.

HILDER, BRETT. 1963. Primitive Navigation in the Pacific - II. In *Polynesian Navigation: A Symposium on Andrew Sharp's Theory of Accidental Voyaging*. Jack Golson, ed. Pp. 81-97. Polynesian Society Memoir,

No. 34. Wellington: The Polynesian Society.

HOFFMAN, CARL. 1983. Punan. Ph.D. Dissertation, University of Pennsylvania. Ann Arbor:University Microfilms International. International.

HSU, CHO-YUN AND KATHRYN M. LINDRUFF. 1988. *Western Chou Civilization*. New Haven: Yale University Press.

HUANG, SHIH-CH'IANG. 1989. A Discussion of Relationships between the Prehistoric Cultures of Southeast China and Taiwan. In *Anthropological Studies of the Taiwan Area: Accomplishments and Prospects*, edited by Kwang-chou Li, Kwang-chih Chang, Arthur P. Wolf, and Alexander Chien-chung Yin, pp. 59-97. Taipei: Department of Anthropology, National Taiwan University. Institute of Archaeology.

HUMBOLDT, WILHELM VON. 1936-39. *Über die Kawi-Sprache auf der Insel Java*. 3 vols. Berlin.

HUNT, TERRY L. 1989. Lapita Ceramic Exchange in the Mussau Islands, Papua New Guinea. Unpublished Ph.D. Dissertation, Seattle: Department of Anthropology, University of Washington, Seattle.

HUTTERER, KARL L., editor. 1977. *Economic Exchange and Social Interaction in Southeast Asia: Perspectives from Prehistory, History, and Ethnography*. Michigan Papers on South and Southeast Asia, No. 13. Ann Arbor: The University of Michigan

INSTITUTE OF ARCHAEOLOGY CASS. 1984. *Xin Zhongguo de Kaogu Faxian he Yanjiu (Archaeological Excavation and Researches in New China)*. Beijing: Wenwu Press.

IRWIN, G. 1985. *The Emergence of Mailu as a Central Place in Coastal Papuan Prehistory*. Terra Australis 10. Canberra: Department of Prehistory, Research School of Pacific Studies, Australian National University.

—. 1991. Pleistocene voyaging and the settlement of Greater Australia and its near Oceanic neighbours. *In* J. Allen and C. Gosden (eds) *Report of the Lapita Homeland Project*. Occasional Papers 20, pp. 9-19 Canberra: Department of Prehistory, Research School of Pacific Studies, Australian National University.

—. 1992. *The prehistoric exploration and colonization of the Pacific*. Cambridge: Cambridge University Press.

—, SIMONE BISKLER AND PHILIP QUIRKE. 1990. Voyaging by Canoe and Computer: Experiments in the Settlement of the Pacific Ocean. *Antiquity* 64:34-50.

KAOGU XUEBAO. 1978. Hemudu yizhi diyiqi Fajue Baogao (First Report of the Excavations of the Hemudu Site). *Kaogu Xuebao* 1:39-93.

KAWAMOTO, TAKO. 1977. *Towards a Comparative Japanese-Austronesian 1*. Bulletin of the Nara University of Education 26: 23-49.

KEEGAN, WILLIAM F., AND JARED M. DIAMOND. 1987. Colonization of Islands by Humans: A Biogeographical Perspective. In *Advances in Archaeological Method and Theory*, Vol. 10. Michael B. Schiffer, ed., pp. 49-91. New York: Academic Press.

KIRCH, P. V. 1984 *The Evolution of the Polynesian Chiefdoms*. Cambridge: Cambridge University Press.

—. 1986. Rethinking East Polynesian Prehistory. *Journal of the Polynesian Society* 95:9-40.

—. 1988a. The Talepakemalai site and Oceanic prehistory. *National Geographic Research* 4:328-342.

—. 1988b. Long-distance exchange and island colonisation: the Lapita case. *Nowegian Archaeological Review* 21:103-117.

—. 1989. Second millennium B.C. arboriculture in Melanesia: Archaeological evidence from the Mussau Islands. *Economic Botany* 43:225-40.

—. 1993. "The Lapita Culture of Western Melanesia in the Context of Austronesian Origins and Dispersals." *Bulletin of the Institute of History and Philology,* Taiwan. Academia Sinica.

—. 1995. The Lapita Complex of Western Melanesia in the Context of Austronesian Origins and Disprsals. In P.J-K. Li, C-H. Tsang, Y-K. Huang, D-A. Ho, and C-Y. Tseng (eds), Austronesian Studies Relating to Taiwan. Symposium Series of the Institute of History and Philosophy, No. 3, pp. 355-294. Taipei: Academia Sinica.

— AND JOANNA ELLISON.1994. Paleoenvironmental Evidence for Human Colonization of Remote Oceanic Islands. *Antiquity*.

— AND R. C. GREEN. 1987. History, phylogeny, and evolution in Polynesia. *Current Anthropology* 28:431-458.

— AND T. L. HUNT, eds. 1988. *Archaeology of the Lapita Cultural Complex: A Critical Review*. Thomas Burke Memorial Washington State Museum Research Report No. 5. Seattle: The Burke Museum.

— AND T. L. Hunt. 1988a. The spatial and temporal boundaries of Lapita. In P. V. Kirch and T. L. Hunt, eds. *Archaeology of the Lapita Cultural Complex: A Critical Review*, pp. 9-31. T. Burke Memorial Washington State Museum Research Report No. 5. Seattle.

—. 1988b. Radiocarbon dates from the Mussau Islands and the Lapita colonization of the southwestern Pacific. *Radiocarbon* 30:161-169.

— , T. L. HUNT, M. WEISLER, V. BUTLER, AND M. S. ALLEN. 1991. Mussau Islands prehistory: results of the 1985-86 excavations. *In* J. Allen and C. Gosden, eds., Report of the Lapita Homeland Project, pp. 144-63. *OPP*, No. 20. Canberra: Department of Prehistory, Australian National University.

—, AND DOUGLAS E. YEN. 1984. Tikopia: The Prehistory and Ecology of a Polynesian Outlier. *Bishop Museum Bulletin*, No. 238. Honolulu: Bernice P. Bishop Museum

KYSELKA, WILL. 1987. *An Ocean in Mind*. Honolulu: University of Hawaii Press.

LANGDON, ROBERT AND DARRELL TRYON. 1983. *The Language of Easter Island: Its Development and Eastern Polynesian Relationships*. Institute for Polynesian Studies Monograph Series, No. 4. Laie, Hawai'i: Institute for Polynesian Studies, Brigham Young

University-Hawai'i Campus.

LAW, G. R.1994. The Likelihood of Multiple Settlement in Eastern Polynesia—A Stochastic Model. *In* Douglas G. Sutton, ed. Pp. 77-95.*The Origin of the First New Zealanders*. Auckland: University of Auckland Press.

LEPOFSKY, D. 1988. The environmental context of Lapita settlement locations. *In* P. V. Kirch and T. L. Hunt, eds. *ALCC,* pp. 33-48.

LEWIS,DAVID. 1966..Stars of the Sea Road. *Journal of the Polynesian Society* 75:85-94.

— . 1972. *We the Navigators*. Honolulu: University of Hawaii Press.

—. 1977. Mau Piailug's Navigation of *Hokule'a* from Hawaii to Tahiti. *Topics in Cultural Learning*, Vol. 5:1-23. Honolulu; Culture Learning Institute, East-West Center.

LI, PAUL JEN-KUEI. 1992. *The Internal and External Relations of the Formosan Languages*. Taitung: National Museum of Prehistory, Planning Bureau.

LIN, CHAOQI. 1973. A Shellmound Site at Fuguodun, Jinmen. *Bulletin of the Department of Archaeology and Anthropology, National Taiwan University* 33/34:36-38.

MACDONALD, DONALD, 19-07. *The Oceanic Languages. Their Grammatical Structure, Vocabulary, and Origin*. London: Henry Frowde.

MCGRAIL, SEAN. 1975. Models, Replicas and Experiments in Nautical Archaeology. *Mariner's Mirror* 61:3-8.

MAGLIONI, RAFAEL.1975. *Archaeological Discovery in Eastern Kwangtung*. Journal Monograph II, Hong Kong Archaeological Society.

MAHDI, WARUNO. 1994. Some Austronesian Maverick Protoforms with Culture-Historical Implications - I. *OL* 33:167-229.

MANSUY, HENRI. 1924."Stations prehistorique dans les cavernes du massif calcaire de Bac-Son (Tonkin). *Bulletin de la Service Geologique d'Indochine* 11(2).

MARSHALL,B. and J. ALLEN. 1991. Excavations in Panakiwuk Cave, New Ireland. *In* J. Allen and C. Gosden (eds) *Report of the Lapita Homeland Project*. Occasional Papers 20, pp. 59-91. Canberra: Department of Prehistory, Research School of Pacific Studies, Australian National University.

MURDOCH, GOERGE PETER. 1967. *Ethnographic Atlas*. Pittsburgh: University of Pittsburgh Press.

THE MUSEUM OF ZHUHAI CITY et al. 1991. *Discoveries and Researches of Archaeology in Zhuhai*. Guangdong Renmin Press.

NORMAN, JERRY AND TSU-MEI LIN. 1976. The Austro-Asiatics in Ancient South China: Some Lexical Evidence. *Monumenta Serica* 32:274-301.

OLIVER, DOUGLAS L. 1974. *Ancient Tahitian Society*. 3 Vols. Honolulu: University of Hawai'i Press.

ORBELL, MARGARET. 1985. Hawaiki: A New Approach to Maori Tradition. Christchurch, New Zealand, University of Canterbury.

PARKIN, ROBERT. 1991. *A Guide to Austroasiatic Speakers and their Languages*. OL Special Publications No. 23. Honolulu: University of Hawaii Press.

PAVLIDES, C. 1993. New archaeological research at Yombon, West New Britain, Papua New Guinea. *AO* 28:55-9.

and C. GOSDEN 1994. 35,000 year old sites in the rainforests of West New Britain, Papua New Guinea. *Antiquity* 68:604-610.

PAWLEY, ANDREW AND ROGER C. GREEN. 1975. Dating the Dispersal of the Oceanic Languages. *OL* 12:1-67.

—. 1984. The Photo-Oceanic Language Community. *The Journal of Pacific History* 19:123-146.

PAWLEY, A. AND M. ROSS. 1993. Austronesian historical linguistics and culture history. *Annual Review of Anthropology* 22:425-459

PEARSON, RICHARD. Taiwan and Its Place in East Asia Prehistory. In *Anthropological Studies of the Taiwan Area*, edited by Kwang-chih Chang, Kuang-chou Li, Arthur P. Wolf, and Alexander Chien-chung Yin, pp. 111-142. Taipei: Department of Anthropology, Taiwan National University.

PETERS, HEATHER. 1983. The Role of the State of Chu in Eastern Period China: A Study of Interaction and Change in the South. Ph.D.Dissertation, Yale University. Ann Arbor, MI: University Microfilms, International.

—.1986. Chu Elegance in the Land of the southern Barbarians. Unpublished manuscript.

—. 1990. *Tattooed Faces and Stilt Houses: Who Were the Ancient Yue*. Sino-Platonic Papers no. 17. Philadelphia: Department of Oriental Studies: University of Pennsylvania.

PIDDINGTON, RALPH. 1956. A Note on the Validity and Significance of Oral Traditions. *JPS* 65:200-204.

PORTER, DAVID. 1822. *Journal of a Cruise made to the Pacific Ocean by Captain David Porter in the United States Frigate Essex*. 2 vols. New York: Wiley and Halsted.

QUIROS, PEDRO FERNANDEZ DE. 1904. *The Voyages of Pedro Fernandez de Quiros, 1595-1606*. 2 vols. Trans. and ed. by C. Markham. London: Hakluyt Society.

REID, LAWRENCE A. 1984/85. Benedict's Austro-Tai hypothesis - an evaluation. AP 26: 19-34.

—. 1994a. Possible Non-Austronesian Lexical Elements in Philippine Negrito Languages. *OL* 33:37-72.

—. 1994b. Morphological evidence for Austric. OL. 33: 323-344.

RIVERS, W. H. R. 1914. *The History of Melanesian Society*. 2 vols. Cambridge: Cambridge University Press.

RIVET, PAUL. 1925. Les melanéso-polynésiens et les australiens en Amérique. Anthropos 20: 51-54.

—. 1926. Les malayo-polynésiens en Amérique. Journal de la Société des Américanistes de Paris 18: 141-278.

ROE, D. 1992. Investigations into the prehistory of the central Solomons: some old and some new data from northwest Guadalcanal. *In* J-C. Galipaud (ed.) *Poterie, Lapita et Peuplement*. pp. 91-101. Noumea: ORSTOM.

ROLETT, BARRY. In press. *Hanamiai: Prehistoric Colonization and Cultural Change in the Marquesas Islands, East Polynesia*. New Haven, Connecticut: Yale University Publications in Anthropology.

ROSS, M.D. 1988. Photo Oceanic and the Austronesian Languages of Western Melanesia. *Pacific Linguistics* C-98. Canberra: Research School of Pacific Studies, Australian National University.

RUNCIMAN, STEPHEN. 1960. *The White Rajahs; A History of Sarawak from 1841 to 1946*. Cambridge: Cambridge University Press.

SAGART, LAURENT. 1993. Chinese and Austronesian: evidence for a genetic relationship. Journal of Chinese linguistics 21: 1-62.

—. 1994. Proto-Austronesian and Old Chinese Evidence for Sino-Austronesia. OL. 33: 271-308

SAHLINS, M. 1981. The stranger king; or, Dumezil among the Fijians. *Journal of Pacific History* 16:107-132.

—. 1985. *Islands of History*. Chicago: University of Chicago Press.

SAND, C. 1992. La differenciation des chronologies ceramiques de Polynesei occidentale a partir d'une tradition culturelle commune issue du complexe culturel Lapita. *In* J.-C. Galipaud, ed., *Poterie Lapita et Peuplement, Actes du Colloque LAPITA*, pp. 207-218. Noumea:ORSTOM.

SAPIR, EDWARD. 1968 [1916]. Time perspective in aboriginal American culture: a study in method. Selected writings of Edward Sapir in language, culture and personality, ed. David C. Mandelbaum: 389-467. Berkeley: University of California Press.

SAUSSURE, FERDINAND DE. 1959. [1915]. *Course in general linguistics*. Edited by Charles Bally and Albert Sechehaye, in collaboration with Albert Riedlinger. Trans. by Wade Baskin. New York: McGraw-Hill.

SHARP, ANDREW. 1956. *Ancient Voyagers in the Pacific*. Polynesian Society Memoir, No. 32. Wellington: The Polynesian Society.

—. 1961. Polynesian Navigation to Distant Islands. *Journal of the Polynesian Society* 70:219-226

— . 1963. *Ancient Voyagers in Polynesia. Berkeley*: University of California Press.

—. 1964. Polynesian Navigation. Navigation: *Journal of the Institute of Navigation* 11:75-76.

SHENON, PHILIP. 1994. Yichang Journal: Digging up the Ancient Past, Before the Deluge. *The New York Times*, Sept. 10: 2.

SHEPPARD, P. J. 1993. Lapita lithics: trade/exchange and technology: a view from the Reefs/Santa Cruz. *AO* 28:121-137.

— AND R. C. GREEN. 1991. Spatial analysis of the Nenumbo (SE-RF-2) Lapita site, Solomon Islands. *AO* 26:89-101.

SIERS, JIM. 1978. *Taratai II: A Continuing Pacific Adventure*. Wellington: A.H. and A.W. Reed.

SMITH, S. PERCY. 1898. *Hawaiki: The Whence of the Maori*. Wellington: Whitcombe and Tombs.

SPRIGGS, MATTHEW. 1988. The Hawaiian Transformation of Ancestral Polynesian Society: Conceptualizing Chiefly States. In *State and Society*. John Gledhill, Barbara Bender and Mogens T. Larsen, eds., pp. 57-73. London: Unwin and Hyman.

—. 1989. The dating of the Island Southeast Asian Neolithic: an attempt at chronometric hygiene and linguistic correlation. *Antiquity* 63:587-613.

—, ed. 1990 *Lapita Design, Form & Composition*. Occasional Papers in Prehistory No. 19 Canberra: Department of Prehistory, Australian National University.

—. 1990a. Dating Lapita; another view. In M. Spriggs, ed., *Lapita Design, Form & Composition,* pp. 6-27. Occasional Papers in Prehistory, No. 19. Canberra: Department of Prehistory, Australian National University.

—. 1990b. The changing face of Lapita: Transformation of a design. *In* M. Spriggs, ed., *Lapita Design, Form & Composition,* pp. 83-122. Occasional Papers in Prehistory, No. 19. Canberra: Department of Prehistory, Australian National University.

—. 1991. Nissan, the island in the middle. Summary report on excavations at the north end of the Solomons and south end of the Bismarcks. *In* J. Allen and C. Gosden (eds) *Report of the Lapita Homeland Project*. Occasional Papers 20. pp. 222-43. Canberra: Department of Prehistory, Research School of Pacific Studies, Australian National University.

—. 1993 Island Melanesia: The last 10,000 years. *In* M. A. Smith, M. Spriggs, and B. Fankhauser, eds., *Sahul in Review: Pleistocene Archaeology in Australia, New Guinea and Island Melanesia*, pp. 187-20. Occasional Papers in Prehistory, No. 24. Canberra: Department of Prehistory, Australian National University

STEADMAN, DAVID W. 1989. Extinction of Birds in East Polynesia: A Review of the Record, and Comparisons with other Pacific Islands Groups. *Journal of Archaeological Science* 16:177-205.

STEINER, J. T. 1980. The Climate of the South-West Pacific Region. *New Zealand Meteorological Service Miscellaneous Publication*, No. 166. Wellington: New Zealand Meteorological Service.

SUGGS, ROBERT C. 1961a. The Archaeology of Nukuhiva, Marquesas Islands, French Polynesia. *Anthropological Papers of the American Museum of Natural History*, No. 49, Part 1. New York: American Museum of Natural History.

—. 1961b. Methodological Problems for Accidental Voyagers. *Journal of the Polynesian Society* 70:474-476.

SUMMERHAYES, G. R. and J. Allen. 1993. The transport of Mopir obsidian to Late Pleistocene New Ireland. *AO* 28:144-148.

SUNG, MARGARET M. Y. 1989. The Languages of the Taiwan Aborigines. In *Anthropological Studies of the Taiwan Area: Accomplishments and Prospects*, edited by Kwang-Chih Chang, Kwang-chou Li, Arthur P. Wolf, and Alexander Chien-Chung Yin, pp. 37-58. Taipei: Department of Anthropology, National Taiwan University.

SUNG, WENHSUN AND CHAO-MEI LIEN. 1989. Table of stratigraphy of prehistoric culture in Taiwan. *Historical Monthly* 81:66-67.

SUTLIVE, RICHARD H., JR. 1978. *The Iban of Sarawak*. Arlington Heights, IL: AHM Publishing Corporation.

SWADLING, P., J. CHAPPELL, G. FRANCIS, N. ARAHO AND B. IVUYO. 1989. A Late Quaternary inland sea and early pottery in Papua New Guinea. *AO* 24:106-9.

—. 1991. Settlements associated with the inland Sepik-Ramu sea. *In* P. Bellwood (ed.) *Indo-Pacific Prehistory* 1990, pp. 92-112. Bulletin of the Indo-Pacific Prehistory Association 11.

—, N. ARAHO, AND B. IVUYO. 1991. Settlements associated with the Sepik-Ramu Sea. *In* P. Bellwood, ed., *Indo-Pacific Prehistory 1990: Proceedings of the 14th Congress of the Indo-Pacific Prehistory Association*, pp. 92-112. Canberra: Indo-Pacific Prehistory Association.

—, B. H. SCHAUBLIN, P. GORECKI, AND F. TIESLER. 1988. *The Sepik-Ramu: An Introduction*. Boroko: National Museum of Papua New Guinea.

TANG, CHUNG, AND JIAFA QU, co-editors 1991. *Archaeological Finds from the Pearl Delta in Guangdong, China*. The Chinese University of Hong Kong Press.

TERRELL, JOHN. 1994. The Postponed Agenda: Archaeology & Human Biogeography in the 21st Century. Paper read at the meeting of the Society for American Archaeology.

THOMAS, STEPHEN D., 1987. *The Last Navigator*. New York: Henry Holt.

THURGOOD, GRAHAM. 1988. Notes on the Reconstruction of Proto-Kam-Sui. In J. A. Edmondson and D.B. Solnit (eds), *Comparative Kadai: Linguistic Studies Beyong Tai*, pp. 179-218. Summer Institute of Linguistics and the University of Texas at Arlington Publications in Linguistics, No. 86.

—. 1994. Tai-Kadai and Austronesian: the Nature of the Historical Relationship. *OL* 33: 345-368.

TORRENCE, R. 1992. What is Lapita about obsidian? A view from the Talasea source. *In* J-C. Galipaud (ed.) *Poterie, Lapita et Peuplement,* pp. 111-26. Noumea: ORSTOM.

TSANG, CHENG-HWA. 1990. On the Fine Corded Ware Culture of Taiwan. *Field Archaeology of Taiwan* 1(2):1-31.

—. 1992. *Archaeology of the P'eng-Hu Islands*. Institute of History and Philology, Academia Sinica, Special Publication No. 95. Taipei.

VAN HEEKEREN, H. R .1972. *The Stone Age of Indonesia*. The Hague .

VAN HINLOOPEN LABBERTON, D. 1924. Preliminary Results of Researches into the Original Relationship between the Nipponese and the Malayo-Polynesian Languages. *JPS* 33: 244-280.

VAN TILBERG, JOANNE. 1994. *Easter Island: Archaeology, Ecology, and Culture*. London: British Museum Press.

VON DEN STEINEN, KARL. 1988. Von Den Steinen's Marquesas Myths. Trans. by Marta Langridge from *Zeitschrift für Ethnologie* 1933-34, 65:325-373; 1934-35, 66:191-240. Jennifer Terrell, ed. Canberra: Target Oceania and the Journal of Pacific History.

WALTER, RICHARD. 1990. The Southern Cook Islands in Eastern Polynesian Prehistory. Unpublished Ph.D. dissertation, Auckland: Department of Anthropology, University of Auckland.

WANG, GUNGWU. 1958. The Nanshai Trade: A Study of the Early History of the Chinese Trade in the South China Sea. *Journal of the Malay Branch of the Royal Asiatic Society* 31(2):1-135.

WANG, ZHENYONG, et alii, 1983. The Second Season of Excavations of the Neolithic Site of Xitou, Minhou. *Fujian Wenbo*, 1:30-46.

WARNER, J. N. 1962. Sugar Cane:An Indigenous Papual Cultigen. *Ethnology* 1:405-411.

WEISLER, MARSHALL IRWIN. 1933. Long-distance Interaction in Prehistoric Polynesia: Three Case Studies. Unpublished Ph.D. Dissertation, Berkeley, Department of Anthropology, University of California.

—. 1994. The Settlement of Marginal Polynesia. *Journal of Field Archaeology* 21:83-102.

WENWU. 1977. Guangzhou Qin Han Zao Chuan Gongchang Yizhi Shijue (A Test Excavation of a Qin and Han Period Boat-Making Workshop in Canton). *Wenwu* 4:1-16.

WHITE, JOYCE C. 1995. Modeling the Development of Early Rice Agriculture: Ethnoecological Perspectives from Northeast Thailand. *AP* 34:37-68.

WHITE, J. P. and J. F. O'CONNELL 1982. *A prehistory of Australia, New Guinea and Sahul*. Sydney: Academic Press.

WHITE J. P., T. F. FLANNERY, R. O'BRIEN, R. V. HANCOCK AND L. PAVLISH 1991. The Balof shelters, New Ireland. *In* J. Allen and C.Gosden (eds) *Report of the Lapita Homeland Project*. Occasional Papers 20, pp. 46-58. Canberra: Department of Prehistory, Research School of Pacific Studies, Australia National University.

WICKLER, S.1990. Prehistoric Melanesian exchange and interaction:recent evidence from the Northern Solomon Islands. *AP* 29(2):135-54.

WILLIAMS, JOHN. 1838. *A Narrative of Missionary Enterprises in the South Sea Islands*. London: John Snow.

WINKLER, CAPTAIN. 1901. On Sea Charts Formerly Used in the Marshall Islands, with Notices on the Navigation of these Islanders in General. In *Annual Report of the Smithsonian Institution*, 1899, pp. 487-509. Washington D.C.: Smithsonian Institution.

YAN, WEN-MING. 1991. China's Earliest Rice Agriculture Remains. *Indo-Pacific Prehistory Association Bulletin* 10:118-126.

YEN, DOUGLAS E.1973. The Origins of Oceanic Agriculture. *Archaeology and Physical Anthropology in Oceania* 8:68-85.

—. 1974. The Sweet Potato and Oceania: An Essay in Ethnobotany. *BMB*, No. 236.

—. 1990. Environment, agriculture and the colonization of the Pacific. *In* D. E. Yen and J. M. J. Mummery (eds) *Pacific production systems: approaches to economic prehistory*. Papers from a symposium at the XV Pacific Science Congress, Dunedin, New Zealand. 1983. OPP No. 18. pp. 258-77.

ZHAO, SONGQIAO AND WEITANG WU. 1986-87. Early Neolithic Hemudu Culture Along the Hangzhou Estuary and the Origin of Domestic Paddy Rice in China. *AP* 27(1):29-34.

INDEX

NOTE: The personal names of people whose work is cited and which appear in the bibliography are omitted from the index, except in a few instances where their historic role is discussed or there is an acknowledgment of thanks to them.

www.ingramcontent.com/pod-product-compliance
Lightning Source LLC
LaVergne TN
LVHW081602100826
845153LV00004B/440